Marlboro
The Real Cowboy

Marlboro

The Real Cowboy

Produced by Simplified Travel Limited
by arrangement with
Philip Morris Incorporated

BARRIE & JENKINS
COMMUNICA-EUROPA

Published by **Simplified Travel Limited,**
Heron House, Chiswick Mall, London W4 2PR

ISBN 0 214 20203 8

Editor:
Tessa Clark
Art Director:
Peter Town
Editorial Consultant:
Ramon F. Adams
Editorial Adviser:
Dennis Bailey
Specialist Consultants:
Dave Gelly (music)
Sonia Allison (cookery)

Copy Editor:
Michael Wright
Sub-editor:
Tom Link
Editorial Assistant:
Maggi Renshaw
Writers:
Drayton Bird; Alastair Clark;
Dave Gelly; Rodney Hyde-Thompson;
Christopher Maynard; Phillip Riley
Designers:
Tim Fitzgerald; Bruce Gill
Text Researchers:
Sue Adderley; Rozina Adler;
Christopher Maynard; Gilbert O'Brien;
Mike Petrovitch; Malcolm Stewart;
Hilary Thomas
Picture Researchers:
Tony Alston; Annette Gallagher;
Miles Karpman; Pat Kornberg;
Pat Miller; Lynn Petersen;
Anne Summer
Indexer:
Hilary Bird
Production Consultant:
John Cleary

Contents

The Cowboy and the West

'The cowboy was the right breed of man in the right country at the right time, doing the right job. He was—and still is—the essence of the American ideal of freedom and self-reliance.'

The American cowboy's heyday scarcely spanned 30 years—from the 1860s, when the first great herds of cattle were driven along the trails from Texas to Kansas, to the 1890s, when barbed wire and ploughed fields, windmills and homesteads replaced the wide-open freedom of the range. Yet those few years gave birth to one of the world's most enduring heroes.

Other cowboys in other parts of the world—the *gardians* of the Camargue in southern France, the *arats* of Mongolia, the *gauchos* of Argentina—share the American cowboy's way of life. But they've never matched his universal appeal. He rode into, and survived, the American West—one of the last great frontiers. It was virgin territory, a new planet of mountains and plains, forests and rushing rivers, withering sun and killing cold. He travelled light, his bedroll and saddle—and perhaps his horse—his only possessions. He lived life his way—the only limits were his honour and the never-defined code of the West.

The cowboy was the right breed of man in the right country at the right time, doing the right job. He was—and still is—the essence of the American ideal of freedom, self-reliance and a man's right to choose how he lives: an ideal that continues to grip, and hold, the imagination of people all over the world.

Strangely enough, this all-American symbol was the product of two entirely different European cultures. The American poet Archibald MacLeish isolated the factors that led to his birth when he wrote, 'The Spaniard trekked his long-horned, gaunt Andalucian cattle into Mexico, then to Arizona, New Mexico and California. The English landed on the North Atlantic seaboard with Red Devon milch cows and fat yellow Danish oxen. It was like lighting two fuses, 2,000 miles apart, that would splutter along over two centuries and finally explode into the fireworks display of the trail drives and the Western range after 1850.'

The Spanish fuse was lit in 1519 when Hernando Cortés landed in

Spanish soldiers and the settlers who followed them laid the foundations of the beef bonanza: 'Cattle Coming into Texas' by José Cisneros

Mexico with 16 Andalucian horses. Two years later, Gregorio de Villalobos followed with six heifers and a young bull. They were the vanguard—settlers followed with more livestock and soon small ranches appeared along the water courses that led north to what is now Texas. The climate of the New World was congenial, and the country was rich in grazing lands. What had been a handful of cattle and horses soon grew into vast herds. As early as 1555, Robert Tomson, an English trader, reported: 'There is in New Spain [Mexico] a marvellous increase of cattel which dayly do increase and are of greater growth than ours.'

Spanish priests and military captains opened up the southern part of North America. From Mexico the settlements swept north along the Pacific coast, north-east up to the Rio Grande, and east into the coastal plains of Texas. In 1582 an expedition pushed as far north as the site of Jerome, Arizona. Several boatloads of settlers arrived from Spain in 1598 and put down roots near what is now Santa Fe, New Mexico. Nearly 100 years later, in 1690, a community of Franciscan friars settled in Texas close to the present-day Louisiana border.

Cowboys today live more settled lives than their predecessors, but they still symbolize freedom and independence to people all over the world: modern cowboys in Texas

These mission stations, established to win men's souls, became increasingly involved in managing their livestock. By the beginning of the 18th century the Espiritu Santo mission alone had 40,000 cattle. The good fathers hired Mexican Indians to tend the herds, and taught them the ancient cattle-handling skills of Andalucia. These *vaqueros* were the first American cowboys. Many later moved across the Rio Grande and settled in what became Texas. (Until about 1850, all Texan cowboys were called *vaqueros.*)

Before he became a cowhand, the *vaquero* had lived on the range, his only shelter a hide-roofed lean-to, open on three sides. He rode his mustang bare-legged, and lived off water, corn meal and any game he could catch. A sombrero kept the fierce sun and stinging prairie grit from his eyes; sandals protected his feet from flinty soil. As a horseman he was more than a match for the Apache, Comanche and Navaho Indians, his natural enemies. His skill with the rope was legendary. Brave and loyal, he was content to spend weeks tracking and rounding up the ever-growing herds of stray cattle.

Northern cowboys were mainly descendants of the pioneers who had first edged onto the range from the eastern seaboard in the early 18th century. Many of these settlers crossed the grasslands, threaded their way through the Rockies, and settled in Oregon and California. They sold their exhausted cattle en route for cash and stores from the scattered trading posts. The cattle grew fat again on the rich grazing land and were resold.

North and south met and mingled on the Western range immediately after the Civil War; in 1866 the long cattle drives from Texas to the north had started, and the West seethed with new arrivals. The professional cowhands were joined by freed Negro slaves and Confederate veterans, steamboat gamblers on the run from the law, and farm boys on the run from home—young men in their early 20s, attracted by the challenge and freedom of life on the range. Later, Scotsmen and Englishmen joined their ranks, some of them the black sheep of noble families who paid them a remittance to stay away from

Britain. The original *vaqueros* worked the ranches only for about 15 years. Though the Texans respected their skills, they thought the Mexicans treated the stock unfeelingly.

Despite old antagonisms, Confederate veterans and Negro slaves bunked together, ate together, drank together and rode together. Lingering prejudices soon disappeared. Some authorities say that one in three cowboys was a Negro; others suggest a ratio of one in ten. Famous Negro cowboys include Boss Ikard, of whom rancher Charles Goodnight said, 'I have trusted him further than any living man'; George Glenn, who brought his boss's embalmed body from Abilene, Kansas, to Texas for burial—a tough 42-day journey; and 'Nigger Add', whose superb horsemanship made him a legend from Mexico to Canada.

Cowboys were expected to work long hours in tough conditions, and had a better than average chance of being injured in an accident, or of falling ill. The Spur Ranch, Texas, records show that of 901 hands employed from 1890 to 1901, only 3 per cent worked as many as five seasons; 64 per cent left after one. Although wages depended more on length of service and reliability than on skills, on average a skilled cowboy received $30 a month, top hands $35 to $45, trail bosses $50 to $60, and range foremen $50 to $65. Keep and board were free. These figures compare with a national wage for labourers in 1860 of $25 a month and $50 for craftsmen. By 1880, these two groups were earning $32 and $60 respectively. Though wages were higher farther north in Montana, Wyoming and Colorado, cowboys had to bear the extra cost of heavy winter clothes.

Cowboys in the northern states like Montana and Wyoming stayed close to their ranch headquarters during the long winters: riding home in the snow

A cowboy's board cost his employer about $3 to $4 a month. Beans, bacon and strong black coffee were staples, and were eaten rapidly, in total silence. The cowboy was so accustomed to bolting his food that lingering over a meal gave him indigestion. Cowboys ate heartily, yet they remained slim and tough. A fat, or even plump, working hand was a rarity—his long hours and tough work made it almost an impossibility.

In the early boom days work was easy to come by. All a cowhand had to do was ride in out of the blue just before the busy season started, and ask the foreman for a job. But this free-and-easy attitude changed in the late 1880s: the bonanza was over, and jobs were scarcer. Many hands applied in December for work the following spring. In Texas the slack period was December to March. If a cowboy was staying on for the next season's work he spent the winter 'riding grubline'—making the rounds of ranches, eating free meals and staying until he wore out his welcome. In return, he'd do odd jobs, for which he received no pay.

Northern cowboys were less nomadic than the trail-driving Texans. They spent the long weeks of the winter snows close to the log-built home ranch. If a man was chosen to 'ride line'—watch over the herds on the range—he'd live in a log cabin or sod house well stocked with food for his winter vigil.

Ranch discipline was strict. A man who broke the rules could find himself without a job; Charles Goodnight and his neighbours, for

Modern ranchers use technical skills and scientific methods that would astonish the first cowboys; some even have diplomas in agriculture: cattle being fattened in a Texas feedyard

instance, made a pact never to hire a man who'd been discharged for theft or gambling. (Goodnight fired his brother-in-law for the latter offence.) Holidays were few and far between. Men on the Spur Ranch worked seven days a week, except over Christmas when they were allowed three or four days off. The Snyder brothers, who allowed their cowboys to relax on Sundays, were exceptional.

Today most cowboys work on small, family-owned ranches, and tend sheep and crops as well as cattle. They're members of a skilled team, and know as much about internal combustion engines as they do about horses. Many ranchers specialize—some breed cattle commercially, others take and fatten calves and yearlings, others act as feeders or 'finishers' who prepare animals directly for market—so the men who tend the herds need skills undreamt of by their 19th-century predecessors. Some even have diplomas in agriculture.

Though techniques have changed, and the cowboys are older (an average age of 30) and better paid (about $350 a month for a married man, plus house and free beef), their links with the men who first rode the range are strong. They still wear wide-brimmed, high-crowned stetsons, chaps and comfortable levis. Today's cowboy still rides the line, armed with a pair of pliers, a couple of pounds of wire fence staples and a wire-stretcher. Pick-up trucks are widely used—even helicopters on large spreads—but the cowboy's horse is still his main means of transport. Round-ups are the highlights of his working year—and roping and riding skills are still essential tools of his trade.

Cowboys had little in common except their job. But after a few weeks of hard, tough living in the open air members of a ranch outfit became a tightly knit group: cowboys relax by a waterhole

John Chisum: one of the West's biggest 'one man ranchers'. He started as a trail driver taking herds to army posts and Navaho reservations after the Civil War. He eventually owned more than 100.000 head and employed 100 hands on his ranch in New Mexico

Charles Goodnight: scout, Texas ranger and Civil War frontier scout. After his first venture into ranching failed, he became part-owner of the JA ranch. His genius for finding new ranges in Texas, Colorado and New Mexico was phenomenal: he owned ranches in all three states

A. H. 'Shanghai' Pierce: born in Rhode Island he ranched in Texas and was one of the cattle industry's most colourful characters. He carried enormous sums of gold to pay for his cattle—and travelled unarmed. He erected a statue to himself in San Antonio

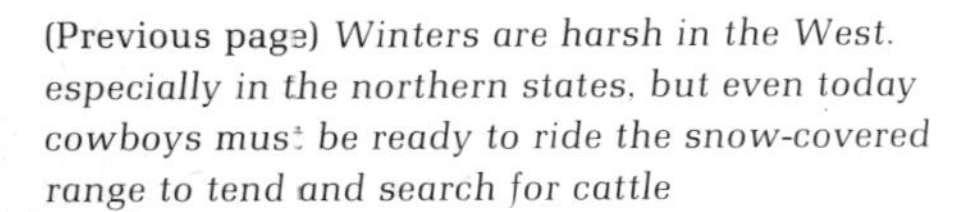

(Previous page) *Winters are harsh in the West, especially in the northern states, but even today cowboys must be ready to ride the snow-covered range to tend and search for cattle*

The Beef Bonanza

Texas was the crucible of the beef industry. Its open plains, lush grass and mild climate were ideal for cattle-raising. And the Spanish authorities, who'd always encouraged American immigration (as did Mexico after the 1821 revolution), loaded the scales heavily in favour of cattlemen. Potential ranchers were given 4,428 acres, whereas farmers were granted only 177. There were 35,000 Americans in Texas by 1835—a melting-pot of hardy settlers, often of British stock, who'd moved on from the Appalachian mountains and across the Louisiana border, and adventurers attracted by the challenge of a new country. The settlers soon adapted to the *vaquero* way of life, and built up herds from the wild Longhorns that roamed the prairies. Ownership in those days was established by brands and ear marks; a stray ('maverick') was the property of the first man who branded it or cropped its ears.

James Taylor White, who arrived in Texas in 1823, was the first American to own a Texan ranch. According to an 1842 account, 'His whole future was three cows and calves, two small poneys, a wife and three children . . . Now he owns about 40,000 acres, upwards of 90 negroes, about 30,000 head of cattle, has 60,000 dollars deposited in New Orleans . . . and what is extraordinary, he cannot read or write and has made his fortune raising stock alone.'

The cattle boom started immediately after the end of the Civil War. By 1865, the Texan herds had increased to over three million head—and steers worth $3 or $4 each in Texas could be sold for $40 to $50 in Eastern and Midwestern cities. Ranchers started to look north to these new urban markets. In 1867, when cattle dealer Joseph McCoy established the first great Western stockyard in Abilene, Kansas, cross-country cattle herding became a business proposition. The long drives from the Lone Star State to Kansas started in earnest; the beef bonanza was on its way.

At the same time the discovery that Longhorns could be turned loose onto the prairies, summer and winter, to fend for themselves encouraged cattlemen to graze their herds freely throughout the year, and to move ever northwards. (The cattle actually put on weight

Pierre Wibaux: the son of French bourgeois parents, he ranched—and succeeded—in the Dakotas. He was backed financially by his family and helped by his wife, an English beauty, who ran the ranch singlehanded when her husband was away on business

The Marquis de Mores: a French aristocrat, and a cattle baron who failed, he spent more than a million dollars of his father-in-law's money. His lavish experiments included shipping fresh salmon to New York. For a time he lived in a private railroad car; photo L. A. Huffman

John Wesley Iliff: Colorado cattle king, and once an Oregon cowboy, he started his cattle-raising career in the Indian hunting grounds north-west of Denver. He died in the saddle at 48. His widow (who married a bishop) founded the Iliff School of Theology in his memory

during an average winter as the grass under the snow retained its food value like frozen foods today.) Texan ranchers grazed their cattle in Colorado—where the herds grew from 20,000 head in 1866 to about one million in 1869.

Abilene, the first cow town, was soon joined by others as the network of rail lines spread across the land: Dodge City, Ellsworth and Hays City in Kansas, Ogallala in Nebraska, Julesburg in Colorado, and Cheyenne and Laramie in Wyoming. Other shipping points were established to the north, and by 1875 a belt of free pasture, stretching from southern Texas to the Canadian border, was well served with railheads. By this time, refrigerator wagons were common, canning had been invented, and Western beef, slaughtered in Kansas City or Chicago, could be sold to markets in the East and in Europe.

Steers not sold at the railheads were turned out to graze or sold to established ranchers to be fattened. They interbred with local breeds—and swarmed out over the prairies that had once been the haunt of buffalo. Other Texan cattle were driven north specifically to provide herds for settlers from the East. The grass remained free until the mid-1880s, and the United States government permitted a man who controlled the water to graze his cattle as far as they could range.

Men with the courage to survive a temporary slump in beef prices in the early 1870s went on to make fortunes. Grazing cost nothing—and by the end of the decade a north-western steer could be sold for $60, a Texan steer for about $50. During the early 1880s, a man could make a 300 per cent profit on cattle bought three years previously.

The late 1870s saw the emergence of the 'cattle barons' and their great spreads: Charles Goodnight, former Texas ranger, Indian scout and pioneer trail driver, owned ranches in Texas, New Mexico and Colorado. The Texas JA Ranch (in which his partner was John Adair) covered 1,335,000 acres and grazed 100,000 head. John Wesley Iliff refused his father's offer of a $7,500 interest in a farm in Ohio in favour of $500 and permission to 'go West'—and eventually owned 105 parcels of range land totalling 15,558 acres. Texan John Chisum, another former trail driver, owned more than 100,000 head and employed 100 cowboys on his New Mexico ranch.

Then there was Shanghai ('Shang') Pierce. When a hotel in Hot Springs, Arkansas, was full, he bought it outright, and then booked the best room for himself and his wife. When 'Shang' visited Rome he tried to bribe his way in to see the Pope. Asked on his return whether he'd seen any Papal Bulls in the Vatican he replied, 'Nary a damn critter. Saw some fine old cows just out of town.'

The cattle barons included some genuine aristocrats, foreign noblemen attracted by Western money: the Marquis de Mores, for instance, who providentially married a New York banker's daughter and, backed by a million dollars of his father-in-law's money, settled in Dakota in 1883. He founded the town of Medora (named after his wife), and lived in a private railroad carriage while his 26-room château-style house was being built.

Pierre Wibaux was a Frenchman who did succeed—eventually. His first Western home was a sod house, and he worked as a hired hand. When he and his English wife invited guests to Christmas dinner after their first year on the range, water dripped through its roof and mice scampered above the ceiling—but Mrs Wibaux wore a Paris gown, her husband faultless evening dress. Wibaux bought stock cheaply after the harsh winter of 1886 led to the 'Big Die-Up' (when many thousands of cattle died and the industry slumped) and built up a 60,000-head herd.

Life at the top of the cattle industry had its luxuries—like the splendid clubs that sprang up in the cattle centres. The Cheyenne Club, for instance, would have been more at home in London's Pall

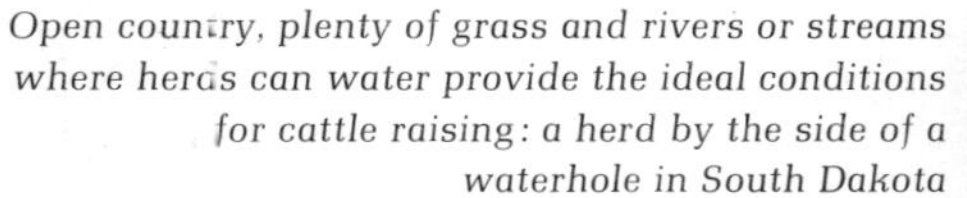

Open country, plenty of grass and rivers or streams where herds can water provide the ideal conditions for cattle raising: a herd by the side of a waterhole in South Dakota

Mall than in a Western cow town. When it first opened in 1880, membership was restricted to 50; later, 200 members were allowed to enjoy its leather-covered chairs, French champagne, and *haute cuisine*. Like its London counterparts, the Cheyenne's rules were uncompromising: a member 'guilty of an act so dishonourable as to unfit the guilty party for the society of gentlemen' was expelled. The Montana Club in Helena, Montana, was a carbon copy of the Cheyenne—but admitted mining men. The Denver Club catered for Colorado's top cattlemen.

A cattle baron's life wasn't all clubs and profit-counting, however. The men who controlled the industry dealt in millions of dollars; inevitably, they stepped on smaller men's toes. As their huge, impersonal ranches spread across the prairies, two cornerstones of the cowboy's existence were eroded: the freedom of the range and his intense loyalty to his employer. When he helped himself to a few cattle that didn't belong to him he was striking back at the new faceless owners—some of whom didn't even visit their ranches—and at the same time building up his own nest egg for the future. In any case, rustling, to the cowboys, was just a variation on the old legal theme that a stray became the property of the man who branded it.

Small ranchers did the same, and rustling grew into a major problem. Some big ranchers offered their hands bribes of $2 to $5 for each maverick branded. Later, some northern barons made a pact to stop paying this commission—they said it was a cowboy's duty to brand mavericks with his ranch's brand. Rustling increased as a result.

The beef industry started on the plains of Texas, but ranchers soon discovered that cattle could also be raised farther north: a modern hand leads a column of cowboys

In 1865 there were 35,000 miles of railroad in the United States. Although the southern and eastern states and the midwestern states of Michigan, Ohio and Illinois were well served, the most westward point reached was St Joseph, Missouri. The Great Plains were untouched. In the eight years that followed, 22,885 miles of track were built across the cattle kingdom. By 1890 five separate railroads spanned the continent, with a criss-cross network of local lines linking small communities.

Important 'cattle' lines were the Union Pacific railroad which ran from Omaha, Nebraska, to the Californian border, linking Ogallala, Julesberg and Cheyenne; the Kansas Pacific, from Kansas City to Denver, Colorado, through Abilene, Ellsworth and Hays City; and the Atchison, Topeka and Santa Fe railroad which linked Newton and Dodge City, Kansas, before running south.

In the northern Great Plains area two other railroads added to the cattle story. The Northern Pacific ran from Minneapolis across the Badlands of Dakota, and through Montana; just south of the Canadian border, the Great Northern Pacific linked Duluth on Lake Superior to the ports of Oregon.

About 1,000 miles farther south the Southern Pacific sent its shining tracks through south Texas, New Mexico and Arizona to San Francisco.

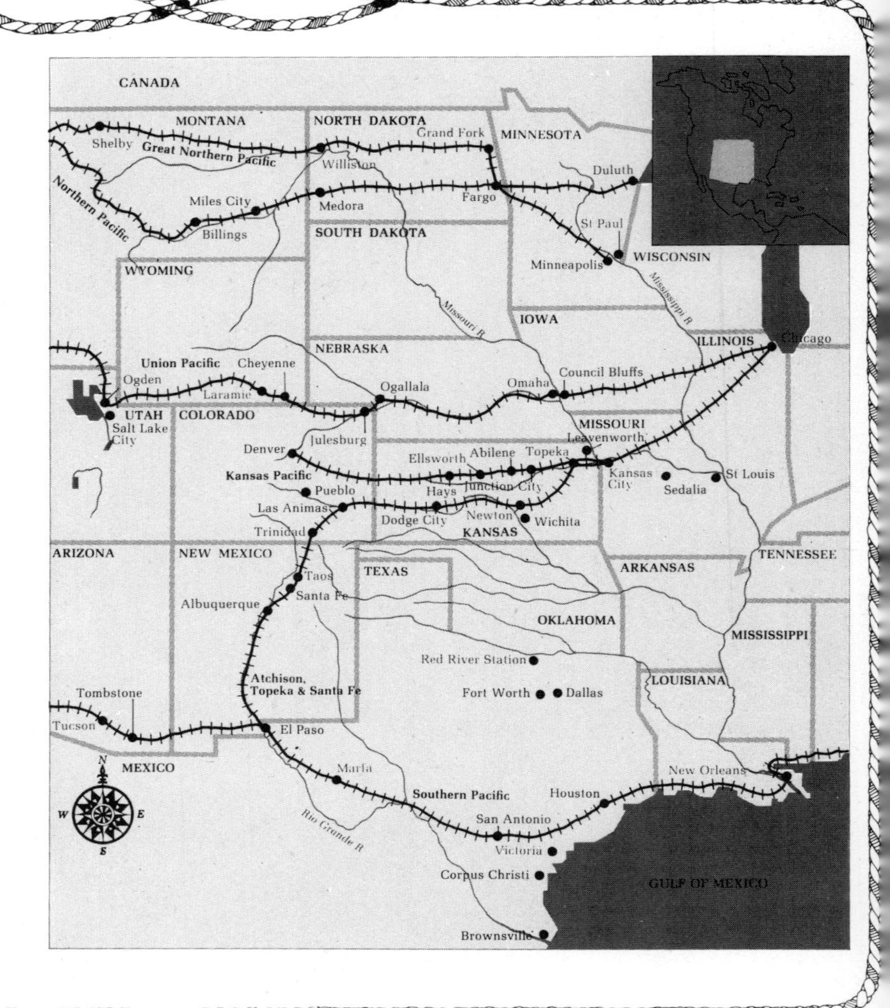

Livestock associations were the main weapons in the owners' anti-rustling armoury. In Texas, small groups formed protective associations in 1868 (a state association was established nine years later). During the 1870s the associations spread north with the cattle—the Montana Stock Growers' Association came into being in 1879. State laws decreed that mavericks belonged to the associations and not to individuals; in Wyoming, range detectives and cattle inspectors were appointed. Eventually, the livestock associations regulated every aspect of ranching: round-ups, disagreements about ownership, stock management. With their development, a respect for brands and for private ownership replaced the old freedom of the range.

Banks started to invest in beef soon after the first long drive; by 1870, the First National Bank of Kansas had opened a branch in Abilene. And in 1873 Charles Goodnight and some friends started one in Pueblo, Colorado. In those days, agreements were sealed with a handshake. The cattleman's security was his character. When a rancher or cowboy gave his word it was an unbreakable bond—even when transactions ran as high as hundreds of thousands of dollars.

Foreign capital started to flow in during the late 1870s. In 1879, an English Royal Commission reported that cattlemen's average profits were as high as $33\frac{1}{3}$ per cent—and much of the floating capital in the world's richest country went West. By 1880, Britain had invested $45 million, most of it in Texas, Wyoming and Montana. In 1881 a Scottish syndicate bought the XIT Ranch in Texas for $253,000; in 1882 the Texas Land and Cattle Company of Scotland paid $1 million for the Los Laureles Ranch in Texas. By 1888, 36 cattle companies with a total capital value of $37 million had been floated in Britain. Of this, $20 million went to America for investment.

For once, American businessmen lagged behind their British colleagues. They only joined the rush in 1883, when a Kentucky corporation was formed to operate a large Texas spread. New York brokers published persuasive brochures extolling the profits to be made in cattle investment—only to find the public's appetite had already been whetted by a book written in 1881 by General James Brisbin. Its encouraging title was *The Beef Bonanza: or How to Get Rich on the Plains*. Syndicates and corporations took over the greater part of the cattle business. By 1885, it was said, only two men continued to operate as individual ranchers in the whole of Wyoming.

Then, in 1886, the Big Die-Up, the most savage winter in American history, hit Montana, Wyoming, Kansas, the Dakotas, Nebraska and parts of Arizona and Colorado. A three-day blizzard, and the long months of cold that followed (temperatures averaged 11 degrees of frost), ruined all but three or four of the soundest corporations. The Swan Land and Cattle Company, for example, lost 5,400 head, the OS Ranch in Kansas lost 11,000, the Circle M 5,000. The catastrophic winter was followed by a drought—then an early winter with heavy snows. Money was expensive; Eastern bankers drew in their purse strings. Corporations, cattle barons and large and small ranchers alike sold out for what they could get.

A few outfits survived. Shareholders who stayed with corporation ranches despite the scare of the Big Die-Up recession left handsome inheritances for their descendants. The Matador Ranch, for example, paid a 30 per cent dividend in 1948; two years later when it sold out, shares were worth 30 times their original cost. The King Ranch in Texas also rode the slump successfully. Established by Richard King in 1853, in 1962 it grossed $15 million in cattle shipments alone. It covers over a million acres in the torrid, flat land west of Corpus Christi, and has its own private railroad and loading pens. It also has branches in Pennsylvania, Arizona and Australia.

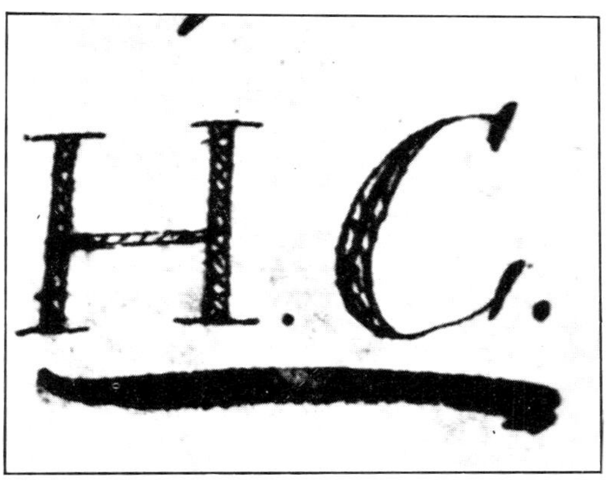

A brand was a rancher's mark of ownership, proof that an animal belonged to him: the HC brand, the first one registered in Texas

By the mid-1850s, although some cattle were shipped live to far-off markets, including Europe, most beef was refrigerated: an early refrigerator wagon

The Decline of the Range

The seeds of the independent cowboy's destruction were sown four years before the start of the beef boom, when the Homestead Act of 1862 opened the prairies to free settlement. The 160-acre parcels the government offered were too small to support cattle profitably (an 1878 report suggested a minimum pasturage of 2,560 acres) and were suitable only for farming. This Act was the first of a series of laws loaded in favour of farmers, and against cattlemen. They were made in the East by men brought up on the tradition of small, owner-run farms, who believed that opening the West to agriculture would bring increased prosperity to the nation—and increased revenue to the government. To them, the cattleman was an obstacle to this settled way of life. (It wasn't until 1916 that Congress admitted that cattlemen existed in the West—and even then, the maximum acreage allowed for grazing was 640 acres fit only for grazing, with no timber, irrigation facilities or minerals.)

As a result of the Homestead Act, thousands of homesteaders (also known as 'sodbusters' and 'nesters') poured onto the open range from the East. In their bib overalls they were scorned by the free-riding cowboys. As one old trail driver put it, 'Those fellows . . . "the bone and sinew of the country" as politicians call them—have made farms, enclosed pastures and fenced in water holes until you can't rest; and I say damn such bone and sinew!'

He had a point. The push of settlement snapped at the stockman's heels, particularly in the north. The cattlemen fought back when they could, and turned laws like the 1877 Desert Land Act to their advantage. This Act leased potential settlers 640-acre parcels at 25 cents an acre. If a man irrigated a portion of his land within three years he could buy it freehold from the government for a dollar an acre. Cattlemen saw their chance to own large tracts of good land, safe from the stealthy approach of the nesters—and registered thousands of dummy claims in their cowhands' names. But the ranchers were fighting a losing battle. For example, in 1885, in Indian Territory (Oklahoma), cattle were expelled from an area as large as the state of Ohio to make room for homesteaders. Between 1862 and 1900, 80 million acres of government-leased land was registered by homesteaders; another massive 520 million acres was sold by land companies, railroads (who advertised for settlers to buy land alongside their tracks) and state offices.

Ranchers were in a stronger position in the south-west, where they held the titles to their grazing lands, and weren't dependent on public decisions. In New Mexico, Arizona and California, grants were of Spanish origin. In Texas, the land belonged to the state and not the federal government; it was cattle country—and remained so.

If cowboys heartily disliked all settlers, they positively hated sheep farmers. These men had as much right as the cattlemen to free grazing, and for many years cowhands believed (quite wrongly) that a glandular secretion from sheeps' hooves made grass unpalatable to cattle. (In fact, sheep did destroy grass—by eating the roots.) Some cowboys were so set against the 'woollies' that they wouldn't wear wool next to their skin, nor eat mutton.

Ranchers laid down 'dead lines' patrolled by cowboys; a shepherd who crossed one of these lines was in danger of being shot. In Wyoming the cattlemen scattered saltpetre around water holes; cattle weren't affected by it, but sheep who tasted it died. Cowboys were so incensed when flocks encroached on 'their' ranges that they sometimes resorted to 'rim-rocking'—driving the sheep over the nearest convenient cliff. In 1884, on the Little Colorado range in Arizona, cowmen drove more than 4,000 sheep into the river. In the same year, in Arizona's San Francisco Mountain country, cowboys rounded up

Barbed wire was patented in 1873, and within a few years ranchers were able to enclose their spreads in hundreds of miles of fencing. The modern West was born: 'Fence Builders' by Peter Hurd

more than 100 wild horses. They strapped cowbells to some, rawhides to the tails of others and, yelling and shooting, drove them into four herds of sheep. Only a few 'woollies' died, but it took the herders a week to gather the terrified animals together and sort them into herds.

The battle between cowboys and sheepmen reached its height in Tonto County, Arizona, in 1887, with the feud between the cattle-raising Graham family and the sheepherding Tewkesburys. It lasted for 15 years, and ended with the death of the last Tewkesbury. The toll was fearsome; 26 men shot and one lynched.

Big business, homesteaders and sheepmen all played their part in ending the cowboy's nomadic existence. Barbed wire was the final blow. Before its coming, cattle had wandered from one range to another, freely and by consent. Disputes about numbers or trespassers were settled amicably among neighbours. Line riders kept constant vigil to prevent the herds mingling. A method of mass-producing barbed wire was patented by Joseph Glidden in Illinois in 1873, and it eventually divided the open range into a chequerboard of huge stock farms, changing the face of the West.

A salesman called John 'Bet-a-Million' Gates demonstrated this new invention to sceptical Texans in San Antonio in 1875. He corralled some lively Longhorns, then challenged all and sundry to stampede them under, over, or through the wire. The Longhorns ran into the barrier every time; they finally refused to stampede.

Barbed wire was cheap, and it was easy to install. By 1883, the Washburne and Moen factory in Illinois was spinning it at the rate of 600 miles of fencing each day. Several ranchers were sent to prison for enclosing land that wasn't theirs. (The Swan Land and Cattle Company put up 175 miles of illegal fencing.) And the new fences led to clashes between large concerns like the XIT Ranch, which enclosed its acres with 781 miles of barbed wire, and small ranchers who saw their range rights disappear, their cattle cut off from water. These clashes culminated in the fence-cutting wars of the 1880s.

By then, the range was divided by a network of railroads and barbed wire fences. Windmills sprang up on the prairies, and water troughs replaced the old waterholes; cowboys no longer had to search for natural sources of water. Trail driving was replaced by railroad shipments, and enclosed pastures were safe havens for improved, and more expensive, breeds of cattle: dollars on the hoof to the new, money-conscious ranchers. Land values soared and cattlemen added to their profits by selling off pieces for town sites. The spirit of adventure was replaced by a sense of business, and by 1900 agriculture was supreme in the West.

Cowboy Country

The land west of the 98th meridian was a harsh, wild region whose challenges and dangers moulded the gritty, self-reliant character of the men who settled it. Roughly 1½ million square miles in area, the West is about the combined size of Britain, France, Germany, Denmark, Holland, Belgium, Austria, Italy, Spain, Portugal and Ireland—plus a substantial slice of European Russia. It can be divided into three parts: the Great Plains, which extend over the western parts of

The West is 1½ million square miles of plains and mountains, deserts and rivers. The men who settled it had to be courageous and tough to overcome the hardships of life on this new frontier: the cattle kingdom

Cowboy Country
CANADA
NTANA
Shelby
NORTH DAKOTA
Williston
Missouri R
Grand Fork
Missoula
Medora
Fargo
Miles City
Billings
Yellowstone R
Butte
Virginia City
SOUTH DAKOTA
AHO
Sheridan
Powder R
WYOMING
Belle Fourche R
Belle Fourche
98th MERIDIAN
St Paul
Minneapolis
WISCONSIN
Mississippi R
MINNESOTA
IOWA
Fort Laramie
Fort Fetterman
Lander
NEBRASKA
Missouri R
UTAH
Cheyenne
Laramie
North Platte R
Ogallala
Platte R
Ogden
Salt Lake City
Julesburg
COLORADO
South Platte R
MISSOURI
Denver
KANSAS
Junction City
Ellsworth
Leavenworth
Leadville
Kansas R
Hays
Kansas City
Topeka
Sedalia
Pueblo
Arkansas R
Abilene
Las Animas
Dodge City
Newton
Wichita
Trinidad
Cimarron R
Caldwell
ARIZONA
NEW MEXICO
OKLAHOMA
TEXAS
North Canadian R
ARKANSAS
Taos
Santa Fe
Fort Union
Canadian R
Arkansas R
Albuquerque
Las Vegas
Red R
Washita R
Fort Sumner
Pecos R
Red River Station
Phoenix
Fort Worth
Dallas
Red R
Tucson
Tombstone
El Paso
N
E
S
MEXICO
Marfa
Houston
Rio Grande
San Antonio
Victoria
Corpus Christi
ULF OF
LIFORNIA
GULF OF MEXICO
Brownsville

Texas, Oklahoma, Kansas and the Dakotas plus the eastern parts of New Mexico, Colorado, Wyoming and Montana; the Rockies, which spread into parts of Colorado, Wyoming and Montana; and the Great Basin and Plateau, which includes Utah, Nevada, Idaho, south-west Texas, New Mexico and most of Arizona.

The terrain was as varied as the men who settled it, but there was one common ingredient: grass, the fuel that fired the cattle industry. The grama grass of the Great Plains dried in winter to form a natural hay. Horse-high in the hollows, it was pale and jointed. Buffalo grass was grey and grew in bunches; bluestem grass was tawny. The grass grew taller in the central Great Plains than in the northern Plains states.

From east to west, the grass changed from tall fronds, to a short thick carpet, to tufts. The grass area was never the same from one year to another: tall grass encroached on short grass in wet seasons, and short on tall when it was dry. One of the higher skills was to be able to 'read the grass' and judge the best pastures.

In *Life on the Range* John Clay described the Little Missouri River country of South Dakota '. . . what a wondrous country it was for grass. There was nothing but grass and then more grass; the blue joint with its ripening heads, good as corn for fattening. Mossy stretches of buffalo grass made unexcelled winter feed. Never before or since have I seen such fat calves, steers, and heifers; all were fat.'

The cowboy had to contend with extremities of climate—broiling, blistering heat in summer and numbing bone-chilling cold in winter: tending a herd in a Western blizzard; photograph by Charles Belden

At particular times in particular places, the West is an idyllic paradise: relaxing in the West Boulder River Valley, Montana

Another witness quoted a stockman who said in 1867, 'The grass was everywhere from one to three feet high, and the range could support 300 head of cattle to the square mile.' (Overgrazing soon put an end to this ranchers' Utopia; only 30 years later, this same witness observed, it was unusual for land to support even one head to every five acres.)

The grass of the Great Basin and Plateau was sparser mesquite grass, intermixed with scrub, sage and cactus. Most of the Great Plains consisted of level tracts of grassland, but it also included highland areas like the Black Hills and the Badlands of Dakota. The Great Basin and Plateau contained vast tracts of desert, great canyons and gorges, and surrealistic buttes (isolated hills) carved out by ancient rivers.

Pioneers of the West encountered weather that spanned the thermometer. Over the year, temperatures in North Dakota can range from a searing 120°F (49°C) to a frigid −60°F (−51°C). And whether the mercury soars or plummets, the winds are constant. On the Great

Plains they blow uniform and high, at a steady 10 to 12 miles an hour, month after month. Then, overnight, they can change to a howling torrent of air that whips up dust and sandstorms in summer, frigid blizzards with temperatures of 30 to 40 degrees below in winter.

'Hang a log chain on a post. If the wind raises it straight in line, it's a calm day; if the links of chain start snapping off, expect rough weather,' was one laconic guide to the weather. A ranch visitor once asked a cowboy, 'Does the wind blow this way here all the time?' 'No, mister,' came the reply, 'it'll maybe blow this way for a week or ten days, and then it'll take a change and blow like hell for a while.'

In the south, summer winds can frizzle crops like a gust from an open furnace. The worst months are usually July and August, when the temperature often soars to 110°F (43°C), but the furnace can build up as early as June and last through September. In the desert, the annual rainfall is sometimes less than five inches. 'It was so dry the bushes followed the dogs around,' remarked one cowboy. Another said, 'If a man died there and went to Hell, he'd wire back for blankets.'

Come September, cowboys in the south awaited the stunning arrival of the 'blue northers'. These winds from the far north could drop the temperature by 50°F (28°C) in the space of a few hours. When this happened, the cowboy scanned the horizon anxiously. If the sky 30 miles away darkened suddenly with a solid sheet of black cloud, a wet norther was on its way. A solid wall of swirling dust a hundred feet high meant a dry norther that would engulf everything before it in choking clouds. Northers sometimes lasted three days—and always closed the furnace door with a bang.

Cowboys of the northern Great Plains faced winter blizzards that lasted for days. With visibility zero and shouts for help muffled by the snow, men caught out on the prairie could freeze to death. The frigid cold, intensified by the howling winds, froze whisky—carried as medicine and cold-beater—in the bottle, and jammed guns fast. Pneumonia was the most common cause of death after riding accidents. Occasionally, the cold weather was interrupted by freak warm winds, 'chinooks' which sent temperatures soaring by as much as 44°F (24°C). Within hours, melting snow turned the ground into a sodden morass. A chinook was often followed by a freeze that transformed the melted water to ice again.

Cowboys were also at the mercy of gigantic thunderstorms that boiled up over the Rockies and the Dakota highlands and, fed by the hot air currents that rose from the Plains, rumbled and flashed their way south. When one of these storms struck, the cowboy had his hands full soothing uneasy cattle, watching for the first signs of a stampede. As the forked lightning came nearer, cowboys threw off their guns, unfastened their spurs, and got rid of any other iron on themselves or their horses. They'd seen the skeletons of men and animals who'd been struck by lightning. Torrential rain sometimes turned the dusty ground into a quagmire; hailstones the size of eggs could beat men and horses to the ground. Storms like these also brought the danger of swollen, swift-running rivers and flash floods that transformed streams into torrents.

Types of grass: little bluestem (right); *curly mesquite* (centre); *black grama* (far right)

Early cattle men inherited a natural bonanza—the grass that grew so lushly in the West: cattle graze in Wyoming

Tough, hardworking and self-reliant, the cowboy's character has changed little over the years: two Cherokee strip cowboys

Danger didn't only come from the elements. The grasslands abounded in poisonous plants—and horses and cattle weren't fussy eaters. It was a real struggle to keep cows from eating the 'wild parsnip' (water hemlock) that grew alongside streams and rivers. Locoweed (*loco* is Spanish for *crazy*) flourished in western Texas, western Oklahoma, New Mexico, western Arizona and southern Colorado. An animal who ate its purple blooms behaved as if drunk, and leapt into the air to avoid imaginary obstacles. Luckily, locoweed doesn't bloom every year, and is at its worst after a wet winter and an early, wet spring—which happens about every seven years. Larkspur was another poisonous danger. Many ranges were out-of-bounds to cattle until August when the larkspur had bloomed and died. The alternative was for the men to pull the plants out by hand—a laborious, never-ending job. In 1930 William MacLeod Raine and Will C. Barnes calculated that total range losses from poisonous plants were about $20 million a year.

A cowboy who saved his stock from the worst the weather and the vegetation had to offer still had to face the animal pests that roamed the range. There were rattlesnakes, wolves, coyotes, prairie dogs, grizzly bears, jaguars, pumas, scorpions, lizards, tarantula spiders, wild cats, lynxes and skunks. Clouds of buffalo gnats and buffalo crickets swarmed all over men and cattle; there were plagues of grasshoppers, disease-carrying mosquitoes, centipedes and ticks.

The Texan diamond back is the king of rattlesnakes. Often as thick as a man's arm and eight to ten feet long, its bite means painful death. A cowboy who'd shot one treasured its skin and often wore it as a hatband. In the north, grizzlies abounded in the mountain areas; once one had developed a taste for sheep or cow meat, it became a menace. Hunts were organized and a bounty offered for its skin. Occasionally a grizzly was so notorious that cowboys spent what little spare time they had hunting it down—and celebrated the killing with a feast.

The puma (also called the cougar or mountain lion) generally attacked colts; the wild cat and lynx killed only sheep. Wolves were probably the cowboy's deadliest animal enemy. Savage and clever, they seem to know when poisoned bait has been laid. They were most common in the timber lands of the northern mountains, but roamed as far south as New Mexico.

Out in the West, small didn't mean safe. Skunks and coyotes, for instance, carried rabies. No antidote was discovered until 1885, and in a single summer in the Dodge City and Hays City area of Kansas there were 30 fatal cases of rabies caused by skunk bites. The grey, burrowing squirrels known as prairie dogs were the West's most numerous pests. In 1901, in Texas, 800 million of them ate as much grass as 3,125,000 head of cattle. Spur Ranch records registered $70,000 spent on poison to annihilate them. The jack rabbit, a hare that 'eats as much as a horse' was a particular nuisance in California, where 494,634 were killed in organized drives from 1888 to 1897.

The old West is now just a memory, but its traditions live on. More than a hundred years have gone by since the first cowboy rode the range—years of technological developments that would astonish the men who founded the cattle industry. But the cowboy's life has changed surprisingly little. Today he still tends cattle for a living, and rides the remote pastures and plains of the West. And independence and freedom are as precious to him as to his forebears.

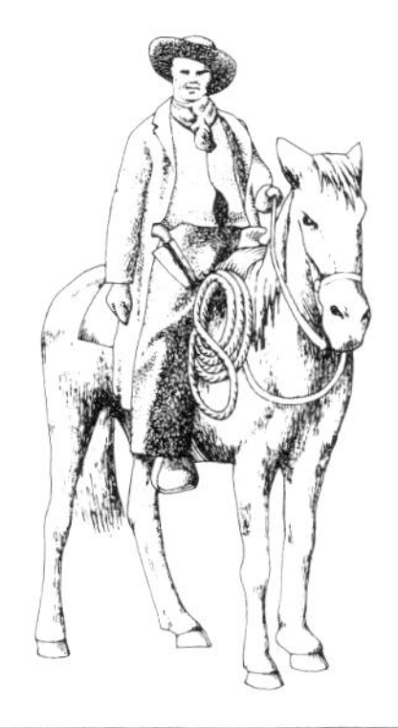

The Long Drive

'Trail driving was the peak of a cowboy's experience. There was hardly a tough young Texan who didn't long to "go up the trail" and participate in exploring his country.'

In the 20 years from 1866 to 1886, America witnessed an annual series of events of improbable and epic proportions—the long cattle drives. These journeys through hardship took place across the rolling plains, raging rivers and unforgiving weather that separates Texas from the Kansas territory. Thousands of herds were driven up to 1,500 miles from the Lone Star State to the railroad shipping stations of Kansas, bound eventually for the dinner plates of Chicago and New York. From a comparative trickle of a few thousand, the torrent of mobile beef swelled to nearly a million head in 1871 and earned the ranchers millions of dollars in that year alone. The flood continued unabated despite market slump and cattle loss until the natural laws of commercial progress combined with natural disaster and brought the drives inevitably to an end.

During this 20 years more than five million head of cattle were driven over some of the world's harshest and most varied terrain, often through some of the world's worst weather. About 30,000 cowboys took part in these drives, and death from disease (pneumonia was the most common), riding accidents, lightning bolts and other tricks of fate and nature was no stranger to them.

Trail driving was the peak of a cowboy's experience. There was hardly a tough, lean and raw young Texan who didn't long to 'go up the trail'—and, along the way, to outwit or outgun his first hostile Indians, see his first railroad head and cow town, and participate in exploring his virgin country. In the space of four months, the many hardships, the tragedies and beauty, the brushes with death and the comradeship of the trail turned boys into men and seasoned trail bosses into philosophers.

The trail boss was responsible for driving as many as 3,000 head of cattle safely—and profitably—across the American West

Trail drivers were mostly sons of the Lone Star State. They were, said cattle entrepreneur Joseph McCoy, clannish and shrewd, loyal to their comrades, and free spenders. They had a strong sense of justice and their word was their bond. Another observer described

Stampedes were the cowboy's greatest challenge. Once a herd had scattered he might have to ride 15 miles to retrieve just one head: 'Stampede' by Robert Lindneux

them as looking like 'a species of centaur, half horse, half man, with immense rattling spurs, tanned skin and dare-devil, almost ferocious faces'. Yet others say they were wild, ribald and hot-tempered, heavy drinkers and tobacco chewers. All agree that they were loyal and straightforward.

Cattle baron and pioneer trail blazer Charles Goodnight wrote: 'If a man was trained to it and liked to work, it was glorious work.' But a cowboy needed more than training. He needed natural reserves of courage, loyalty and patience. He had to be able to work 18 hours a day, seven days a week. He had to survive Arctic blizzards that could plaster him to the saddle. He had to work in temperatures of over 100°F (38°C), blistered and blackened by the sun, sweat-soaked in a dust storm, sucking a bullet to soothe his thirst. He had to live in mud-caked clothes and sleep under wet blankets, ignoring the wail of the prairie winds.

At all times he had to put his cows and his comrades before himself. He had to be able to read the stars, know how to locate water and cure a crippled steer. He had to have the courage to stop a stampede of plunging, maddened cattle, outface hostile Indians and fight off angry farmers. For all these qualities, at the end of a three- or four-month drive he received $100. After he had bought new clothes and spent a week in the dance halls, saloons and gambling dens of Dodge City, Abilene or Wichita he was lucky if he had enough money to go back home to Texas.

Goodnight admitted the debt he owed his cowboys: 'I wish I could find words to describe the companionship and loyalty of the men towards each other,' he wrote. 'It is beyond imagination. They were as brave and chivalrous as it is possible to be. Bullies and tyrants were unknown. They kept their places round a herd under all circumstances. If they had to fight, they were always ready. Timid men were not known among them—the life did not fit them.'

Texas was 'lousy with cows' before the drives north started. (The ranchers were called the 'cattle poor'—they had the herds, but were

1
2
3
4
6
7
8
1 Frank Pierce
2 Jim Gorman
3 Unidentified
4 Bob Drennan
OLD TIME COWBOY GROUP, 188
Photo was made at San Angelo,

Trail drivers were tough, skilful and daring: they were also very young: cowboys photographed in Texas, 1884

unable to sell them.) Even before the Lone Star State became independent in 1836, the year-round lush grasslands were reckoned to support six cows for every one human being. The main trade then was in tallow, hides and horns to the north, and beef to Missouri and New Orleans in the east.

There were some trail drives in those early days. Ranchers took their cattle up through Tennessee and Kentucky to the east in the 1820s and 1830s, and to California in the 1840s. In 1846, Edward Piper pushed 1,000 head all the way to Ohio. Ten years later he took a herd to Chicago. Tom Candy Ponting went even further. In 1852 he drove 700 head to Indiana, and went with them in box cars to New Jersey. Two years later he pushed a herd from Texas clear across the country and into the cattle pens of inner New York City. Other pioneers set their sights on different destinations. A rancher named Dawson drove a herd to the Colorado gold fields in 1859, and in the same year Harry Hunter took 1,200 head to Omaha on a government contract.

The long drives north started in earnest in 1866. During the four years of the Civil War, between 1861 and 1865, the herds of Texan cattle had increased mightily, and though some Longhorns were driven to feed the Confederate Army and others were skinned for leather, by the end of the war the total had swollen to 3,100,000 head. Of these, two out of three were mavericks—unbranded and unclaimed grazers on the open range. The ranchers culled these animals and branded them with their own marks.

With the South demoralized, Mexico impoverished and no other markets ready to hand, Texan ranchers were forced to look farther afield. Most of the big ranchers—men like George Slaughter, Abel Pierce and Dudley Snyder—turned north to the developing urban markets of the Midwestern and Eastern cities. Some, like Goodnight and his partner Oliver Loving, chose to try the gold mines in Colorado and the military posts that burgeoned to the west in New Mexico and Colorado. Goodnight knew that 7,000 Navaho Indians were held captive by the army in Fort Sumner, New Mexico—and they had to be fed.

The partners set off with 2,000 head and a mobile kitchen laden with water barrels and drawn by ten oxen—the first chuckwagon. Warlike Comanche along the trail were a threat, and to avoid them Goodnight first drove south. Here he met the real obstacle—a waterless, 96-mile stretch of bone-dry desert that stretched from the Middle Concho to the Pecos River. Three days there turned the cattle into stumbling, gaunt skeletons; the horses were little better. By the fourth morning all the water barrels were empty. But the Pecos River lay just ahead. The weary cattle smelled the water and ran the last 12 miles to salvation. Goodnight rested the herd and his cowboys by the river for a few days and later sold the steers at Fort Sumner and points beyond for a large profit.

This was the start of the Goodnight-Loving trail, and in blazing it two lessons had been learnt: lack of water wasn't an insuperable obstacle (only 300 cattle were lost in the desert crossing), and markets for beef were wide open to bold cattlemen.

The long drives to the north tested the endurance of men and cattle; those 'journeys through hardship' are now part of America's legendary past, but the country itself is much the same

Joseph McCoy: cattle dealer and entrepreneur. he established the first railhead at Abilene and opened the floodgates to a torrent of men. cattle and horses

While Goodnight and Loving went south-west, Nelson Story drove north on the longest-ever cattle drive—nearly 2,000 miles. Story, who'd tried his luck in the Montana gold fields without success, realized that there were profits to be made in fresh meat. He made his way to Texas, rounded up 600 head and drove north to Baxter Springs, Kansas, in the spring of 1866. But the locals were hostile, and he decided to make for Montana and test the market potential of the mining camps. He finally reached Fort Laramie in Wyoming, then headed for Fort Phil Kearny—only to find himself in the midst of a full-scale Indian uprising. The army commander forbade him to go farther. Story asked his riders to vote on whether they should disobey the order or stay; all but one voted to drive on.

They moved silently out on the night of 21 October and headed through Sioux territory. Although the Sioux were on the warpath, only one cowboy was killed and two seriously wounded—thanks to the new, rapid-fire Remington rifles they carried. Travelling by night and grazing by day, Story and his men reached Virginia City, Montana, on 9 December.

Nelson Story wasn't the only cattleman to come into conflict with the Indians. Hostile tribes poised on the borders of Oklahoma (then called Indian Territory) and Texas were a constant danger on the early drives. During a Goodnight drive in 1867 one of the herders had an arrow driven through his neck when Comanche attacked the herd; Goodnight pulled it out again with a pair of pincers. 'Jay-hawkers'—federal soldiers turned homesteaders who'd settled in the Ozark Mountains, Missouri and Kansas—were also hostile. They were named after the pro-Union marauders who'd rampaged through the territories before the Civil War and resented the Confederate cowboys' incursions into their land. Some were robbers and cattle thieves who levied money from trail bosses in return for the herd's safe passage.

Nelson Story: cattleman and pioneer. he faced hostile Sioux to drive his herd to Montana. He eventually made a fortune of about half a million dollars—and invested his money in city property

Drivers were also hindered by armed farmers who feared that Texas fever (or Southern or Spanish fever) would ruin their stock. The Longhorns carried the tick that transmitted the disease, and although the Texan cattle were immune this didn't apply to local cattle who used the same bedground or feed. By 1867, parts of Missouri and Kansas had passed quarantine laws that made it difficult to market Longhorns. These laws were often enforced by vigilante bands of local farmers or grangers, gritty, self-reliant Yankees intent on carving out new lives for themselves after the Civil War. As a result the trail drives had to veer west—'Bend 'em West, boys' was a common command when a herd entered Kansas.

Railroads were still in their infancy when the drives began. Only the Union Pacific had pushed its iron tracks to the edge of the Plains, and the herders had to trail farther east than they wished. The first drives in 1866 crossed the Red River, then went past Fort Smith, Arkansas, then north to Baxter Springs, and Sedalia on the Missouri Pacific railroad. That year 270,000 head were moved—and all arrived at St Louis, Missouri, their ultimate destination, in poor condition.

The Texans were discouraged by their first year's efforts, and it took an adventurous young cattle dealer from Chicago to add beef

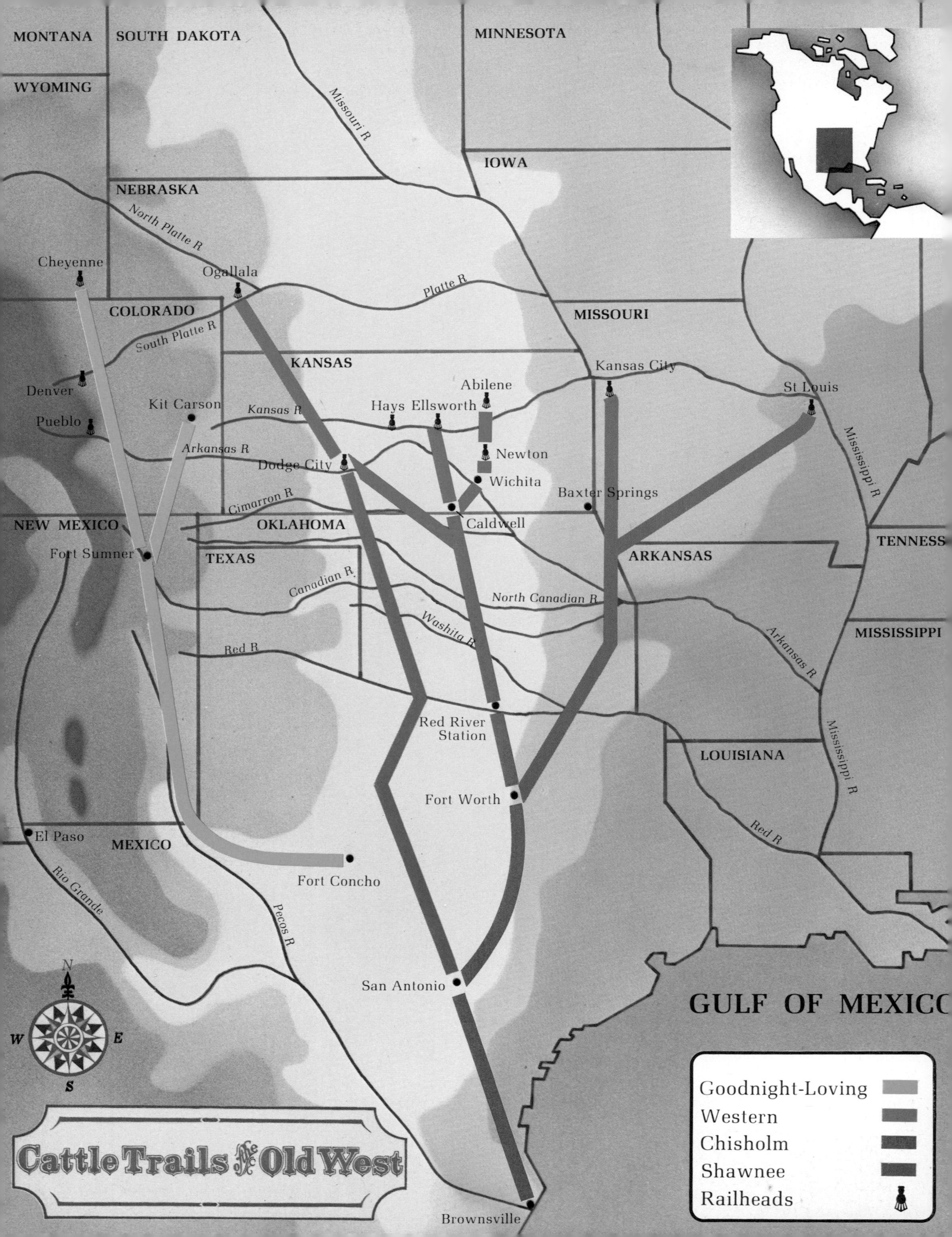
Cattle Trails of the Old West
MONTANA
SOUTH DAKOTA
MINNESOTA
WYOMING
Missouri R
IOWA
NEBRASKA
North Platte R
Cheyenne
Ogallala
Platte R
COLORADO
MISSOURI
South Platte R
KANSAS
Kansas City
Abilene
St Louis
Denver
Kit Carson
Kansas R
Hays
Ellsworth
Pueblo
Newton
Mississippi R
Arkansas R
Dodge City
Wichita
Baxter Springs
Cimarron R
Caldwell
NEW MEXICO
OKLAHOMA
TENNESS
Fort Sumner
TEXAS
ARKANSAS
Canadian R
North Canadian R
Washita R
MISSISSIPPI
Red R
Arkansas R
Red River
Station
Mississippi R
LOUISIANA
Fort Worth
El Paso
MEXICO
Red R
Fort Concho
Rio Grande
Pecos R
San Antonio
GULF OF MEXICO
N
W
E
S
Goodnight-Loving
Western
Chisholm
Shawnee
Railheads
Brownsville

The trails were 'highways' along which the cattle were driven from Texas to the railheads at Dodge City, Kansas City, Cheyenne and other cow towns.

The main trail north was the Chisholm trail, blazed by an eccentric half-Scots, half-Cherokee stockman and trader from Texas. For 600 miles it ranged over mountain and valley, beaten into the bare earth by millions of hooves. The trail often sank below the level of the surrounding ground, was only 200 to 400 yards wide in places—and was scattered with the bleached bones of man, steer and horse.

When Dodge City became the cattle capital, the Chisholm threw off a western offshoot before Caldwell that took it straight to Dodge. It ran in a straight line from the point where it entered Kansas to the shipping station—and was signposted.

The other trail was the Shawnee which led mainly from Texas to Baxter Springs and Kansas City. The Goodnight-Loving trail went west through Texas, then through New Mexico and Colorado to Cheyenne in Wyoming. The Western trail, between the Chisholm and the Goodnight-Loving, led from Texas to Dodge City and Ogallala. Some individualists made their way across country, but these trails took the vast bulk of the herds during the years of the long drive.

to rail and make sense and money. Joseph McCoy realized that the herds should meet the railroad west of the quarantine area of Kansas and Missouri—where they would also be clear of the jayhawkers, and nearer to Texas. Typical of the forceful entrepreneurs who were to bring big business to the West, he declared: 'If I can make money out of the Texas trade, I'm not afraid of Texas fever, but if I can't, I'm damned afraid of it.'

McCoy set out to find a suitable site for a railhead. At first he was unsuccessful. The citizens of Solomon City and Salina turned his proposition down flat. Then he asked officials of the Kansas Pacific and Missouri Pacific railroads to back him. Both boards declined at first, but when he finally decided on Abilene, 165 miles west of Kansas City, the Kansas Pacific agreed to put in a switchline. The actual shipment of cattle was the responsibility of the small-time Hannibal & St Joe line that ran to Chicago.

McCoy hired gangs of workmen to erect sidings and pens big enough to hold 120,000 head. And with typical forethought he despatched a lone rider to contact the Texas trail herders as they wandered dispiritedly in search of a buyer for their cattle, and 'sell' them Abilene.

The first herd into Abilene was brought by a rancher named Thompson, and on 5 September 1867 the first 20 rail wagons rolled out towards Chicago. That night, ranchers, bankers and stockmen sat down to a gigantic celebration arranged by McCoy. But even he couldn't have foreseen the tide of cattle, cowboys and commerce he'd released. Within three months, 1,000 wagons had left for the East with 36,000 cattle on board. The ranchers were delighted with this arrangement—and so were McCoy, the railroad and the increasingly prosperous citizens of Abilene.

From now on the horned armies descended on Abilene. In 1868, 75,000 head were shipped out; in 1869, 350,000 head; and in 1870, 300,000. The Chisholm trail was crammed for many miles with separate herds moving close behind each other under a pall of trail dust. In 1871, an unparalleled 700,000 head of cattle arrived at Abilene; another 400,000 went to Baxter Springs and Junction City. But providence had been tempted. That year's glut lowered prices disastrously. In Wichita, herds were sold for losses of between $7,000 and $10,000—and worse was to come. The frosts of the winter of 1871/72 were exceptionally severe, and herds were savagely depleted. Out of one herd of 4,000 cattle, only 100 lived through the winter. Nevertheless the ranchers made some profit by skinning the dead beasts for hides.

Abilene's bad year coincided with a new railroad link. The Atchison, Topeka and Santa Fe railroad bisected the Chisholm trail south and west of Abilene at Newton, and the new railhead rapidly took over Abilene's trade. (It also gained a reputation as the wickedest town in America—'There ain't no Sundays west of Newton.') Wichita, just south of Newton, also began to take a big share of the trade; 450,000 cattle were shipped from its pens in 1873. Julesburg, Ellsworth, Hays City, Ogallala, Cheyenne and Laramie also burgeoned into boom towns as the railroads moved ever west.

Dodge City, Kansas

For the first few months of their existence, cow towns were rip-roaring places where cowboys could relax and let off steam. But local tradesmen and their wives, in league with local preachers and homesteaders who disliked cowboys and cattle, soon put their moral foot firmly down.

The towns were divided into respectable and disreputable areas. In Abilene, for example, 'low life' was confined to Texas-Abilene, named in honour of the Texan cowhands. Tascoosa's seamier side was known as Hogtown. Caldwell, Ellsworth and Dodge City also had their 'pink light' districts; brothels were on the extreme outskirts of the towns.

In 1870 the citizens of Abilene formed a local chapter of the Independent Order of Good Templars, and charged brothel and casino owners a minimum licence fee of $100. In Dodge City there was violence between card-sharps, pimps and prostitutes, and the town's do-gooders. The businessmen, 'decent' women and the self-styled Law and Order League won. In Caldwell in 1881, saloons and gambling rooms were banned, and in the same year Kansas went officially dry. It was a victory for Carrie Nation, a granite-jawed, strong-minded fighter for temperance; her strategy included charges into saloons where she smashed bottles—and sang 'John Brown's Body'.

In 1872 the Atchison, Topeka and Santa Fe reached Dodge City. This 'beautiful, bibulous Babylon of the Plains' became, and remained, the acknowledged centre of cattle shipments until the era ended in 1886. In Dodge's first violent years as a cow town 64 men were buried on Boot Hill, the town's cemetery. It was always, as one cowpuncher said, 'a town with the hair on'; imported lawmen like Wyatt Earp, 'Bat' Masterson and Luke Short could never tame it.

Although Dodge became the favourite place for trail hands to let off steam at the end of an arduous drive, cattle owners complained that they lost more cows to the friendly, local Tonkawa Indians than to all the raiders and rustlers of the hostile tribes in Indian territory. The Tonkawas believed that the cattle were restitution by the gods for the vanished buffalo, and gratefully appropriated these gifts.

Not all the beef went straight to market. Herds were also sold to farmers in the northern Plain states of Iowa and Illinois, and the big ranchers regularly drove cattle to Wyoming and Montana to fatten them on these states' excellent pastures. Colorado, too, was splendid grazing country. Longhorns trailed up from Texas put on as much as 200 lb in one season—on pastures that cost the rancher nothing.

Most of these cattle were eventually destined for the abattoirs of Kansas City, Omaha and Chicago. The first wagon-loads rolled east to join the Abilene shipments in 1869.

But even as the bonanza years rolled on (in 1882, Texas steers sold for $6.80 per 100 lb), the range was changing. Barbed wire reached the prairies in the early 1880s and inevitably the farmers and ranchers who settled along the trails used it to enclose their grazing. Townships sprang up and small farmers planted wheat on the old ranges. Although they were known, disparagingly, as 'fool hoe men', their settlements reduced the amount of free grazing land. The trails were no longer wide open; trail driving was on its way out.

There were other, even more significant, developments. After 20 years of popularity, the stringy Texan Longhorns were beginning to lose their market appeal to the growing herds of Shorthorn beef that grazed the Great Plains. Cattle ranching was becoming standardized and structured throughout the region, and the Texas ranchers found it increasingly difficult to act on the old, swashbuckling, *laissez-faire* principle. Lastly, the railroads were beginning to track into Texas, and so bring direct transport to the doorsteps of the ranches.

The final blow was the winter of 1886/87, the Big Die-Up. Ranches reported losses as high as 95 per cent and scores went out of business; one trail boss was paid off with 75 cents at the shipping station after all his horses and all but a handful of his cattle had died. Some herds continued to struggle up the trails from Texas to Dodge and Wichita. But year by year the trickle diminished. By 1891 the profit from the stockyards was drying up. The trail of the Longhorns was moving towards its close.

During the peak years of the long drive, most big ranches and cattle companies drove north every year, sometimes in the autumn but usually in the spring when the herds could keep pace with the ripening grasslands—called 'travelin' with the grass'. The most manageable—and profitable—size for a herd was 2,500 to 3,000 head, but some were as small as 500. A herd of 2,500 required eight to ten cowboys—one to every 250 head—a trail boss, his number two (the *segundo* or 'straw boss'), a wrangler and the cook. The wrangler was responsible for the *remuda*, a herd of 80 to 125 spare saddle horses which the trail hands used by rota. Before leaving on a drive the hands signed an article of agreement. The one that bound Charles Goodnight's men laid down, among other conditions, that if a man shot another on the trail he would be judged by his fellows—and hanged on the spot, if found guilty.

Cattle selected for the drive were cut out from the ranch herds in the morning. Calves were sometimes allowed to accompany their mothers; mother love often took the steam out of a 'spooking' herd. Sometimes, too, other ranches sent some of their steers to join the drive. In the early years the herds were a mixture of yearlings, calves and hoary old steers. Any animal the 'brushpoppers'—cowboys who rounded up the maverick Longhorns—managed to rope was sent up the trail. The market demand eventually levelled out at choice four-year-old steers—but even so the herds were usually well mixed. The cattle were given a road brand, and the herd then moved off; 2,500 to

FIFTY-SECOND ANNIVERSARY

I. O. O. F.

AT THE

DROVERS COTTAGE,

ABILENE, KANSAS,

WEDNESDAY, APRIL 26, 1871.

BILL OF FARE.

SOUP.
Oyster.

ROAST.
Beef. Turkey and Cranberry Sauce.

BOILED.
English Leg of Mutton and Caper Sauce.
Turkey and Oyster Sauce,
Ham,
Tongue.

ENTREES.
Chicken Salad, Escalloped Oysters.
Pigeon Pie. Oyster Pies.

GAME
Woodcock. Quail Larded. Partridge Larded.

RELISHES
Lettuce, Pickles, London Club Sauce,
Cranberry Sauce, Beets, Cucumbers,
Worcestershire Sauce, Horse Radish.

VEGETABLES
Sweet Potatoes. Green Peas.
Irish do Tomatoes. Turnips.
Mashed do Corn. Squash.

PASTRY.
Plum Pudding. Apple Pie.
Blanc Mange. Raspberry Pie.
Squash Pie. Peach Tarts.
Raspberry Tarts. Lady Fingers.
Charlotte Russe. Cranberry Sauce.
Fancy Cake.

DESSERT
Oranges. Apples.
Filberts. Walnuts.
Raisins. Almonds.
Strawberry and Vanilla Ice Cream.
Chocolate, Tea, Coffee.

Chronicle Print.

Abilene boomed as the cattle trailed in to its railhead: menu for a celebration held at the Drover's Cottage in 1871

3,000 head would string out into a line about three-quarters of a mile long, and 50 to 60 feet wide. When they slowed to graze the cattle spread out into an arrowhead with a base a mile wide.

The trail drivers always watched for a dominant steer to emerge as the natural herd leader. Old Blue, who led many Goodnight herds, was treated like a pet, fed cookies by the camp fire—and travelled back to Texas in a private box car. When he died his huge spreading horns were mounted on the wall of Goodnight's office.

For the first 14 days the cattle were herded at a rate of 20 to 30 miles a day to get them 'trail broken'. The harder they were driven, the less chance they had to translate nervousness into trouble. It was at this stage that awkward cows who were forever spooking were killed for food, or were sold. The cowboys themselves were eager to get into the hard country and out of settled Texas. 'Civilization and cows just don't mix' was their motto.

When the drive crossed the Red River at Doan's Crossing or Preston Bend near Dennison, the cowboys collected their mail and checked their gear for the long haul through Indian Territory, the hunting grounds of the Cherokee, Chocktaw and Chickasaw tribes. From now on the grass was to get shorter, the work harder, the

Doan's Store on the Red River was a trading post and post office, and the cowboy's last chance to collect mail and buy provisions before the haul through Indian Territory: photograph, 1889

weather fiercer. But this was the time the cowboys loved best. The real drive had started.

No two days were quite the same, although the framework was unaltered. At about three in the morning the cook woke the sleepers with hot black coffee, meat, dried fruit and sourdough bread. After breakfast the trail boss rode off to look for water holes on either side of the trail, and to select the next camp site. But before he went, he and another man counted off the cattle, dropping a pebble or coin into their pockets for every 100 head. Widely differing totals meant they they had to start again. Once the trail boss had decided on the next evening's camp site, the cook and his chuckwagon followed.

The herd was allowed to graze at leisure in the morning, then turned onto the trail for a steady walk of eight to ten miles—timed to arrive at the new camp at about five o'clock. Each trail hand had his position on the column—and he kept to it like a soldier going into battle. At either side of the head of the column were two *point* or *lead* riders, the most seasoned men in the outfit. They scouted, tested fords, and directed the cattle; they made sure the dominant lead animals kept to a pace suitable for the rest of the column. These riders changed sides every morning.

At the start of a trail, drivers waited for a dominant steer to emerge and lead the herd: cattle following a bull across a stream

Moments of relaxation were rare on the trail. Even during the night cowboys took turns to guard the cattle: hands eating their dinner; photograph by L. A. Huffman

Behind the point riders came the *swing* men, who took the place of a point rider if he rode ahead. The *flank* riders were next. These men rode close to the herd to make the cattle move faster; to slow them down, they moved slightly out. Swing and flank men rode more miles a day than anybody else on the trail; their job was to patrol the column constantly, drive stragglers back, and scare off foreign cattle.

At the rear were the *drag* or *tail* drivers whose job was to 'keep the corners'. With rope and whip they forced weak tail-enders to keep pace, and kept the column orderly. Usually novices, the drag riders lived in a permanent cloud of trail dust, 'eatin' drag dirt'. Another of their jobs was to stop the cattle from bunching. Steers jammed together generated heat which lost them pounds in weight.

After the long day on the trail, the cowboys turned the cattle off to graze again around the camp site, in the early twilight. As darkness gathered, they gradually worked the animals into a compact mass on a bedground and waited patiently until they settled down.

The bedground was chosen with great care. Off the trail proper, it was a good distance from ravines and washouts—and from timber. It was not unknown for a cow to take refuge in a thicket and furiously fight the cowboy who tried to move it. One cowboy, threatened by a cow that tried to gore him when he tried to dislodge it from a thicket, killed it with a stone. When he was accused by the trail boss of killing the cow he pleaded self-defence—and was acquitted. Dry, high ground made the ideal bedground. Here the cattle were cooled by breezes and could be rid of plaguing insects.

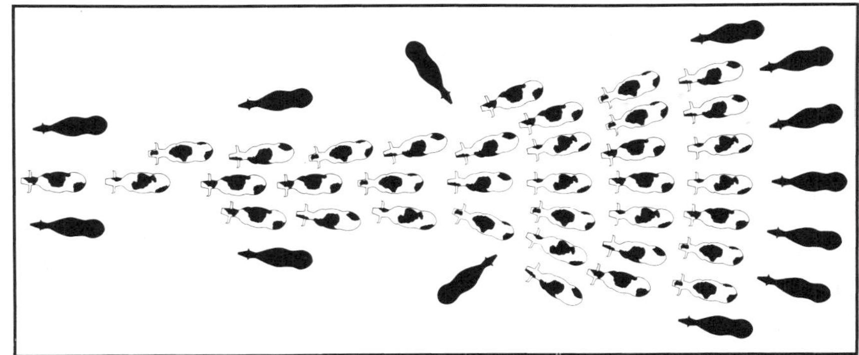

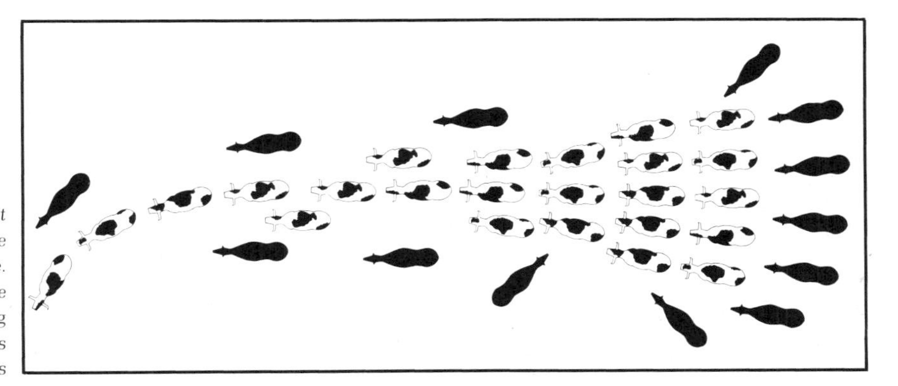

Every cowboy on a drive knew his position, and kept to it like a soldier going into battle (Above) On the trail the point riders accompany the lead cattle, followed by the swing men. Behind them are the flank riders and, at the end of the line, the drag riders. (Right) To change direction, a point man rides on one side of the leading animals

If the cows had been well watered and fed they settled quietly and easily enough—for about four hours. Then they would get up, wander about for a few minutes, and settle down again—lying on their other sides. During the night, the night herders circled the herd in opposite directions, crooning softly to the cattle if the animals seemed restless; for some reason hymns always seemed to be popular with the animals.

Before the camp bedded down, the trail boss fixed his direction by the North Star and pointed the chuckwagon tongue in the direction set for the next day. This was known as 'following the tongue'. Next morning the lead steers would be 'headed up', or pointed in the right direction, and the herd strung out. Another day of grazing and walking the cattle to the next night's camp site would follow. The choice of camp site and watering-place was all-important; as Charles Goodnight said, 'The science of the trail is in grazin' and waterin' the cattle, but the waterin' is the most important of the two.'

Every man except the cook and the wrangler took his turn on night duty. (Some big outfits had permanent night riders or 'hawks' who allowed the day men to enjoy uninterrupted sleep; but this was a rare luxury.) The first guard from sundown to eight o'clock was called the 'killpecker' or 'bobtail' guard; the midnight to 2 am shift was known as the 'graveyard', and the last watch before sun-up the 'cocktail' guard. This last shift was the most disliked because there was no rest period for the guards afterwards. Few cowboys owned watches, and the passing of the hours was calculated by the position of the constellation of the Plough.

The night herder's worst fear was a stampede. Sudden and violent, there was little warning of its coming. Anything—or nothing—could spook a herd: a clap of distant thunder, the clanking of a spur, a crackling twig on the camp fire, the whinny of a horse. Seasoned trail hands reckoned that two-year-old heifers were the most nervous, and most likely to spook. Once spooked, the whole herd would move in a split second, in unison and with explosive violence, 'jarring the earth like an earthquake'. Cattle that were apparently resting peacefully on the ground would leap straight onto all four feet like cats—and take off.

Cowboy Frank Collinson wrote how 'distant thunder could be heard and phosphorus would shine on the long horns of the cattle and on the horses' ears. Then we knew a storm was brewing. Suddenly like a streak of lightning every steer jumped to its feet and was away on the run. The entire herd seemed to move like one animal.' Charles M. Harger described other causes of a stampede: 'A flash of lightning, a crackling stick, a wolf's howl, little things in themselves, but in a moment every horned head was lifted, and the mass of hair and horns, with fierce, frightened eyes gleaming like thousands of emeralds, was off.'

The cry 'Boys, the cattle's running' got sleeping cowboys onto their saddles in a matter of seconds, to ride hell-for-leather after the bucking sea of maddened steers. 'The noise of the stampeding hooves was engulfing,' said one seasoned trail hand. 'It sounded like hell migratin' on cartwheels.'

In the days of the open range water was free to all comers. Well-watered cattle bedded down amenably: 'Longhorns Watering on a Cattle Drive' by Sanchez y Tapia

The trail boss rode ahead of the herd in the early morning to select the night's camp site. Later he returned to watch over the cattle: 'The Trail Boss' by Edward Borein

The cowboys on their sure-footed saddle ponies tried to turn the head of the thundering column into a U-shape. Then by whooping and hitting out with their ropes they forced the cattle into a circle. The bellowing steers, 'revolving with lightning ferocity', would mill themselves to an exhausted standstill and stand shivering. The weary cowboys, plastered with mud, had to stand guard for the remainder of the night—and pick up strays from a radius of up to 15 miles. In 1871 a sudden storm spooked several large herds waiting to cross the Red River. Thirty thousand head and 6,000 horses stampeded, and it took 300 cowboys ten days to sort them out. A herd that had stampeded was never taken back to its old bedground because it would inevitably spook again.

It was a favourite trick of Indians and settled farmers to stampede herds—in broad daylight—so that they could pick off the strays. Even if the trail boss paid them the levies that they demanded—usually of ten cents a head—this was no guarantee of peace. Another trick was to stampede the herd during the night, then ride into camp in the morning and offer to retrieve the strays at a dollar a head. 'I knew they had done it,' said one trail boss, 'so I paid them just 50 cents each.' Aside from their nuisance value, stampedes reduced the value of the cattle when they reached their journey's end; a steer could lose as much as 50 lb in weight in a long stampede.

Stampedes were the cowboys' greatest challenge. When they finally stopped the plunging cattle—after hours of riding at breakneck speed, in imminent danger of being trampled to death—they were the happiest men on earth.

When the drive reached a river or water hole, the cattle were cut out into small groups, or herded along the banks. Cattle could smell water from miles away, and if the drive had been dry for some days the trail hands had all their work cut out to prevent the herd from massing together on the banks and muddying the water. If the banks were steep, huge 'dugways' were cut down to the water's edge.

River crossings could be dangerous for man and beast. High waters, quicksand that dragged men, horses and cattle down, undercurrents: these were some of the hazards. There were many treacherous streams between San Antonio, Texas, and Abilene, Kansas. The Red River could be a torrent a mile wide even when the nearby Colorado was easy to cross. The Washita and the North Canadian were narrow but swift-flowing. The Cimarron had an especially bad reputation because of its quicksand. A cloudburst at the head of any of the rivers sent water down in solid sheets that made them impossible to swim. One cowboy told how he camped one night on the bank of a stream and woke the next morning to find that it had risen 19 feet. Flooding (when the water was 'over the willows') could delay a drive for days; as many as 20 outfits might have to wait at a crossing until the water subsided.

Flooded or not, the water was sometimes too deep for the herd to wade through. Some bigger drives carried flat-bottomed scows on their chuckwagons, and floated food, bedding and equipment across on these. In smaller outfits, the men had to carry the equipment when they—together with the horses and cattle—swam the river. A couple

A flooded river could delay an outfit for days, and even when conditions were ideal skill and persistence were needed to urge the cattle into the water (Above) *Crossing Powder River; photograph by L. A. Huffman* (Below) *A herd wades across the Rio Grande*

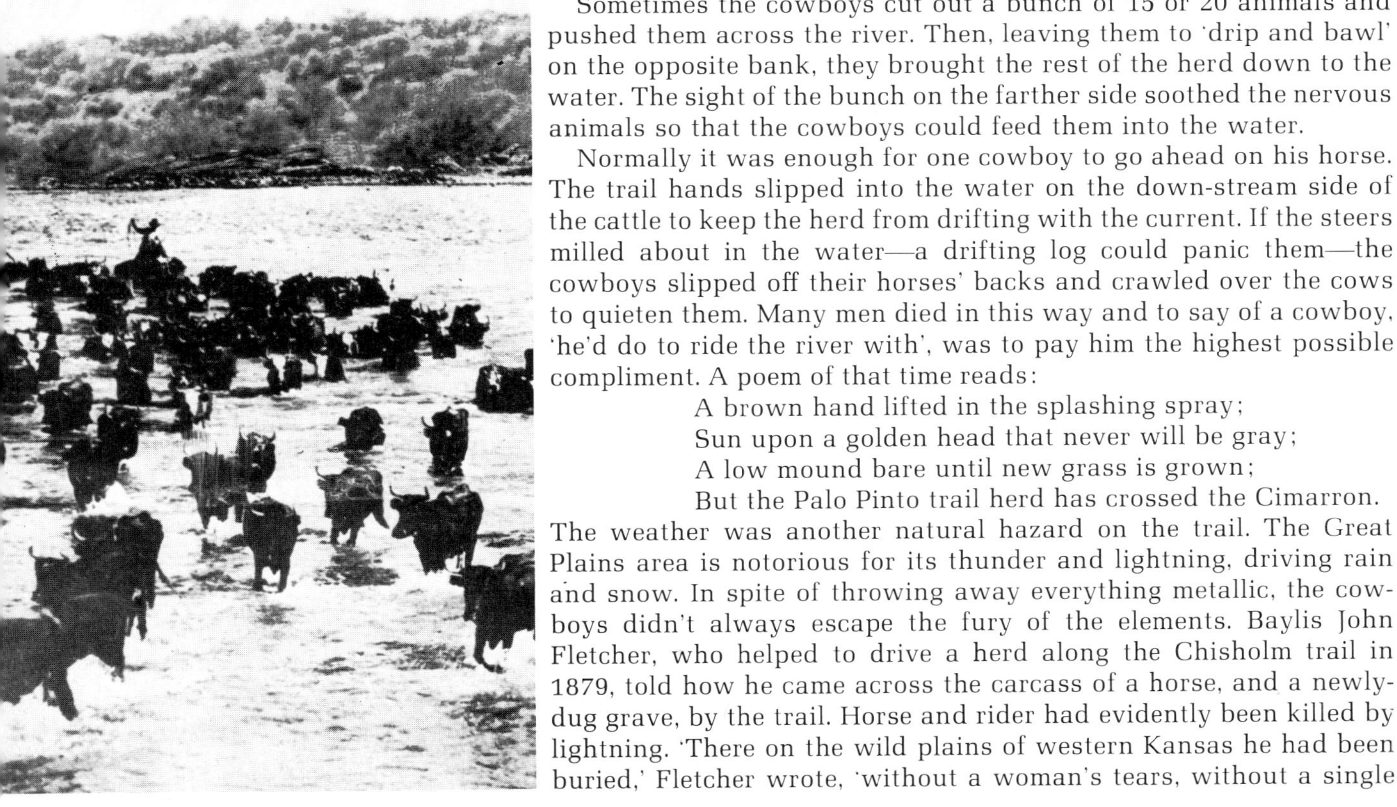

of big cottonwood logs would be lashed to each side of the all-important chuckwagon to float it across safely.

If the cattle were scared for any reason (they might baulk because the sun in their eyes prevented them from seeing the opposite bank), the remuda was driven across before the lead steer; cattle always follow horses. Two men stayed at the head of the herd to keep it moving, and the men behind stopped the cattle turning back.

Sometimes the cowboys cut out a bunch of 15 or 20 animals and pushed them across the river. Then, leaving them to 'drip and bawl' on the opposite bank, they brought the rest of the herd down to the water. The sight of the bunch on the farther side soothed the nervous animals so that the cowboys could feed them into the water.

Normally it was enough for one cowboy to go ahead on his horse. The trail hands slipped into the water on the down-stream side of the cattle to keep the herd from drifting with the current. If the steers milled about in the water—a drifting log could panic them—the cowboys slipped off their horses' backs and crawled over the cows to quieten them. Many men died in this way and to say of a cowboy, 'he'd do to ride the river with', was to pay him the highest possible compliment. A poem of that time reads:

> A brown hand lifted in the splashing spray;
> Sun upon a golden head that never will be gray;
> A low mound bare until new grass is grown;
> But the Palo Pinto trail herd has crossed the Cimarron.

The weather was another natural hazard on the trail. The Great Plains area is notorious for its thunder and lightning, driving rain and snow. In spite of throwing away everything metallic, the cowboys didn't always escape the fury of the elements. Baylis John Fletcher, who helped to drive a herd along the Chisholm trail in 1879, told how he came across the carcass of a horse, and a newly-dug grave, by the trail. Horse and rider had evidently been killed by lightning. 'There on the wild plains of western Kansas he had been buried,' Fletcher wrote, 'without a woman's tears, without a single tribute of flowers, and doubtless without a coffin.' He added: '... here was a solemn admonition to the cowboy that death lurked in the storms that swept over the plains with vivid flashes of lightning.'

'Foxfire', or St Elmo's Fire, gave warning of a storm and was familiar to trailherders; blue flames shimmered around the steers' and horses' heads and sometimes danced around a cowboy's hat. The heavens would open—and the herd often broke into a stampede. Egg-sized hailstones were recorded at Cheyenne in August 1876. But most persistent—and, some said, worst of all—was the ever-present cloud of choking dust that hung for days over the drive. No wonder the barber-shop bathrooms had first call on the cowboys' hard-earned money when they hit town.

Official stock inspectors were another burden to the harassed trail hands. These men were entitled to stop the herd and 'cut the trail'—look for strays and brands that didn't match the owner's mark. As the sale of these cattle went towards paying their salaries, the inspectors were understandably diligent. Farmers whose lands had been crossed by the herd also had the legal right to inspect the drive and make sure none of their animals had drifted along the trail. Many of the settlers took full advantage of this regulation simply to express their hostility to the great columns of Longhorns who grazed their way across farming country.

The herds sometimes met huge flocks of sheep being driven between California and Oregon and Wyoming or Montana. Sheep drovers had once included mighty figures like Kit Carson, who was as tough as they come. But the cowboys who rode the trails despised sheepmen—and were equally hated in return: hence the armed skirmishes that sometimes broke out.

The end of the trail drive meant a welcome opportunity to enjoy some of the pleasures of town life: cowboys gallop into a cow town

But there were days on the cattle trail that were free from human—and natural—interruptions. The herd grazed contentedly under blue skies and fleecy clouds, a soft fragrant wind relaxed the cowboy, the sun warmed him, and the grass undulated to the horizon. Then the great adventure could be enjoyed. 'It was', said Fletcher of Indian Territory, 'the cowpuncher's paradise . . . no more lanes, no more obstructing fences, but one grand expanse of free grass.'

The first sign that the drive was nearing its end was the arrival of 'drummers' from a cow town's stores galloping out to meet the herd and give the men free samples of whisky and cigars. Understandably, journey's end was an opportunity for the men to cut loose, 'see the elephant and hear the owl hoot'. They had lived hard on the trail, sometimes for months, with only their fellow punchers for companionship. Liquor had been forbidden, and by nightfall they were too tired to play poker. Little wonder that when the herd had been bedded down in the pens outside town and the guards chosen for the night, the off-duty men were ready for a spree. First, though, they stopped off at the barber-shop for a bath and to have their shaggy hair and unkempt beards cut, then bought new clothes 'from the skin out'.

In the words of Alfred Henry Lewis, the cowboy then became . . . deeply and famously drunk. Hungering for the excitement of play he collides amiably with faro and monte and what other deadfalls are rife in the place. Never does he win; for the games aren't arranged that way. But he enjoys himself; and his losses do not prey on him.' Joseph McCoy described the cowboy's dancing technique, declaring that it would put the French Can-Can to shame. 'The cowboy enters the dance with a peculiar zest,' he wrote, 'not stopping to divest himself of his sombrero, spurs or pistols . . .'

The long drives were an important and adventurous chapter in American history. The thousands of young men who rode the long trails knit the nation together. They played an essential part in forging the American West and expanding the American identity. The Texas cattle drives were the most important element in cementing the union between North and South. The cowboys, with their special code of comradeship, toughness and loyalty gave the West its individual stamp.

The Working Cowboy

'The cowboy's work was dangerous and exhausting. It covered a range of activities, climates—and above all, challenges—depending on the area, the time of year, and the period.'

The cowboy worked from 'see to see'—from first light of dawn to last light of dusk—and that's not counting night watches. His day in the saddle could start as early as 4 am and end at 9 pm, to be followed by two hours' night guard. Night guard could mean that a man staked his night horse at 9 pm, slept for three hours, was woken at midnight, worked till two, then went back to bed for another 90 minutes till the cook yelled 'Roll out' at 3.30. Some cowboys used to rub tobacco juice in their eyes to keep awake at night.

The cowboy's work was dangerous and exhausting. It covered a range of activities, climates—and above all, challenges—depending on the area, the time of year, the period. But it was a way of life men loved, and it still is. 'No man who has ever worked the JA ranch will overcome the urge to return there,' said the Hon James Wadsworth Jnr, an early cowboy. In the same spirit, in 1973, 69-year-old Andy Jauregui, a retired rodeo rider and small rancher, was still exercising his skill with a rope (despite an arthritic shoulder), on a round-up in South Dakota. He couldn't keep away.

An understanding of men and animals, a thorough knowledge of his range and the ability to win and keep his hands' respect were essential qualities of a good foreman: Pink Murray, foreman for the Green Cattle Company

In 1865, in Texas, a man would have to round up half-wild cattle and drive them 1,000 miles to market across unfenced and probably unowned range. In Montana, 30 years later, his son could be mowing hay and mending fences. His great-grandson, today, might be working in Colorado, trying to master the problems of artificial insemination or keeping a look-out for stray cattle from a light aeroplane. Nevertheless, today's cowboy has much in common with his forebears.

Cowboy Fat Alford was well described in the 1950s as having all the skills of his forebears, and much of their self-reliant character, although he'd never shot a man, chased a rustler across the Rio Grande, nor rescued a beautiful girl from ruthless bandits. Alford, it was said, could 'rope a cow out of a bush patch so thick a Hollywood cowboy couldn't crawl into it on his hands and knees'. He had an astonishing range of abilities. He could break in a horse, doctor wormy sheep, make a petrol engine pump water for thirsty cattle, punch a string of post holes across a rocky ridge—all this under the worst of conditions, with poor gear, bad food, in freezing winter or under a blazing sun 'hot enough to raise blisters on a boot heel'.

When a cowboy was hired, his first job was to spend four to six days breaking in his horses (each man needed at least five or six). The cowhand lived in the saddle; his horse imparted dignity. He would never walk if he could ride, and even the couple of hundred yards from bunkhouse to corral was considered quite a stroll. Significantly, when a foreman took the top horse of a man's string from him, he was saying—plainer than words ever could—that he wanted him to quit before he had to fire him.

The foreman was, and still is, absolute monarch of all he surveyed on the ranch. He had to be able to control and win respect from men who were courageous, dedicated and indifferent to suffering. He had to be talented in man-management, an outstanding horseman, skilful with the rope, and have an encyclopedic knowledge of his range. Above all, he needed a deep understanding of cattle and horses. Such a man could remember one cow out of many thousands after seeing it but once. A good look at a horse would fix the animal in his memory forever. This is still true today. Only a few years ago, a writer told of a veteran rancher who could tell the parentage of individual calves at a glance, and predict their disposition accurately.

Like some medieval wizard, a foreman had to be able to divine the hidden presence of animals on the range. He had to be able to devise the strategy for a round-up or take thousands of cattle through unknown country for hundreds of miles; he had to be able to bring back more steers than any of his men, though he may have had the poorest mounts. He had to bear the prime share of risk and fatigue. And, last but not least, he had to be honest.

Roping a calf (top) and throwing an animal for branding are still essential cowboy skills as these hands demonstrate

Apart from the cowboys and their foreman, there were other specialists around the ranch. The *wrangler* was in charge of the horses. Responsible for them 24 hours a day, he rounded them up as often as three times each day. Each cowboy chose the horse he needed for a particular job—bog riding, cutting out, fence riding or night riding.

On one ranch, as well as the wrangler, there was a man whose sole job was to break in new mounts. In 13 years he was never seen to be thrown from a horse; he was happy only on untrained animals, and once a horse had been trained, he lost all interest. (In fact, he fell asleep on anything but a half-wild animal!) There were also itinerant horse-breakers, who went from ranch to ranch, charging about five dollars for every horse they broke in, plus their keep.

The cook was always an important feature on ranch life. One cowboy recalls how, when he was away from the ranch, the one moment he looked forward to was the cry of 'Come and get it before I throw it out'. This was not because the average cook was a great chef, but because the average cowhand was even worse, subsisting, when on his own, on a basic diet of fried sowbelly pork and homemade sourdough biscuits, often rolled with an empty beer bottle.

Attempts to improve stock by cross-breeding started early. By 1880 the 'White-Face' Longhorn, bred from Longhorn cows crossed with Hereford and Angus bulls, was common. So was the Shorthorn, a cross between the Longhorn and the Durham cattle brought over from England in the 17th century by the Pilgrim Fathers.

Some cattle barons imported European cows and bulls, to see if the purebred result would adapt to life on the Great Plains: British Red Devons and Welsh Blacks, French Charolais and Limousin, Fleckvie and Melbvieh of Germany, Chicanina of Italy, the Swiss Simmental —and even shaggy Highland cattle. The Hereford finally triumphed; by the 1920s it had proved to be the best beef cow.

There were many curious hybrids en route. One was the Brangus, a cross between the Angus and the humpbacked Brahman bull which had first been seen in the West in 1906. Even more curious was the 'Cattalo': half-cow, half-buffalo. In 1888 its creator, Colonel Charles J. Jones, hailed it as 'the perfect animal for the plains'. He was wrong. The Cattalo was extremely ugly and, though it had the Longhorn's independence, it also had the buffalo's evil temper. It was almost a hundred years before a buffalo-cow cross —the 'beefalo'—became a viable commercial proposition.

Breeding experiments are still carried out in the West. One stockman, Ed Lasater, has crossed Brahman bulls with Hereford and Shorthorn cows. The result, the Beefmaster, thrives on his Texas and Colorado ranges.

Half-buffalo and half-Hereford hybrid cross

The cowboy's job knew no hours, no times, no certainties, and this remains true to this day. Over the 150 years since the birth of the cowboy, his working life can be divided into three periods. First, the glorious days of the free range and the long drives, when men were herdsmen, and the cowboy was truly the cavalier of the Plains. Fences were unknown, the sea of grass was so immense it seemed it could never be denuded, and it was unthinkable that the cowboy would ever become a cultivator.

Second, there was the period of settling down when barbed wire made it possible for men to fence in the range to protect their stock and territory. Cowboys found themselves doing work they'd once considered demeaning. Cattle needed hay, for instance, and one cow-hand in Texas recorded ruefully that he had just built the biggest haystack ever seen on the Rio Blanco Division: 79 footsteps long.

Line riders patrolled ranch boundaries in the early days to keep the cattle in and watch over the animals' welfare

The third period, one of increasing sophistication, saw the introduction of modern machinery: cars, trucks, even helicopters. The cowhand had become almost a farmhand, and had to learn new skills. Cattle had to be vaccinated as well as branded. Weakened calves were injected with caffeine, or fed milk fortified with vitamins. Increased skills, new discoveries and new breeding techniques can change many things. For example, in the 1870s a rancher was well satisfied if his cows had a 70 per cent calving rate. Today the figure is 95 per cent. But the basic challenge of life on the range has never lost its fascination.

The cowboy's daily assignments covered a bewildering variety of jobs. As a *line rider*, he lived in lonely, rough solitude, miles away from the home ranch. This was a job which only existed in the early days before barbed wire fencing was introduced, when the only way to supervise the outlying range was to have men continually patrolling the borders of the ranch. Their job was to keep the cattle within the boundaries of the range, and to look after them. They watched the condition of the beasts, made sure that they always had sufficient grass and water, and acted as nursemaids when necessary.

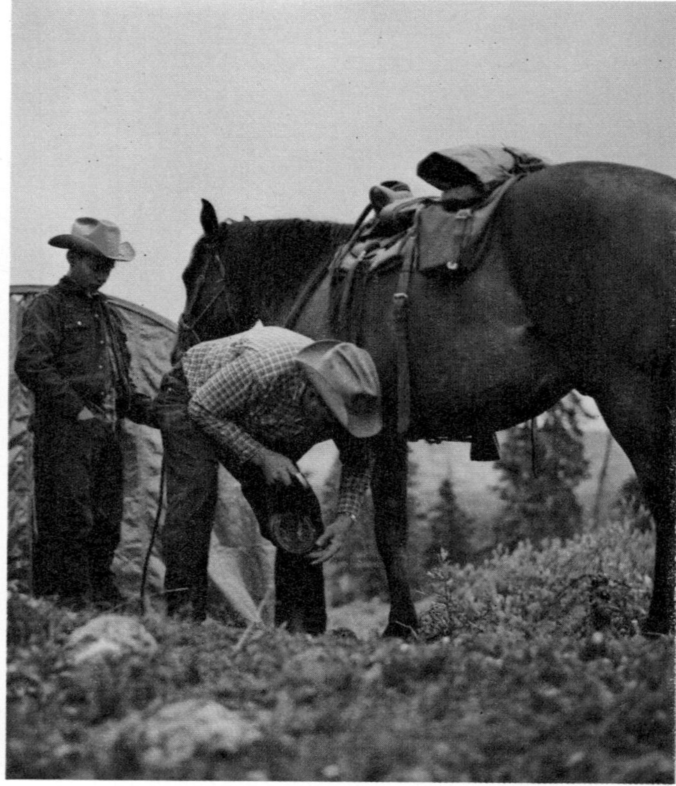

(Above) *The line rider's lonely job is no longer necessary, but cowboys still spend—and enjoy—many hours riding the range* (Right) *Even today a horse is often a cowboy's main means of transport; a hint that it may be lame signals potential trouble*

The line rider (or the *outrider*, who had a similar job on the remoter stretches of the range) had to be well able to endure his own company. He had to live on his own or with one other companion in a primitive wooden or sod-walled hut, chinked with mud, sometimes hewn into the side of a hill. Furnishings were simple: a few rickety chairs, a wooden table, a couple of cheap iron beds, a small wood-burning stove, a blanket or an old cowhide for a door. It was often called a 'boar's nest', because there were so few civilized amenities.

After the invention of barbed wire, the line rider was replaced by the *fence rider*. Instead of moving cattle within the rough boundaries of the ranch, he spent his days mending fences. The fence rider was armed with pliers, wire-cutter and hammer plus a coil of wire. He watched for breaks in the fence through which cattle might struggle. Lightning could destroy whole sections; heavy rain could wash away the 'dead men'—the uprights—or create gullies that allowed the cattle to struggle through. Gates were accidentally left open. The fence rider was a busy man.

Perhaps the most unpleasant job was *bog riding*. In the spring, when cattle were weakened by poor winter feed, they were tormented by swarms of voracious heel flies. They would find relief standing in

deep mud holes. But because of their weakness, they were often trapped. It was the bog rider's job to dig them out. Two men usually went 'riding bog' together. One man roped the trapped cow; the other went in to the mud hole and started to dig out its feet with a shovel. He had to be careful he didn't end up in the same predicament himself; 'gumbo', as the mud was called, was tenacious. Today it traps pick-up trucks, and the cowhands have to dig *them* out.

One of the most perilous aspects of the bog rider's task was rescuing animals from quicksand. Anyone who struggles in quicksand is gripped even tighter, so a cowhand had to be very, very careful. He took his boots and trousers off and approached the animal gently. Then he would tramp down the sand between its forelegs, while his partner's horse pulled back on a rope attached to the animal's horns. The same laborious process was repeated with the back legs, then with the forelegs again, and so on, until the animal was released. It took patience, teamwork, a well-trained horse and luck. When rescued, the cow was not in the least appreciative. 'Ungrateful as a cow fresh pulled from a bog hole' was a common turn of phrase in the old West. If the animal had any strength left after its ordeal, it'd often as not try to gore its rescuers.

The old Longhorn cattle, apart from being very stupid, were not at all like today's tame animals; they were half-wild, and acted it. It took a tough man to dig a cow out of the bog; it took a tender man to nurse a young calf back to life. Considering how troublesome the old Longhorns could be, and how strong they were, it's amazing how much nursemaiding they needed. 'Tailing up' a cow—lifting an

Firefighting was yet another skill that cowboys had to master. Prairie fires were sometimes started by Indians, or by rustlers who hoped to stampede a herd and give themselves the opportunity to cut out a few choice head in the confusion that followed. Or a greenhorn cowboy might start a fire by tossing a smouldering cigarette butt into the bone-dry scrub. Whatever the cause, the whole community recognized the danger. Even townsfolk helped when there was a fire.

Two techniques were generally used. One, the 'back fire', meant starting another fire which was fanned forward to meet the oncoming blaze. It was a risky procedure that could easily get out of control. The other, 'the drag', was effective—and dangerous. A steer was killed and skinned, and the carcass was dragged, flesh side downward, over the fire. Two brave cowboys rode swiftly along, each holding one side of the carcass. At the end of each run they changed side to prevent their horses' hooves being too badly scorched.

Cowboys were expected to turn their hands to many jobs including tending to sick animals

The fence rider spent his days maintaining the all-important barbed wire fences that enclosed his ranch: 'Riding the Line of the Wire Fence' by Frederic Remington; from Harper's Monthly Magazine, *1890*

animal that had lost its footing by its tail until it was on all four legs again—was typical.

The one sure thing about the range rider's day was its uncertainty. One moment he might be driving cattle to new grass because they were overgrazing a certain section. An hour later he might have to bring in a calf that had lost its mother, to be reared on a bottle at 'headquarters'—the central ranch house. Later on in the day he could well find himself pulling porcupine quills from the nose of an over-curious cow.

He had to be prepared for any emergency. If a cow had lost her calf, he had to rope her, tie her down and milk her to keep her udder from spoiling. Some calves fed from their mothers for too long and weakened them; when this happened the cowboy would 'blab' the calf—place a thin board over its nose to prevent it suckling, but allow it to graze, thus sparing the mother's health. Sometimes he would find an animal with the gaunt flanks, drooping head, and swollen jaw that signified a rattlesnake bite. He could only cut open the wound and hope for the best.

The cowboy had to be constantly alert, narrowed eyes ceaselessly searching the horizon, as he looked for the tell-tale signs that meant trouble. Many of his day-to-day activities were known as 'riding sign'. It involved recovering animals that had strayed, turning cattle from patches of locoweed or bog holes, and keeping them away from poisonous alkaline waterholes. To an outsider, a cowboy riding sign might seem to be dozing in the saddle. In fact, he couldn't be more wide awake. If he saw cattle spread out, grazing peacefully, he knew all was well. But a bawling calf, a trapped cow, a lost stray: these drew immediate action. Some cowboys could even tell from a great distance whether another rider was a white man or an Indian, just by the way he rode.

Men expert at riding sign were the famous 'trackers' associated with cowboy films, and their skill was greatly admired and described with colourful phrases: 'He could track a bear in running water,' or 'He could track bees in a blizzard.' A man unskilled at the basic skills of riding sign was dismissed contemptuously: 'He couldn't find a baseball in a tomato can,' or 'He couldn't track an elephant in three feet of fresh snow.'

A good cowhand's ability at riding sign could save his ranch time, money and trouble. When following rustlers, for example, a good man could tell as clearly as if it were printed in a book how many horses there were, how fast they were travelling, where they had stopped to graze.

As ranches grew more sophisticated, new jobs appeared. *Mill riding* was one of them. This was the job of making sure that the windmills installed to pump up underground water for stock to drink did not break down—keeping them well oiled and in good order. The mill riders' primary task (they usually rode in pairs) was to scramble up the ladders bolted to the mills' legs and coat the bearings and gears with grease. Most mills were about 30 feet high, but there were exceptions. Those on the Yellow Houses Ranch in Texas included one as high as a 13-storey building.

Cowboys were always alert, looking for signs of trouble, even when they seemed to be relaxing: a horse wrangler watches over his remuda

Over the years the cowboy's life changed in many ways. Today he must know as much about machines as he does about cattle: modern ranch scene

One story that reflects the innate scepticism and wit of the cowboy comes from the early days of the windmill. A Texas rancher called his boys round to watch the operation of his newly-built mill. When the first water appeared he was as 'happy as a dog with two tails'. One of his men eyed the thin trickle produced by the new-fangled invention and observed cynically: 'Hell, boss, I could get behind a bush and do better than that myself.'

The brush rider was a very specialized cowboy. His job was particularly difficult, and his skill was much admired by other cowhands. Where the Plains cowboy had great freedom of movement, the brush rider had to work where the ground was covered with thick underbrush and thorny thickets. This required superlative horse-management, as the rider dodged and weaved from one side of his horse to another to avoid being slashed. It also called for rope-work of a high order. He used a 25-foot rope—much shorter than the 45-foot one used by the Plains cowboy.

Many cowboys also had to be amateur vets. Throughout the summer, cows had to be doctored for screw-worm, caused by the blowfly, which laid its eggs in open wounds or sores on the animals' bodies. A tiny parasite like a maggot some three-quarters of an inch long, the screw-worm caused agony and even death if untreated. The treatment was as drastic as the disease (and sometimes even more dangerous). Powerful ointments made from such fiendish ingredients as axle-grease mixed with carbolic acid were smeared into the affected part.

One cowboy sprayed a group of animals suffering with a mange-like infection with kerosene. All would have been well if one animal hadn't run through a branding fire and become a living torch. Some 20 head died as a result. The foreman's comments aren't recorded.

Other doctoring jobs included dehorning and castrating. Dehorning was performed on young Longhorns to stop them goring each other; castrating to make them fatten into beef cattle or steers. If a calf was caught young—preferably in its first week of life—and its horn buttons rubbed with caustic potash, they would never start growing again. But if there was any delay the operation was painful and dangerous—for cowhand and animal. The horns had to be sawn off, or cut with cumbersome dehorning clippers. In either case, the animal had to be held down bodily. And it might bleed to death if the wound wasn't cauterized immediately: this is one of the reasons why men were constantly alert to catch young calves soon after they were born.

The most serious disease that ever struck the cow country was Texas fever. Carried by ticks, it produced fever, paralysis and death, and dipping was a regular chore. When the process was introduced, the hardy ranchers objected violently—and sometimes dramatically. In Shelby County, eastern Texas, 69 dipping vats (out of a total of 70) were dynamited in one night. One old lady in the same area made her point more personally. After her herd of Jerseys had been dipped by the Sanitary Commission inspector, she produced a gun and pushed him under the foul-smelling dip with his own cattle prod. He was sick for several days.

In the early days, when ranching was seasonal, a man might be employed only during the two great round-ups, from April until mid-June and from the end of August to the end of October. At the end of each round-up, many cowboys drifted into the towns and spent all their money, before returning to the ranch for the next round-up. Those who remained employed did an astonishing variety of jobs, apart from cattle-minding.

Ranch tasks were cordially disliked—and it's not hard to see why. Over one three-week stretch, Texas cowhand Blue Stevens did nothing but collect dried cow manure for fires. A Colorado puncher, 'Lasso' Bill Sears was reduced to milking cows and raising chickens—though he did make a profit on the job! C. H. Hanbury on the XIT ranch in Texas was assigned the nautical task of building traps for turtles that had over-populated a lake which the rancher used to water his stock. On a ranch in the Dakotas, the boys mined coal from a small seam on the spread during winter.

One of the most exciting jobs in winter was wolf-hunting. In cold months, when other game was sparse, the wolves became unusually predatory, and packs of them stalked the cows. One man was hired by a Texas ranch to shoot wolves at a salary of $35 a month, plus $5 a scalp bounty paid by the county government. He also received his keep, rifles, a Colt 45 with free ammunition, and between four and eight horses. One Wyoming ranch kept Russian wolfhounds; others kept greyhounds, deerhounds and stag hounds, and the wolf-hunting cowboys rode to hounds like English gentry. Many cowboys caught wolves with their lariats.

Wolf-hunting not only provided winter sport for the cowboy, it also helped ensure the herd's safety: a gray wolf is caught in Wyoming

There was always a risk that cattle might freeze to death during winter. Cowboys had to search for stranded beasts and herd them to more sheltered spots where they could graze: 'Rescue'; photograph by Charles Belden

Among the most demanding of winter assignments was the gruelling task of riding out to make sure the cattle didn't either starve or freeze to death. Rather than look for food, cows stood miserably huddled together. The marooned beasts were often covered with snow, their eyes frozen shut, icicles drooping from their muzzles. The cowhand had to bundle himself up in his buffalo coat, seek a place where the wind had blown the snow from the grass, then drive the cattle to it. The chore of breaking ice on ponds was also an infuriating one; cattle didn't have the sense to eat snow for moisture. If they did freeze to death, all that could be done was get the hide off before the animal was frozen too hard for skinning.

By late November, two out of every three cowhands were normally laid off. But the cowboy was resourceful by nature and experience. Some took up that most respected (and respectable) of Western professions, gambling. Others moved into town with friends, and did odd jobs like housepainting or carpentry, bartending or blacksmithing.

But the most famous of all out-of-work pursuits was 'grublining': riding from ranch to ranch, doing odd jobs in return for free meals and lodging. There was no shame attached to this. People welcomed cowboys who were honestly out of work, and owners of outlying ranches were glad to see a new face, and hear the latest news. This old-time friendliness was mourned recently by Vern Torrance, a present-day Wyoming cowboy, who reminisced: 'Forty, fifty years ago, you could ride a couple of hundred miles, and never worry about having a place to eat or sleep. Now you can hardly ride beyond your own outfit, because nobody's going to offer to put you up.'

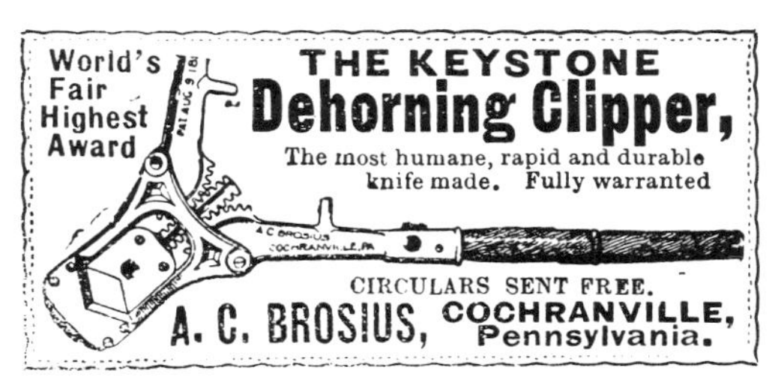

A calf's horns were usually treated soon after birth to stop them growing. If this wasn't done they had to be cut down or sawn off—a dangerous process: advertisement for dehorning clippers

The cowboy's year centred on the round-ups. They took place in spring and autumn and were the culmination of all the previous few months' work; every man co-operated with his neighbour to gather together and sort out the vast herds on the open range. (There were also other, small, affairs when a man sorted out his own cattle—these 'private' round-ups are still held today.)

Of the two round-ups, the biggest was in the spring. A whole territory would co-operate to round up as many as a million beasts, so that they could be branded, sorted—and tended—before those to be sold began the long trail north. The autumn round-up was usually a more local affair. Each rancher rounded up animals that he had missed in the spring, branded calves born during the summer and sorted out animals for market. Even these smaller round-ups required co-operation between neighbours.

Some authorities say the round-up started among the mountain men of Kentucky, Tennessee, Virginia and the Carolinas, who, back in the early 1800s, rounded up their cattle once a year. Others point to the Mexicans and their *rodeos*. In those days the rodeo was not a show, as it is now. It was—as the word infers—a 'surrounding'. With Latin disregard for commercial niceties, the Mexicans often planted tall poles coated with salt and tallow at various points; the cows came to lick them of their own accord. This relaxed and easy-going attitude was not for the hard-headed cattle barons of Texas or Montana. Their round-ups were rough, tough and superbly organized.

Round-ups today are highly organized and no longer the prelude to a long drive north. But herding and branding the cattle require all the old skills (Right) *Cowboys move a herd of Herefords towards pens before separating mother cows and their calves* (Below right) *A roped calf is dragged towards one of three branding crews*

Cowboys were adept at separating a single calf from the herd, and 'cutting out' contests were held: a cowboy trains his horse for a competition, using goats which are much more agile than cows

Round-ups, when ranch owners co-operated to drive all the cattle in their district together, were the highlights of the cowboy's year: 'Going to the Round-up'; photograph by L. A. Huffman

The early American round-ups were called 'cow hunts' or 'cow drives', and were casual affairs where a few neighbours gathered together to sort out their animals and look over each other's herds for strays. With the birth of co-operative stockmen's associations in the late 1860s these developed into vast joint endeavours that were looked forward to with interest and eagerness. There men would meet old friends, and make new ones. Each ranch would send 'reps' to other ranches' round-ups. They were responsible for bringing back their ranch's strays. A rep could easily end up driving as many as a hundred head of cattle back to his own ranch.

At the height of the open range system in the 1880s the organization was elaborate, with an exact set of rules. Each state governor appointed a commission of three herd owners—the *round-up commissioners*—for each round-up district of some 100 to 150 square miles. These men decided on the programme for the round-up, fixed the date, and made sure the 'laws' of the round-up were carried out.

Once the commissioners had decided on the date of a big round-up, notices were published in the newspapers. In large areas, there were 'handbill round-ups'. In Wyoming, for example, handbills were printed and distributed throughout the vast territory to be covered. (The organization eventually became so sophisticated that daily figures of cattle rounded up were published in the press.) Nobody was allowed to start branding calves before the date set by the commissioners. Men who tried to jump the gun—'sooners'—might be ruled out of the round-up; if they were small ranchers this could

mean ruin. Men suspected of being dishonest were also ruled out. Everyone had to play the game; if not, the entire system, based on mutual trust, would break down.

The round-up district was divided into smaller districts by the commissioners; each was about 10 to 15 square miles, and each had to be worked in a day. The commissioners appointed a *captain*, generally a very experienced small herdowner or foreman. He had to be thoroughly acquainted with his district, down to the smallest creek, ridge, and fold in the ground. He had to know all the many brands involved, and understand the peculiarities of cattle. He was absolute head of the round-up.

A ranch outfit on round-up consisted of 10 to 15 cowboys, a chuck-wagon—and, as life became more easygoing, a 'hoodlum' wagon for the men's kit. There was also a cook, horse wrangler (and remuda), and a wagon boss (sometimes called a 'circle boss' because he was responsible for organizing the daily circle the riders made). A wagon boss was judged by his skill at distributing his men in a given area, to bring in the greatest possible number of head; when he had completed this job he had 'covered his dog'.

The men who drove cattle in from the farthest edge of the daily circle were called *lead drive men*. Those who worked the inner periphery were *inside circle men*. If men got behind on the job, they sometimes had to go on a 'greasy-sack ride': pack provisions in small cotton bags and ride on ahead of the others to get started earlier. Working in country too rough for wagons was called 'moonshining'.

By law ranchers had to register their brands in the county where their cattle were expected to graze, and branding was the main purpose of a round-up: an 1888 branding scene

Forcing a calf into position for branding—and keeping it there—is still one of the cowboy's toughest tasks: modern branding scenes

Hands worked long, hard hours on round-ups, but they also had a rare opportunity to meet hands from neighbouring ranches: chuckwagon at a round-up, from Marvels of the New West *by W. M. Thayer. 1888*

There were moments of relaxation before the round-up proper started. Men sauntered over to other ranches' camps, to sample their cooks' specialities or exchange tales and reminiscences. Sometimes they held 'kangaroo courts', mock trials where men were found guilty of meaningless or ridiculous crimes. The 'criminal' might be sentenced to ride on a wild young steer or a notorious bucking horse from some nearby outfit. Or he might have to hand over some of his precious tobacco. But he knew it was all in fun, and that his fellows would repay him.

The first part of the day was spent rounding up the cattle. While the men worked, the wagon moved forward to the next point on the round-up. Rounding up could be over by 10 am if only a small number of cattle—700 or 800 head—was involved; 2,000 or more head would take till noon. Then the cow 'wrastling' began. Two or three men mounted their 'cutting' horses, which were trained to cut out selected cattle, some to be branded, some to be castrated, some to be marketed. (Johnnie Martin of Texas recounts that he changed horses six times a day.)

Branding a calf was no easy task, and took a team of two 'wrastlers'. First the animal had to be forced into position. Cowboys agreed that this was one of their most physically demanding jobs. One wrastler roped the calf; the other lifted the animal bodily off the ground and flipped it onto its side, ready for brand or knife. The pace of branding was astonishing. The average was about 300 calves in one afternoon, and in 1885 a crew at Marias River, Montana, branded 130 calves in an hour.

Today the 'squeeze' makes the job a lot simpler: the calves are run through chutes and caught between parallel bars. Small squeezes, 'cradles', tip over so that the calf, lying prone, can be treated more easily. The team has also changed—to six men. Two cowboys drive calves into the chute; one brands, one inoculates, one castrates, and one keeps the irons hot with butane gas. (Even electric branding irons have been tried.) Today, a branding team can work some 500 calves a day—but it's still a big job and calls for tough men.

Round-ups varied from place to place, and from time to time. In the south, enormous spreads like the XIT in Texas held their own private round-ups. But co-operation was always essential, as in the winter of 1880, when storms mixed up the cattle so badly that 80 men and 10 wagons worked together west of Forth Worth to sort them out. Wherever the round-up was held, the skills that were most prized did not vary, nor did the challenges lessen. A cowboy was judged by his skill—not in roping and branding, but in bringing cattle in from the roughest, most difficult country. Each one represented hard cash.

The round-up reached its peak of sophistication in 1886, with the famous Miles City, Montana, round-up. It had all the complexity of a military campaign, and 175 members of the Montana Stockgrower's Association met in the city to plan the operation. Cowboys from as far south as Texas, as far west as the state of Washington—and even from beyond the Canadian border—were at the round-up. Famous cattle barons—John Clay, Granville Stuart, the Marquis de Mores among them—attended. So did railroad officials, and stockyard men from St Paul.

A grand opening luncheon was held in Miles City's new civic centre—the pride of the town, with its roller skating rink. There was a Stockgrowers Ball. Military officers from the fort attended in glittering full dress, so did the local belles, including the lovely half-Indian daughters of Granville Stuart. More than 4,000 brands were involved in the round-up, and more than a million cattle. Some of the districts into which the area was divided were as big as the states of Rhode Island or Connecticut. Yet only 50 to 100 men were needed to handle each vast area.

Men needed toughness and endurance to work at this pace—and handle maybe 150 cattle apiece. The modern cowboy has inherited these qualities. His meals may be served—hot—from a pick-up truck. He may have a diploma in agriculture, and drive a tractor. But, like his predecessors, he still has 'a way of meeting life head on, with a recklessness and wildness of spirit and a real relish for conquering it'.

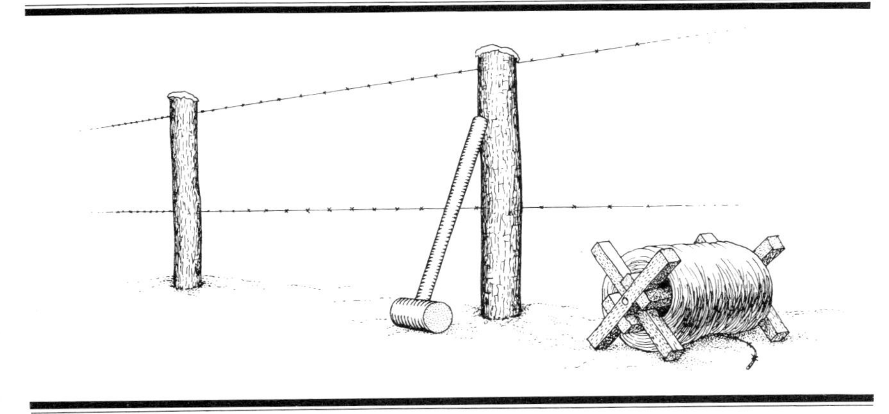

At Home on the Range

'In the early years, ranch furniture was spartan. Trunks doubled up as wardrobes, boxes became improvised tables, cupboards and benches. Barrels that had held nails served as seats.'

During the early years of the cattle industry, most ranches were relatively small family concerns that were run on a financial shoestring as their owners begged, bought and 'borrowed' cattle to build up their herds. At its most basic, a ranch was an isolated outpost consisting of the bare necessities of water, pasture, a primitive log or sod dwelling for the men and a corral for the horses. At first, one rancher said, ranch headquarters was 'more habitation than real home, beyond the reach of close neighbours, beyond the reach of mail delivery, beyond the reach of city facilities, and almost beyond reach'.

Most cattle families arrived at their ranch site with no possessions other than the wagon they came in and the tools and furniture loaded inside. Until a home could be built, they camped out rough, living in a canvas or sheet tent or lean-to—or even in (and under) the wagon itself. Families who established themselves in open country, where timber was in short supply, improvised with the only plentiful material on hand, the thick prairie sod (known as 'Nebraska marble' in that especially flat and treeless state).

The simplest home to build was a dugout—a glorified pit cut horizontally into a sloping rise of ground. After the rear walls had been excavated, a front extension of sod bricks or, less frequently, logs was added. A strong, flat roof of logs and poles was placed across the top of the walls, and covered over with successive layers of brush, prairie grass, sod and packed earth. It was angled downwards into the slope of the hill to prevent water flowing over it and cascading into the doorway.

Dugouts leaked like sieves. During a serious rainstorm muddy water streamed from the roof and the dirt floor rapidly turned to a sea of mud. And they were invariably dark and dirty. Even when dry, they perpetually drizzled dirt clods, roots, worms and even field mice from the ceiling. The only real advantage of a dugout, compared to living under the stars, was that it was cool in the summer and

In the days before piped water, ranches had to be close to rivers, streams or waterholes: lone ranch perched above its water supply; photograph by L. A. Huffman

warm in the winter, when a fireplace dug into the earth wall at the rear kept the family snug. A chimney, made from mud-plastered sticks, drew off most of the smoke. A typical one-room Nebraska dugout measured 10 by 12 feet, and an entire family and all their worldly possessions crowded inside this tiny living area.

The sod house was a far more comfortable alternative. Unlike a dugout, it bore some relation to a proper home. It was built from sod bricks, made by turning over long furrows of thick prairie sod with a heavy breaking plough, then cutting them into two- to three-foot strips. These were reinforced with long wooden stakes. A ridge pole and rafters were covered over with brush, grass and a layer of sod. If the family could afford wood, a board roof was built and sheeted over with tar paper and sod. Most sod houses sprouted luxuriant roof pastures of weeds, grass and bright sunflowers. The walls might be left rough or shaved smooth with a serrated hay-knife. Plastering them over on the inside added a civilized touch.

In the early days, most houses had dirt floors. Wooden ones singled out a family for envy by their neighbours. Writing of his childhood life, Charley O'Kieffe noted that all his neighbours had '. . . dirt floors, which meant that they had plenty of fleas also. Because of our fine [wood] floor, our home became the mecca for square dances and many were held there over the years.'

Most sod homes had two rooms at the most. One room was used for sleeping and the other for cooking, eating and all the general activity of daily life. At one end of the living area was a huge fireplace built of clay-coated sod bricks baked rock-hard by the fire's heat. The chronic shortage of wood on the Plains forced the families to turn to dried cow and buffalo dung for fuel, or else they burned great quantities of prairie grass or cornstalks and cobs.

The log cabin remains an American legend: a typical example of a ranch in its earliest days

Small windows meant that a sod house was dark and poorly ventilated. (In any case, glass was a rare luxury; greased paper made a poor substitute.) And dirt was always becoming dislodged from the sod roof and dropping onto the family (a cheesecloth net under the ceiling was of some help). When it rained, leaks were inevitable. One housewife recalled how one of her neighbours slept under an umbrella. In her own house, she wrote, 'Hats on our heads and rubbers on our feet kept those two extremities dry—and each night we moved our beds to dryer quarters and were lulled to sleep by the drip of water which constantly ran down the inside walls of the house.'

Along the rivers and streams, where timber was relatively abundant, the first ranch houses were invariably log cabins built in the traditional style of the American frontier. At its most basic one of these cabins was a crude one-room structure, with a huge fireplace made from stone or mud and clay-covered sticks at one end. The roof was made from 'shakes' (wooden shingles) fastened to the rafters in overlapping layers. It kept out the rain, but driving snow tended to sift through the cracks; as E. N. Dick wrote, 'It was not at all uncommon . . . to awake . . . to find snow drifted about the room.'

The homes of established ranchers were more comfortable: ranch in Arizona; light and airy, it was luxurious compared to the sod houses and log cabins that many families lived in

Adobes were very like sod houses. Originally Mexican, they spread throughout the arid south-west. Adobe houses were made from sun-hardened clay and straw bricks, with walls two or three feet thick. Mud was used as a mortar. Cheap and simple to make, adobes remained refreshingly cool inside during the blazing summer heat.

Privacy was unheard of in a one-room cabin. Quilts and blankets suspended from the ceiling were the only partitions between the living and sleeping areas. If an attic was built into the cabin, it was divided in the same way to give additional sleeping space.

In the early years, ranch furniture was extremely spartan. Trunks doubled up as wardrobes, and boxes became improvised tables, cupboards and benches. Barrels that had held nails, and packing cases, served as seats until they could be replaced by rickety home-made chairs and stools—noted neither for stability nor comfort. An iron cooking stove was a considerable luxury, and many an unfortunate woman was obliged to cook over a hot and smoky fire. Cooking implements were also limited—typically a couple of big pots, a frying pan, and a large tub for heating water, bathing the family and doing the laundry.

Beds, generally simple pallets on the floor, were feedbag mattresses stuffed with hay or grass ticking—'prairie feathers'. Sometimes simple wooden bunks were knocked together and pushed against a wall. To brighten up their homes wives had the walls plastered and covered over with muslin or cheesecloth. Home-made wallpaper of old magazine and catalogue pictures were often pasted up, as much to hide the dirt and improve insulation as to cheer up the house.

Humans were not the only inhabitants of these rough frontier ranches. Skunks burrowed under cabin walls to get close to the warm hearthstone of the fireplace, and rats and mice nested in sod roofs. One rancher's wife shudderingly recalled how, when she and her husband moved into their first shack, 'mice ran around in the roof at night and dislodged dirt which fell down on our bed. The mice did not last long, however, as bull snakes found them.' Worst of all were the bedbugs. It was impossible to eradicate them once they had infested a house. They hid in innumerable cracks in the walls, and flourished in the dirt floors along with the inevitable fleas and lice. The only way of fighting back was to stand the legs of all the beds in small tins of kerosene.

As a ranch prospered, the first crude home was soon replaced by a considerably more comfortable three- or four-roomed log or frame house, usually in an L or T shape, with a covered porch extending past the front door. Wooden floors, often laid double for extra warmth, were far easier to keep clean, and dramatically reduced the dirt and vermin inside the home. The walls were carefully smoothed, plastered, white-washed, lined with wallpaper and given a final homely touch with hung pictures. Each of the rooms had its own glass windows. Successful ranchers, or those with well-to-do relatives back East, shipped out proper oak and walnut furniture.

After the deprivations of the first years, luxury sometimes came as a shock. One household found that, 'upon moving into a frame house after five years in a sod structure, the change was so great

An established ranch: the main house boasts windows, a sod roof and a near-by well; photograph by L. A. Huffman

Saddles and equipment are neatly stacked outside this wood and stone bunkhouse

from the dark cave-like dwelling to the well-lighted frame building that the family could not sleep on account of the light.'

The original sod shack was sometimes converted into a barn for horses and milk-cows, or became a storage shed and a blacksmith's shop. If the ranch was reasonably prosperous, the owner employed more cowboys and added to his existing riding stock—which involved building suitable living quarters and a mess house for the hired hands. And so the ranch headquarters was gradually transformed into a small community of log cabins, sheds and stables.

The 'saddlebag' or 'Texas' house emerged on the range all the way from Texas to Montana. It consisted of two separate structures connected by a single long roof. Ropes, saddles, bridles, other equipment (and even dogs) were kept in the intervening 'dogtrot'.

On one side of the saddlebag house was a cookhouse and mess hall. Into it were crammed a huge fireplace or stove, all the cook's pots and pans, and the cowboys' long dining table and benches. The other side was the bunkhouse. Beds were ranged all around the walls and a heavy wooden table stood in the centre of the room. A few benches and some stools completed the simple furnishings. Bunkhouses were usually earth-floored wooden shacks, notable chiefly for their untidiness.

The prosperous ranch owner normally built his own home a slight distance away from his employees' quarters. Low-roofed and rectangular, its large open rooms were built in a straight line, like beads on a string, to trap as much sunlight and air as possible.

Although the majority of ranchers had few luxuries to compensate for the hardships of frontier life, a small number of cattle barons enjoyed a relatively opulent—and sometimes even spectacular—life style. The JA Ranch was a sprawling complex established in the Palo Duro Canyon of the Texas Panhandle by Charles Goodnight and his partner John Adair. The ranch headquarters was a small village in its own right. An imposing stone house was erected for the Adairs—but was used only on the rare occasions when they actually visited

The Marquis de Mores' residence, a 26-room house, overlooked the Little Missouri River at Medora, North Dakota; photograph by L. A. Huffman

the ranch. The Goodnight family lived in a two-storey log-and-plank home that had the luxury of running water piped in from a spring over half a mile from the house. There were also a mess hall and bunkhouses for the employees, a blacksmith's shop, a tin shop for making plates and cups, a dairy and a poultry yard, and numerous sheds and stables—a total of about 50 buildings.

Henry S. Mudge's spread near Dodge City, Kansas, was less grand than the JA Ranch, but its comforts were equally impressive. Though Mudge owned a 'mere' 10,000 acres, the ranch house, according to one writer, resembled 'a clubhouse with its dairyman, a bookkeeper and two cooks. A Chickering piano, a fireplace, pipes, tobacco, cigars, English and American magazines and newspapers, and a well-stocked library' completed the atmosphere of gentlemanly ease and comfort.

The most memorable of all the gentleman ranchers was the Marquis de Mores. He settled in the Badlands of North Dakota in a 26-room, French-style château. With 20 servants and a library of German, French and English books, he established a new dimension in elegant frontier living. Pierre Wibaux built his wife a sprawling home complete with sitting room, wine cellar and billiard room. The interior was furnished with elaborately carved wood panelling and luxurious rugs. Landscaped gardens were filled with flowers and shrubs, and—the ultimate touch of class—decorated with statues.

Homes like these were oddities, transplants from another world of gracious and leisured living and quite out of character with the conditions of the frontier ranges. Most ranch families lived close to nature—and the wives bore the brunt of her harsher aspects. The quality and quantity of the water, for instance, directly determined the amount of hardship involved in mundane chores like washing and cooking. Water on the plains was often highly alkaline, with an unpleasant 'mineral' taste. It was almost impossible to dissolve soap in this water, and bedding and garments soon acquired a characteristic yellow dinginess.

The Marquis de Mores named the town of Medora after his wife, a New York banker's daughter

The saying that the frontier was hard on women and cattle was all too true for the first wives who came to the range. If it was hard for men to live in cramped and dirty dugouts, sod houses and log cabins, it was worse still for the women. Many wives burst into tears of horrified dismay at their first sight of their first home.

Their diaries were filled with their shocked reactions. The heart-rending impressions of Alice Baldwin, who arrived in her new home as a recently married young bride, were typical. When her husband pointed to the site of their home, she was just able to make out 'the stub of a stovepipe, although no smoke issued from the top'. Inside, she 'gazed with disgusted disappointment around the bare, squalid room. Its conveniences were limited to one camp chair, two empty candle boxes and a huge box stove, red with rust and grime, its hearth gone and the space filled with a tobacco-stained hill of ashes . . . Canvas covered the ceiling and dirt sides. It sagged slightly in the centre and trembled under the scampering feet of pack rats and prairie mice.' The overwhelming disappointment was too much, and she burst into tears at the evening meal.

Another woman slumped to the floor in despair, buried her eyes in her hands and remained frozen in that position for several hours. But her inner strength and courage was unquenched. She regained her composure and got down to the task of caring for her family.

Washing clothes was in any case a back-breaking weekly chore. Armed with a scrubbing-board, tub and fist-sized chunks of soap, women scrubbed and pounded the laundry mercilessly before spreading it out on the grass or over bushes and fences to dry—and frequently complained that the regular Monday wash was never over until Tuesday. Starch was usually home-made: water in which potatoes, wheat or bran had been cooked was left standing for several hours until a starchy sediment formed. The water was drained off and the residue used on clothing.

Bathing facilities were crude, and the biggest luxury of all was a hot bath. The water had to be fetched and then slowly heated on the kitchen stove. (In winter, the tub was placed next to the stove to keep bathers from freezing to death.) The entire family used the same water, starting with the youngest child.

By modern standards, the list of domestic chores was endless. Clothes always needed mending, the house had to be cleaned, wood chopped, tallow rendered for burning in lamps, chickens, pigs and

Ranch wives found washing day more burdensome than did the cowboys shown here: 'Starting a Laundry' from Marvels of the New West *by W. M. Thayer. 1888*

steers killed and butchered for meat, the small garden patch (where a few tomatoes, beans, squash and melons grew) had to be tended and meals constantly had to be prepared for the rest of the family.

To some extent, the hardships and drudgery were compensated by the exaggerated respect and courtesy with which women were treated. And when a young woman reached marriageable age she was literally besieged by eager young suitors. Courting wasn't elaborate by Eastern standards, but there were certain definite customs. A young man who was interested in a particular lady hired a horse, or preferably a buggy, from the local livery stable, and together the two of them went out riding over the prairie. Or they attended social events.

One historian of the West tells how 'many young men attended Sunday School zealously because they knew the girls would be there; and in a day of limited social activities this became an opportunity for social outlet.' If a couple were frequently seen in each other's company, they became 'obligated' to each other. If the courtship foundered and the young man was rejected, he was faced with the public embarrassment of getting 'the mitten'. In fact, young men were subjected to all sorts of pressures not to get married. Ranch owners, for instance, discouraged hired hands from marrying because the men would want to leave their employment to establish their own family spreads—or move into town and take jobs that kept them near their wives.

There were no major social barriers on the frontier, and love was the main reason for marrying. Preparations were completed with a minimal amount of ceremony; long engagements, elaborate family negotiations before the wedding, calling the banns, were generally considered irrelevant to the couple's needs—and were conveniently ignored.

The typical Protestant wedding ceremony was brief. Afterwards, a riotous celebration was held at the bride's home. Neighbours and friends crowded around the house, beating drums and tinpans, blowing horns and setting up a terrific din until the bridegroom came out and 'stood everyone a treat'. The numerous well-wishers were frank about the sexual pleasures of marriage; 'Health to the groom, and here's to the bride, thumping luck, and big children' was a common wedding toast. As the newly-married couple drove away, they were followed by a shower of old boots and shoes, onions and other assorted junk. The day after the wedding, the husband and wife and the bride's parents attended an 'infair'—the name given to the customary visit to the groom's parents. If they were lucky, the couple set out for a brief honeymoon afterwards. This was usually a few days in the nearest large town to shop for the essential household goods with which to set up their new home.

Ahead of the newly-weds lay the inevitable hardships of frontier life. A woman's most important task was to raise and care for her family. The birth of the first child generally followed the marriage in swift succession. Large families were common, and government incentives encouraged people to have more children. In Tennessee, fathers of triplets were granted 200 acres of government land for each child. As a ranch prospered, it seemed doubtful at times whether its prime purpose was to raise cattle or children. The owner, and quite likely the foreman as well, both had rapidly growing families.

Youngsters on a ranch led a free and uninhibited life. What they lacked in toys they made up for with games and amusements of their own devising. They kept pets like dogs, calves, ponies, and even deer fawns. They played at being cowboys fighting off Indians and rustlers, they staged miniature round-ups and practised their roping skills on dogs, chickens and each other. While boys acquired their fathers' skills, girls imitated their mothers and learned how to cope with the million and one chores of being a ranch wife. Children were expected to be independent at an early age, and to make their own choice about the future.

Education was highly regarded, but schooling was a problem for youngsters on remote cattle ranches. If their parents could afford it, they were sent to a nearby town to board with another family during the school term. More prosperous ranchers employed tutors to come and live on the ranch. Families who couldn't afford to send their children to school had to educate them at home. This was generally the mother's task—prairie women were very much the 'standard-bearers of literature and learning'. Jessie Benton Smith in later years recalled how she longed for the twice-monthly arrival of the stage-coach, with its precious cargo of 'brain rations'—newspapers, periodicals, letters and books. Another ranch wife, Nannie Alderson,

Large families were common in the West, and a woman's most important task was caring for, and educating her children: ranch family

Ranching was a family business and husband and wife were partners economically as well as socially: wedding portrait, Nebraska, 1882

found an unusual use for the catalogue from the mail order firm Montgomery Ward. She tells how her children 'pored over it endlessly; before they could read, the pictures were there to dazzle them . . . In time they learned how to spell words out of it. They never went to school until we moved to Miles City, when Mabel was almost ten years old. All they knew up to that time was reading as taught by Montgomery Ward, and printing block letters, which I taught them.'

If there were enough children in a locality to make it worthwhile starting a school, each parent chipped in with money, logs or timber, and a 'school-raising bee' was held. The first schools were small, battered frame buildings—or sod houses, dugouts or even tents. If a community couldn't afford a schoolhouse, classes were held in a room in somebody's home. Each family provided simple home-made desks and benches for their children. A water bucket with a communal dipper stood at one end of the room and at the other end was a wood stove. In winter it broiled half the children and left the others freezing in the cold. There were often no blackboards or maps, not even a school library. Children brought their own books and in any class there could be up to half-a-dozen different reading texts.

Boys and girls of all ages were crowded into the same room. Occasionally, a few adult students also squeezed onto the benches alongside them. 'When I started Fairview [school] in the fall of 1886 at six and a half years of age,' wrote Charley O'Kieffe, 'I drew as my seatmate one Alexander Gosch, a Bohemian immigrant, aged thirty-four. He was trying to learn his ABC's in English.'

It was a rare event for all pupils to be present at one time. Attendance fluctuated wildly as children stayed home because of bad weather, to help their parents with work—or else because they were ill with one of the epidemics that repeatedly swept the West. These provided a tragic counterpoint to rearing a family. Measles, scarlet fever, typhoid, diphtheria and smallpox were commonplace—and often fatal. Malaria, or 'ague', was so widespread that many people regarded it as a normal fact of life. Disease apart, the conditions of prairie life added danger even to normal events. Childbirth, for instance, was a major ordeal, and babies were frequently born with no medical assistance if the nearest doctor—several days' journey away—was held up by floods or blizzards. Many infants died soon after being born.

Sickness and injury were always major calamities on isolated prairie ranches. If the patient was able to travel, he would be taken to the nearest town that boasted a doctor—which could mean a trip of up to a hundred miles. If he couldn't be moved, a rider was despatched to fetch the doctor, who would arrive many hours later, cold and exhausted from bouncing across the prairie all night in his open buggy. Doctors were expected to perform medical miracles in the primitive and unsanitary conditions of a ranch-house kitchen or bedroom. Unaided, they delivered babies, dug bullets out of gunshot wounds, amputated gangrenous limbs, stitched together gored cowboys, set fractures and sat up nursing the victims of contagious diseases.

Ranchers who needed medical care were faced with a double dilemma: 'You couldn't afford to be ill; and if you did become ill, you couldn't afford a doctor if you could locate one. A good midwife—or even a fat, greasy, complaining one—was hardly more likely to be available than a doctor.' Fees for an emergency visit were high: 50 cents a mile for the ride, in the 1860s, a dollar for the visit, and an additional charge for any medicines prescribed. Doctors usually presented bills of $20 to $25. Very few ranchers had this kind of ready cash, and were obliged to pay their medical bills in kind—a calf or a load of wood—or rely on their neighbours for financial help.

Many doctors had minimal professional qualifications; and some even dispensed with the quick two-year course that constituted formal medical training at the time. In Nebraska there were no laws regulating the practice of medicine until 1880. As a result, a Dr William Browner, practising in Jefferson County, Nebraska, in 1862, could get away with staking his professional reputation on 'August Flower Bitters', a remedy which he loyally claimed could cure coughs, colds, mumps, measles and fevers. Doctors were also renowned for taking a more than professional interest in alcohol. At least one in eastern Montana had to be 'corralled and kept locked up by the male relatives of a prospective mother, just to insure that he would be available and sober when the time of need came.'

Injuries at work were a major cause of death among cowhands: 'Range Burial' by Harry Jackson

Most ranchers relied mainly on home remedies learned from their neighbours and the Indians to see them through illness and injury. The typical contents of a ranch's medicine chest included Epsom salts, calomel, arnica salve, quinine and 'Mustang' liniment. Patent medicines were also popular (their alcoholic content was appreciated as much as their curative powers). Kerosene was used to disinfect minor cuts and burns, and whisky was the universal antidote for everything from rattlesnake bites (it was said to neutralize the venom) to attacks by rabid skunks.

It's not surprising that death was commonplace in the West. Mrs H. A. Ropes tells: 'The graveyard is one of the first apportionments and the soonest to be thickly inhabited. Quite late in the autumn, one of our merchants returned East to bring his wife out here. She died of cholera on the Missouri River . . .'

Undertakers were few and far between. When a member of an isolated ranching community died, he was buried by his friends. They closed his eyes, crossed his arms over his chest, washed the body and carefully dressed it. In the early days of settlement, when timber was rare, bodies were often wrapped only in a sheet. Occasionally the boards of a wagon, a floor or a shelf might be torn up to construct a coffin. The rough casket was blacked over with soot (or even shoe polish) and the corpse, wrapped in a shroud, was laid inside. Children's coffins were covered with white cloth. The body was laid to rest with a prayer and a few short words. At the close of the ceremony, a bunch of wilting prairie flowers were placed beside the gravemarker that identified the lonely little plot.

If a minister was available, he dignified the ceremony with a service in the house and another short one at the graveside. More often the community had to wait several weeks before the next circuit-riding preacher showed up to conduct a funeral service. 'Circuit preachers' were usually Methodists, and made regular rounds of isolated ranch and farm communities. These churchmen on horseback rode enormous distances, in every kind of weather, to keep their preaching appointments. The Rev F. A. Wilson estimated that he travelled 150,000 miles on circuits in east Texas, and preached 7,000 sermons.

Circuit-riding preachers set out from their homes to make regular visits to isolated ranch families: Methodist Mission

The circuit-riding minister held services in any available location. Tents, barns, stores, blacksmith shops, outdoor sites and even stables were all used as temporary churches. In Lawrence, Kansas, the first Sunday School was held in a wooden shack with nail kegs used as seats. The preachers boarded with their parishioners, shared their food, and were expected to lend a hand with chores and to participate in family life. The itinerant minister was a source of news and companionship to lonely ranchers and settlers. He visited and comforted the sick (who often passed their germs along to him in gratitude), held funeral and memorial services, performed marriages and baptisms. And he was an outside mediator in disputes.

Laymen often presided over religious gatherings in the absence of a minister. A passage was read from the Bible and a few prayers were intoned. One old-timer recalled that the local school was used for the infrequent religious services: 'On several Sundays of the year, Old Man Horner, as the unregenerate natives called him, would hold forth and preach to his flock of hard-shell Baptists. Once or twice a year, the Catholics would have a service; there was no local priest . . . We also had Sunday School of a sort, with folks all the way from six to sixty in the same class.'

The cowboy's attitude towards religion was earthy and uncomplicated. His natural forthrightness cut through much of the pretension and pious sentiment that marked established religious convention. J. Marvin Hunter tells the somewhat apocryphal story of a country man who attended church while in town for jury duty and heard his first sung hymn. Back at home, he tried to explain it to his wife: 'If I say, "Ma, the cows is in the corn", that would be no anthem. But if I'd say, "Ma, Ma, the cows—the spotted cows—the Holstein cow—

The majority of cattle owners forbade gambling on their ranches, but most cowboys ignored this rule: a game of blanket dice

the muly cow—the Jersey cow—all the cows—the cows—is in—is in—the cows is in—is in—the corn—the corn—corn; ah, men" that would be an anthem.'

Few cowboys were interested in churchgoing and religion. To men on the open range, Sunday was a working day like any other. When they did relax, they took their pleasures seriously and exuberantly. A pack of dog-eared and greasy playing cards was a standard fixture in every bunkhouse. Whenever there was a lull in the work, somebody was sure to start up a game—usually poker (it even ranked above sleep as the most popular indoor sport on a ranch). Cowhands were also skilled at Mexican monte, seven-up, faro, pitch, cribbage and blackjack, although none of these games was played with the same furious dedication.

The cowboy was an irrepressible gambler, and not only at cards. Any bet that was offered was sure to attract someone's immediate interest: grasshopper-jumping contests, snail races, spitting competitions and horse races. Most cattlemen disapproved of gambling, and expressly forbade it on their ranches, but a sharp pair of eyes posted at the bunkhouse door allowed cowboys to indulge their 'sporting' inclinations to their hearts' content.

There was a certain amount of reckless gunplay inside the bunkhouses—cowboys sometimes felt the need to express themselves forcefully. Taking idle potshots at the walls and ceiling was a favourite pastime. These activities were often generated by the excruciating boredom of being cooped up in a bunkhouse with nothing to do. One old-timer tells how he spent his time 'looking up at his bunkhouse ceiling and counting bullet holes—3,620 of them—put there by bored cowboys shooting at flies overhead.'

Wm A Rogers

Cowboys were prepared to bet on just about anything going (Left) *'Betting on a Bullfight' by W. A. Rogers* (Below left) *A cockfight in Tombstone, Arizona in 1885*

Enforced idleness was a chronic condition of range life, and at times it led cowboys to devise outrageous diversions for themselves. One unfortunate ranch wife was shocked to find that her pet donkey had become the object of the cowboys' playful attentions and had been sheared to resemble a French poodle. The men also staged competitions to show off their professional skills. The horse-racing, steer-riding and calf-roping that later became enshrined in rodeos had their origins in these spontaneous contests. Cowboys were also famous for their skill with their lariats, and spent hours practising the finer points of rope throwing.

These were some of the rough entertainments that men out on the range devised for themselves. In the towns, the West also witnessed the extraordinary craze of the 'Lazy Man's Club' during the 1870s and 1880s. Almost every self-respecting cow town had one of these at some time. The regulations of a Lazy Man's Club prohibited its members from participating in any form of physical and mental labour. Any breach of the rules was punishable by 'standing the treats'—that is, buying a round of drinks—for the other members. This liquid incentive ensured that the club rules were carried to absurd lengths. A member was once charged with having 'borrowed a newspaper and read it himself'.

Visits between ranches were rare special occasions, for frontier families might live miles away from each other. All the children were piled into a wagon (along with flour, meat or other food for 'house gifts'). Guests were welcome to stay as long as they wished. If sleeping accommodation at night was limited, several people crowded into the same bed and, as the expression went, 'the kids would be hung on a nail'. What was intended to be a day's visit could last several

Bunkhouse scene: the walls are lined with newspapers and early 'girlie' calendars

Public holidays—and the spring and autumn round-ups—were the social highlights of the rancher's year: 'Thanksgiving Dinner for the Ranch' by Frederic Remington; from Harper's Weekly, *1888*

days. This gave the two households plenty of time to renew their friendship, exchange gossip and information, and enjoy the rare pleasure of each other's company.

Community celebrations were the high points of frontier social life. Any reason was good enough: a house-warming, a family move, the opening of a new store, a birthday or a holiday. The occasion was planned well in advance, and word of the event soon spread for miles around. Every woman in the district was specifically invited to attend, for the men outnumbered the women a dozen to one. 'No woman, whatever her personal description, needed to fear being slighted at such a ball,' said one observer. 'There were no wall-flowers on the range.' On the smallest and most isolated ranches, where there were virtually no women, some cowboys gallantly offered to balance the discrepancy between the sexes. They tied handkerchiefs around their arms, or wore aprons, to show they were playing the female. This was known as being 'heifer-branded'.

On larger spreads, one of the women would take charge of social activities. Mrs Campbell, wife of the manager of the giant Matador

Ranch, fully realized how lonely the men were without female companionship and took an active interest in organizing entertainment for them. In 1882 she held the first of what was to become a famous annual event, the Matador Christmas dance. Everyone was welcome —on the understanding that Mrs Campbell would allow no drinking or quarrelling, a wish that was largely respected. Guests travelled up to 50 miles to attend her first dance, though there were only 6 women present to more than 50 men. The festivities lasted for two nights and a day, during which there was almost continuous dancing to fiddle music. When the dancers began to collapse with exhaustion, they lay down (the women indoors, the men outside or in the barn) and slept for a few hours. Then the dancing started up again.

The Fourth of July—Independence Day—was always an excuse for a gigantic blow-out, with barbecues, games, competitions and all-night dances. The celebration at Marble Falls, Texas, in 1854 so moved Noah Smithwick that years later he could still recall in mouthwatering detail the feast that was prepared: there was 'a wagonload of roasting [corn] ears, along with loads of other vegetables, water melons, and cantaloupes. Huntsmen brought in venison and wild turkey, and beef and port galore were advanced. There were pound cakes, wildgrape cakes, dewberry pies, and wild plum pies.' As well as mountains of food, there were always calf-roping and rope-throwing contests, fireworks and dancing in the evening to stimulate the senses, and political speeches to numb the mind.

Community entertainment wasn't limited to public holidays. Travelling circuses drew people from miles around. County and state fairs, with their stock shows, horse races, cockfights, fireworks and a host of carnival attractions, were also major events, worth a long trip into town. Any kind of get-together was an occasion for ranch families. Life on the range often seemed to be an unending cycle of hardship and toil; a meeting with friends was a happy break from the drudgery, and proved that other families were meeting—and beating—the challenge of the West.

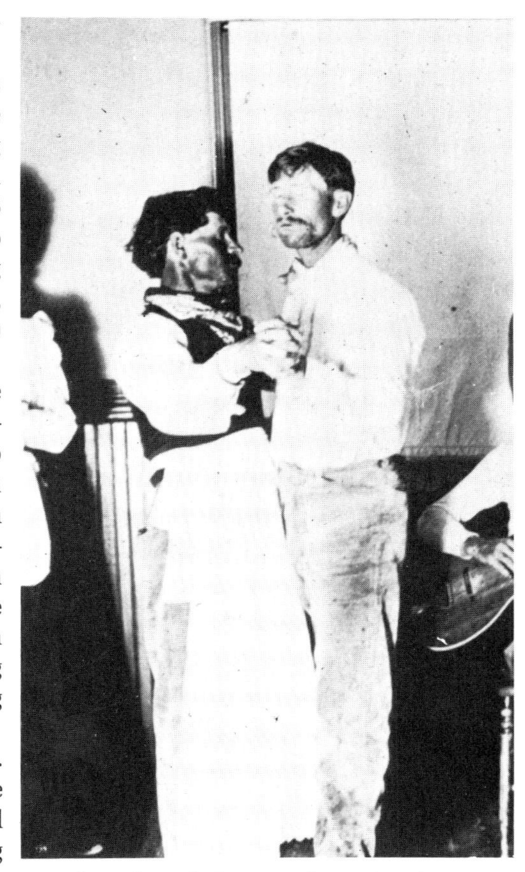

A cowboy who took the woman's part in a dance was 'heifer-branded', often by wearing an apron. At one Christmas dance held at the Matador ranch there were 50 men—and only six women

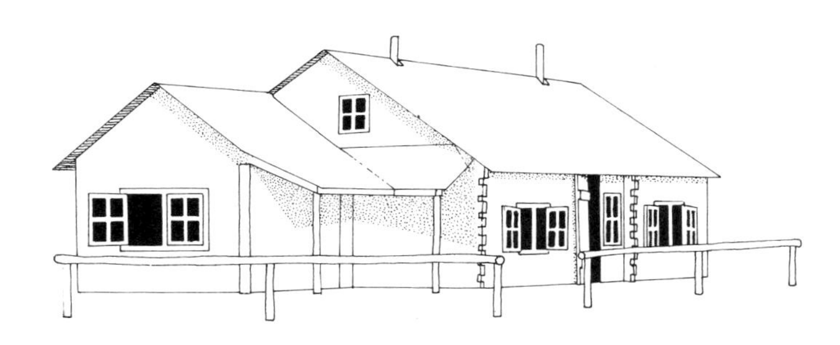

Man and Horse – An Inseparable Pair

'The cowboy depended for his very life on a well-trained horse. In the madness of a stampede, in the heat of the round-up, in the swirl of a river's currents, his horse could save his life.'

The horse shaped the American way of life, with its tradition of 'moving on' to find new pastures, new frontiers, new challenges. Probably the most memorable image of the American West is of the cowboy riding away into the sunset. Yet, curiously, the famous mustang, the horse that did so much to build the old West, wasn't native to America.

Certainly there were horses in America, as far back as 60 million years ago, although the modern *Equus caballus* didn't appear until comparatively recently—about 600,000 years ago. These horses thrived and multiplied until around 9,000 BC, then, inexplicably, they disappeared. Strangely enough, conditions for their existence were ideal at that time, with greater grazing areas than ever before. *Equus caballus* was about 14 hands high (a hand equals four inches), the maximum size for a pony today.

Among the American mustang's ancestors were the 16 horses that Hernando Cortés brought with him to Mexico in March 1519. As recorded for posterity by Bernal Días, they ranged from a 'vicious dark chestnut horse' belonging to Cortés (it died as soon as the expedition landed) to a 'parched sorrel horse, no good for warfare', which was jointly owned by Francisco de Montejo and Alonzo do Avila. *El Arriero* (The Carrier), 'one of the best horses in the fleet', was another. Then there was *La Rabona* (The Bob-tailed), 'very handy, and a good charger'. One dappled horse was unkindly described as 'no good for anything'.

The mere appearance of these horses was responsible for one of the most significant victories ever recorded on American soil. The Mexican Indians, ferocious fighters who feared no man, outnumbered Cortés and his band by about 300 to 1 and the battle went badly for the Spaniards—until Cortés ordered the first, weak charge (of 13 horses) in American history. It was decisive. The Indians imagined the riders and horses to be strange, godlike super-beasts, and fled in disorder. Time and again during their ruthless conquest of the

When the Spaniards sailed to Mexico in 1519 their 11 ships carried 508 soldiers, 100 sailors—and 16 horses: Hernando Cortés, leader of the expedition

Americas, the Spaniards ended their description of a battle with the words, 'after God, we owe our victory to our horses.'

This was only the beginning of the astonishing impact the Barbary horses were to have on the history of North America. Other conquistadores, fired by Cortés's startling success, tried to emulate his exploits in other parts of the Americas. Francisco Coronado, for example, attempted to conquer the mythical cities of the north—in fact, the trackless plains.

He started out with a thousand horses as well as cattle and mules, over 300 Spaniards and hundreds of black and Indian slaves, who were the continent's first cattlehands. He ended up a sick and disheartened man with only a hundred men left. He lost cattle, swine, sheep, mules and slaves. Many horses were also lost, and some were even stolen by enterprising Indians around what is now Albuquerque, New Mexico. These, and horses lost by other expeditions, may well have been the start of the great herds of wild horses who found a perfect home on the Great Plains, already stocked with buffalo, deer, antelope and elk.

Francisco Coronado's expedition into America failed to find the rich cities of legend—but he and his men did discover some famous landmarks, including the Grand Canyon: 'The Coronado Expedition' by Frederic Remington

Some authorities dispute this theory, and believe that the first horses to roam free were stolen by Pueblo Indians who'd been enslaved by the Spaniards and taught the arts of horse management during the 17th century. Be that as it may, two facts are clear. First, in its facial lines the cow pony bore a remarkable resemblance to the beautiful Barbary horses of the Spaniards. Second, the Indians—until then a footbound people—developed an astonishing degree of horsemanship remarkably swiftly.

'Comanche Captures a Wild Horse' by George Catlin

The mustangs were small (14 to 15·2 hands or 56 to 62 inches high) but very powerful and with remarkable powers of endurance. George Catlin, a painter and writer who in 1834 accompanied a US military expedition to the southern plains along the borders of Texas, described how 'they graze over the vast plains . . . and congregate in large bands . . . several hundreds together, presenting many varieties of colours and forms of marks.' He said of the Comanche that they 'had a wide reputation for warlike skills as horsemen.' They were 'the finest riders on earth . . . capturing and subduing the finest of wild horses, and displaying the trickiest methods of riding.'

'Sioux Buffalo Chase' by George Catlin

The Indian technique for catching and training horses was very similar to that used later by the cowboy. The mustangs could detect a man at a great distance, and an Indian might have to pursue one of these horses for several miles before catching it with a leather lariat some 15 to 20 yards long. This was often attached to the girth of his own horse, to take the initial strain of holding the struggling mustang. Heroically, the Indian often allowed himself to be dragged along the ground by his captive until the horse wore itself out.

When the horse came to a halt, the Indian hobbled it and placed a halter round its jaw. Then the battle would begin—and last for as long as an hour—until the mustang was subdued. The final moment came when the Indian advanced slowly and gently, hand over hand along the halter, and placed a hand tenderly over the conquered horse's nostrils. Symbolically, he covered its eyes, and breathed into its nostrils. This exchange of breath between horse and man sealed their friendship.

A famous Comanche feat was for the rider to throw himself down on one side of the horse while galloping at full speed. In the heat of battle, he could fling himself from one side to another, using his horse's body as a screen from his enemy's weapons. At the same time he carried a bow, shield, and a 14-foot-long lance. Catlin claimed that although other Plains Indians practised this trick, none did so with the skill of the Comanche. Some Comanche could even shoot an arrow from under the neck of a galloping horse.

The Indian practice of using different horses for different purposes was later emulated by the cowboy. There were squaw horses, which pulled the *travois*, the litter that was dragged along like a wheel-less barrow and carried belongings when moving camp. There were, of course, war horses, and—the precursor of the cowboy's 'cutting' horse—the buffalo horse. This horse had to be miraculously manoeuvrable; once a buffalo had been approached and speared, or shot with an arrow, the maddened animal could easily impale the rider if his mount didn't swerve instantly away.

Descended from the hot-blooded Barbaries, and hardened by generations of life in the wild, the Indian horse developed a strength, stamina, and sharpness of senses that made it the perfect mount for the cowboy. Perhaps the most striking testimony to its character came from early artist and writer Frederic Remington, who told how he rode a horse 'at a very rapid gallop for twenty four miles during the middle of the day through the desert sand' [of Arizona]. At the end of the ride the horse (which belonged to Chief Ascension Rios of the Papago tribe) was as fit as when he started.

In appearance, the cowboy horse was unprepossessing, and it is interesting that it had, in fact, started out as the Cordoban horse, first bred by the Arabs in the 12th century and famed for its beauty and classic lines.

The cow pony was not entirely the result of random breeding on the Plains. Other breeds had been introduced to America in the East, starting with those of the 17th-century English settlers. They were interbred with the mustangs to add a turn of speed to stamina and endurance. The mustang was generally regarded as a 'cold-blooded' horse: slow, steady, tireless. These new horses were 'hot-blooded' breeds: thoroughbreds and quarter horses (sprinters). They had the qualities of racehorses. As a result of this interbreeding, an animal evolved that combined matchless endurance for the long days riding line, with the speed needed for round-ups.

The typical cowboy horse combined endurance with speed. It often had to carry its rider, and his possessions, over many long miles: a cowboy in the 1920s loads his horse

The first cowboys culled their mounts from the great herds of wild horses that roamed the plains and prairies: 'Wild Horses' by George Catlin

The cow pony was 'close-coupled'—able to turn very sharply. It was small, usually no more than 15 hands (60 inches). It came in a startling variety of colours, a result of endless, unplanned breeding in the wild. It could be roan, bay, or piebald ('paint' or 'pinto')—anything from a golden Palomino (eventually elevated to a separate breed) to black. The Appaloosa was also a separate breed, a blue roan that sported spots and blotches, especially on the rump, and was bred originally by the Nez Percé Indians of Montana. In the taxing terrain of Oregon, Montana and the Dakotas, interbreedings of the Texas cow pony with big, strong Clydesdales and Percherons from the East were used. They were known respectively as Oregon Bigfoots, and Percheron Puddin'-foots because of their big feet.

Most cowboys preferred solid-coloured horses. A cowboy looking for work was influenced by the quality of the horses offered. If they were poor, he often left the job and looked for another. To be fired and have to leave the job on foot was a deeply shameful experience.

'A man with guts and a horse' is an apt description of a cowboy. The relationship between man and horse was typically described by an old cowhand, talking to another as they unsaddled in the corral after a long day's riding: 'You know, Walt, I love that damn horse so much, I like him.' A cowboy relied on his horse to carry him in all kinds of weather: when the footing was so slippery that he wondered how long the horse could stay vertical, when the cold was so fierce that the horse had to paw through the snow to find feed.

Horses were specialists. A trained, intelligent animal with skill in roping and cutting out cattle from the herd was a 'top' horse, the pride of a man's string. An ordinary horse—possibly still half-trained—was used for day-herding and riding circle. A stupid horse was called a 'jughead', 'churnhead' or 'crockhead'. Some animals were ruined during their breaking-in and were called 'spoiled horses' or 'salty broncs'. Others, broken down after years of service, were 'plugs', dismissed by some as 'shad-bellied, slabsided crowbait'.

A horse would not become a top horse until quite late on in life; most great 'cutting' and 'roping' horses were at least ten years old. A man who had a cutting horse in his string was the envy of his comrades. The horse anticipated every turn and twist the animal that was to be cut out might make. What's more, it could spin and turn faster than the cow. Its rider, usually a top hand, needed skill to stay on it. Many of these horses could cut without a bridle.

The roping horse was equally important. Roping from horseback was an essential cowboy skill; even corralled cattle would attack a man on foot. A man who could every time catch a cow, by the heels or head, from a running horse was, in an immortal phrase, 'as scarce as bird dung in a cuckoo clock'. There were many types of roping technique, but they all depended on one vital factor: the horse. From the instant the rope landed around the cow, a roping horse knew when to turn, when to stand with legs braced, pulling against the rope and keeping it taut. This horse was as laconic and relaxed as his master. His head drooped, he moved serenely, his energy was conserved for the moment of action, when his rider had singled out the animal to be dragged from the herd.

Communication between a cowboy and a top cutting horse is silent—and total. The slightest pull on the reins is enough to guide the animal: cowhands cutting out a steer, by Edward Borein

A good roping horse instinctively keeps the rope taut and holds that tension even if its rider dismounts: 'Roping a Calf for Branding' by W. A. Rogers

Roping from horseback is still an essential cowboy skill. Techniques vary, but their success always depends on the horse's speed and dexterity

The 'river' horse was also in a class of its own. Cattle didn't like swimming; they became spooky. A river horse had a mysterious instinct that told him where the bottom was safe, where it was treacherous. Some of these horses would swim high, so that men could stay on their backs; others swam low with their men beside them. To guide the horse, the cowboy splashed water gently on his face. Using the reins was likely to panic him. Every man knew what this could lead to; the graves of cowhands lined many river banks.

Certain horses were trained as 'night' horses. These could detect a single cow straying from the herd, and turn her back without any guidance from the rider. A cowboy could doze safely in his saddle with a horse like this beneath him; the animal would even know within a few minutes when the two-hour night watch was over. Whenever a storm was brewing, or the cattle were restless, the night horses were kept near the camp for emergencies.

Other animals included a quiet, well-behaved horse for the women and children around the headquarters ranch; and, of course, the cook's mule team. Because of the tremendous demands cowboys made on them, the average horse had a working life of only about seven years.

The cowboy depended for his very life on a well-trained horse. In the madness of a stampede, in the heat of the round-up, in the swirl of a river's currents, his horse could save his life. A cowboy who would never be guilty of sentimentality was never ashamed to pour

Cowboys thoroughly appreciated the antics of bucking broncs—an appreciation that's now shared by the public who flock to modern rodeos. Judging is based on the animal's performance as well as the man's

Breaking in horses was an art. The 'bronc-buster' would select the natural leader from among the bunch of horses let loose in the corral. The first trick was to get the noose round it, then anchor that to a deeply sunk post, the 'snubbing post'. Then the creature was forced to the ground by several men while the cowboy, with one knee on the horse's neck, slipped a bridle on it. The next 15 minutes were spent cautiously manoeuvring reins, saddle blanket and saddle into place. Then the cowboy would distract the horse by twisting or biting its ear—and mount swiftly before the animal realized what was happening.

Once he was on the horse's back, all hell broke loose. The horse bucked, curved, reared and leapt into the air. It might try throwing itself backwards. The cowboy had to ride out these manoeuvres. He sat as tight as he could and used his strength, skill—and leather quirt—to make the horse do what he wanted. When the animal's resistance was broken, perhaps after some sulking, it circled the corral relatively obediently. Just to make sure, the cowboy dismounted and mounted again a few times. Eventually, he brought the horse to a stop. Then he patted it, removed the saddle and bridle, and moved on to the next animal. Today, 'bronc-riding' is a standard rodeo event.

out his troubles to the uncomprehending, but sympathetic, ear of his mount. Nevertheless, with typical Western humour, the cowboys gave horses the most disparaging of names. Names like Monkey Face, Rat Hash, Old Guts or Leapin' Lena were common; others were unprintable.

The cowboy's appetite for inventing descriptive horse names reached its height with the famous buckers: Jack Dempsey, Mary's Lamb and Gentle Lizzie; Hoochie Coochie; I Be Damn, You Be Damn and Damnifiknow; Flying Devil; Gut Buster and Dynamite; Widow-maker, Yellow Fever and Leprosy; Red Pepper, Gin Fizz and Bad Whisky. There was Double Tough who, after being a champion bucker for years, suddenly reformed one day and became gentle. And the never-to-be-forgotten Midnight; the cowboys who'd worked with him paid for a monument to his memory. On it they engraved:

> Under the sod lies a great bucking horse;
> There was nary a cowboy he couldn't toss.
> His name was Midnight, his coat black as coal.
> If there is a horse heaven, please God, rest his soul.

Cowboys made large claims for their mounts. A horse was invariably so skilled that 'it could spin on a quarter and give you fifteen cents change', and 'so gentle, you could stake it to a hairpin'. Horses were well-represented in the tall-story department. Like the animal that was so well-trained he could sing—or rather hum—the tunes his owner sang. One old cowboy recalls: 'I went to the ranch this horse came from, in South Dakota, but he was dead. He probably heard I was coming, and being kinda old and not being able to sing with the fervour of youth, the poor old boy just laid down and died with a broken heart.'

There was a world of difference between a cowboy who was a 'rider' and one who was a 'bronc rider'. Any man was a rider; it was part of his job. The bronc rider, besides being a good cowhand, specialized in staying on difficult horses. He might also be a specialist in breaking in horses.

Breaking-in usually took place around the time of the spring round-up. 'There ain't no horse that can't be rode, and there ain't no man that can't be throwed,' went the rhyme. This dual challenge made bronc- (or bronco-) busting fearsome and fascinating. Some professional bronc-busters did the job by sheer brute force; they got on and stayed on until the animal gave up. Others, especially Indians, had a strange, hypnotic effect on horses; it was said that no Indian's horse would ever buck. The average cowhand took great pride in his ability to stay on all the horses in his string (even after breaking, the cow pony was notoriously erratic and bad-tempered). But the professional bronc-buster was exceptional.

'Weak head and strong back for a horse fighter' was the saying. It showed. As the photographer L. A. Huffman wrote, 'The gentleman could almost unerringly be spotted by his swagger, his unfailing weakness for wearing heavy bearskin or llama leggings even in the hottest weather, and his spurs.' The job was so demanding that few men could carry on after they'd reached 30.

A buster like Lee Warren of the Bow and Arrow outfit in Montana could break in six horses in a morning, starting in the grey dawn. His equipment was simple: a plain, single-rigged cowboy saddle, bridle, lariat, spurs, quirt, and short lengths of grass rope for the hobbling. It then took him five days to train the string of six horses. When Warren got married his wife made him give up bronc-busting. Who can blame her? More than one good man was 'kicked into a funeral procession'. A good horse-breaker never lost his temper, always stayed in control of the situation. If a man killed a horse, he lost his job.

No two horses buck in exactly the same way, and a host of colourful expressions described their different movements. 'Bucking on a dime' . . . 'high rollin'' . . . 'weavin'' were simple to understand. 'Fence-wormin'' referred to horses that zig-zagged; a horse that reared high, pawing forward with his front feet, was called a 'cloud hunter'.

Even after a bronc-buster had trained the horse to be ridden, the cowboy had to 'iron out the kinks'; and after a winter of idleness even a horse that was already trained would come out lively. 'Green' horses, fresh from the gentle hands of the buster, had to be taught skills by the proud new owner. First, he completed their training by

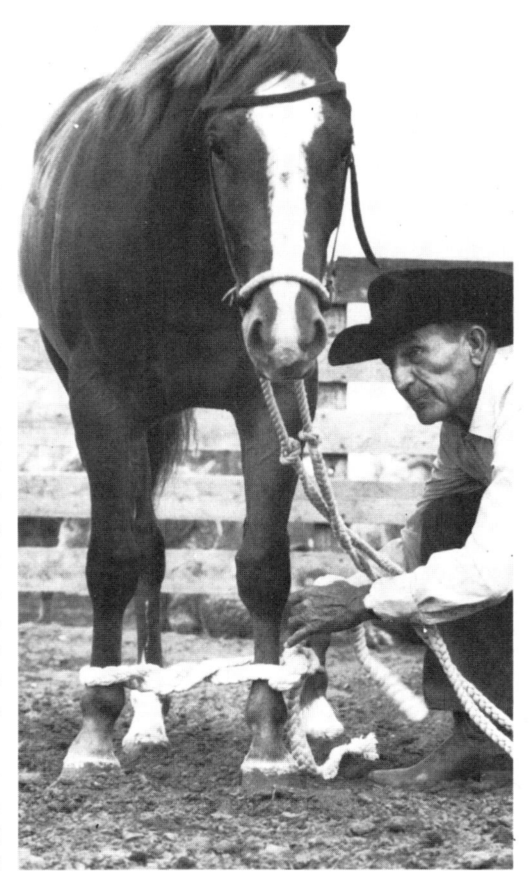

Ideally horses are allowed to move around freely in their pastures, but sometimes it's necessary to hobble them: a cowboy makes sure a horse won't stray

The remuda was always grazed away from the cow camp with the horses brought in at regular intervals for riders to select fresh mounts: a wrangler takes a remuda back to grass

using them for simple jobs, like riding into town. These trips to town gave rise to the popular use of the word 'bronc'. To the cowboy, a bronc was a horse still untrained and fresh from the wild. Townsfolk, hearing him refer to his mount as a 'bronc' during his visits, imagined that he called all horses by this name.

The basic equipment every cowboy needed for riding included the famous high-heeled boots, the fancy big-rowelled spurs (used sparingly by a good rider), bridle and bit, and lariat. The boots were high-heeled to get a comfortable purchase on the stirrups; their pointed toes made it easier to get the foot in fast. Bits were often extremely harsh; they needed to be, with the 'ornery' half-wild manners of many cow ponies. The lariat, between 30 and 60 feet long, was a flying noose; a skilled man could catch any horse or cow, no matter how wayward, with its aid.

The horses were kept in a *remuda*, a group, which might or might not be corralled. North-western ranchers called the remuda a *cavvy*, short for the Spanish *caballada* (horse herd). Many cowboys referred to a 'saddle band', or just 'the hosses'. At the beginning of each season there was a 'choosin' match', when the cowboys selected their strings from the remuda. Top hands chose first, the least experienced last. The 'rep', who went round to other outfits at round-up time and brought back the strays, usually got the finest string. He was the ranch's ambassador.

The horses were looked after by the wrangler, usually a novice or an old man near retirement. The young wranglers were the butt of many practical jokes, and hard-worked by the cook. They had to wash up and chop logs—and were usually given the most broken-down nag in the remuda. The horses were easily contained within a rope corral, even if it was just a couple of feet high, with no strength; every horse remembered his first, traumatic experience with the

Horses raised in the open take longer to mature than ranch-reared animals. As a result they develop stronger bones and muscles, and greater powers of endurance: cowboys round up a remuda

rope. For most of the time the horses were free to forage (they lived almost exclusively on grass in the early days). Some horses who learned to hop along even when hobbled by the forefeet would be cross-hobbled.

Most remudas contained only geldings. Stallions fought too much; mares disturbed the peace of the herd. Much of the time the horses were not shoed. Certainly, during the winter, when many were left to roam free, their shoes were removed to allow them to run barefooted, as nature intended. No cowboy enjoyed shoeing, though if the ranch were not big enough to employ a blacksmith he had to take his turn. One old cowhand observed: 'This shore is hard work, and has wrecked a lot of promising cowboy careers. The young hosses is bad; the older ones is worse; and the idea that cowboys is bowlegged from much ridin's all wrong. Cowboys is bowlegged from holding up nine hundred pounds of kickin' hoss while at the same time raspin' his feet down and putting shoes on him. Shoein' hosses and trying to break some of 'em to ride accounts for all cowboys' most painful and embarrassin' moments.'

While a real bond existed between man and animal, cowboys were never sentimental about their horses: a Cherokee cowboy and his horse

The remuda was replenished from the range herd. This consisted of a number of small bands of brood mares, 20 to 25 head strong, each headed by a stallion. These herds were rounded up, roped and branded in summer. All these horses were corralled several times a year, with some cut out for breaking in each time.

The most spectacular demonstration of horse and rider in action was—and is—the rodeo. This public display of the cowboy's skills originated in the early Mexican round-ups (*rodeo* is *round-up* in Spanish). Unlike the Western round-up, these affairs were often more like fiestas, with roping competitions and horse racing among the men, and dancing and dining among the entire community. A fiesta is recorded in 1792 in San Francisco. (California was always recognized as the first home of roping skills.) Others were held in New Mexico in 1832 and 1847. But the first modern rodeos started in the early 1870s: a steer-riding contest was held in Cheyenne, Wyoming, in 1872. The first real rodeo was organized by Col George Miller of the famous 101 ranch in 1882. This was a Wild West Show in Winfield, Kansas. In December of the same year, a steer-roping contest was held in Austin, Texas; a $300 silver-mounted saddle was the coveted prize.

Today the rodeo is a carefully-organized commercial event, watched by an estimated 30 million people a year. At its best, it represents the only real opportunity that remains for people to see the skills most working cowboys took for granted in the old days. There are demonstrations of cutting, rounding up, and stagecoach and relay races recalling the days of the Pony Express.

The decline of the Western mustang—like many other aspects of Western life—started with the introduction of barbed wire in the 1870s, and the fencing of the range. Men began to do new types of jobs, which either didn't need horses or required different types of horse. A cowboy didn't need a skilled cutting horse when he was riding along a fence; he didn't need an agile horse to go climbing windmills. Furthermore, he didn't need a horse at all to dig post holes. The mustang was exported to swell the ranks of the horses used by the British Army in the Boer War between 1899 and 1902. It was sent to die in France in the Great War (and, the worst indignity of all, when it was killed it was made into meat stew). Eventually, wild mustangs were shot for pet food.

Ranchers demanded new kinds of horses: great plodding Percherons and Clydesdales that could be harnessed together in long teams to pull the cumbersome early combine harvesters. Even the US Army used thoroughbreds—despite the fact that the Indians had demonstrated time and again that their mustangs could outrun army horses any time.

When horses became popular again after the Second World War, this time as pets, people chose the kind of horse that some cowboys still ride on modern ranches out West. The Appaloosa and the quarter horse have both won enormous popularity with the new generation of riders. In fact the Appaloosa, starting with a total of only 339 registered animals in 1946, has grown faster than any other breed—to 126,000 in 1970.

But the relationship between the cowboy and his horse, half tough-minded practicality, half a carefully concealed but very real affection, can never exist in riding stables or on dude ranches. Man and horse were inseparable. Alexander Sweet and J. Armory Knox wrote in *On a Mexican Mustang Through Texas*: 'A cowboy is a man attached to a gigantic pair of spurs. He is generally found on the back of a small mustang pony. This fact has given rise to a widely diffused belief that the cowboy cannot walk. Some scientists, however, dispute this as several specimens have been seen—under the influence of excitement and while suffering from intense thirst—to detach themselves from their mustangs and disappear into business houses where their wants were attended to by a man wearing a diamond breastpin and a white apron.'

Rustlers and Horse-thieves

'Cattle-rustlers were more common than horse-thieves—and more widely accepted. Before the advent of barbed wire, cow country ethics were actually on the rustler's side.'

Law and order in the West was a heady mixture of rough justice and might is right—with a dash of macabre humour. Formally, the law was in the hands of the marshals, sheriffs and their deputies. Most of them were courageous men, eminently capable of keeping order in the towns they controlled. Others were only too aware that as elected officials their jobs depended on the goodwill of the citizens. However, the law officers just didn't have the manpower to police the lonely acres that stretched beyond their town's boundaries. So 'right' was whatever most people agreed was right. Their ideas of rectitude were often inconsistent, but they had a logical basis—and could be light years away from Eastern city ideas of law.

It was right to respect a man's property; but it was also right (or not really wrong) to cock a snook at the anti-rustling laws introduced by the great cattle barons. (Big-business takeovers of the range were fiercely resented by independent ranchers whose livelihood depended on the free movement of cattle.) Equally, it was right for law-abiding citizens to form vigilante committees to track down and execute stock thieves. These groups represented the will of the community and compensated for the established law's failure to protect property and keep order.

This *ad hoc* legal system worked surprisingly well. The vast majority of ranchers, cowboys and citizens obeyed its rules without question. The law-breaking minority were often ne'er-do-wells and criminals who'd come West to escape the law or make an easy living; they were, literally, outlaws. Their crimes ranged from bank-robbing (an attractive occupation when banks were first established —the robbers often outnumbered the lawmen) and stagecoach hold-ups to whisky-running to the Indians and crooked gambling. But by far the most common crimes were horse-thieving and cattle-rustling.

Of the two, horse-thieving was by far the most serious. (It was always called 'stealing' or 'thieving'; cattle thieves were generally

Vigilante groups were active in most parts of the West—and were generally more efficient than elected law officers: a committee of vigilance coin

'rustlers' from 'hustler', meaning anyone active and bustling.) In the East, a horse was merely a piece of property worth perhaps $25, and stealing one was a modest misdemeanour. In the West, a man's horse was his only form of transport. Without it he was at the mercy of any sudden storm, he could die of hunger or thirst, he'd be unable to escape if he was attacked by hostile Indians. In most states of the West horse-stealing was looked on as worse than murder, and the penalty was swift and unquestioned: death by shooting or hanging from the nearest tree.

But the horse-thieves flourished. In 1874 the Fort Worth, Texas, *Democrat* reported that the thieves' boldness had 'aroused the blood of Texans, and new ropes are being prepared for those who love horseflesh not wisely but too well. A few wholesome hangings will soon be in order, and the traffic in horseflesh will be sensibly diminished.' In spite of these strong words, four years later a Houston newspaper estimated that 100,000 horses had been stolen in Texas during the previous three years—and that 750 men were involved. It added that only one in ten had been captured.

Lynching played its part in Western society: the result of a lynch party in 1888

Stealing horses was a serious crime, and owners often gave chase for as much as 500 miles: a horse ranch, a tempting target for thieves

The epitaph on this tombstone stresses that the men it commemorates were legally hanged: Boot Hill, Tombstone, Arizona

A horse was easily recognized by its markings, so the stolen animals were usually sold far from their home range. An enterprising Montana thief used to drive his booty across the border to Canada, sell them there—and then steal Canadian horses to sell in Montana.

There was a good market for stolen horses. A man could sell to Indian agents or military posts, with no questions asked, for the contractors too made fat profits. These same contractors were often involved in selling whisky illegally to the Indians. And this set up a never-ending cycle of theft and drunkenness: to buy the whisky the Indians bartered their horses, their only valuable possessions. When they recovered from the effects of the rotgut booze, they found themselves without any means of transport—and so they had no alternative but to steal more horses; which they later bartered for whisky . . . and so the cycle continued. Greenhorns from the East were also good customers for thieves. If the legal owner recognized the horse, he usually had to refund the purchase price (about half or two-thirds of the normal market price) to the innocent buyer.

Cattle-rustlers were more common than horse-thieves—and more widely accepted. In fact, before the advent of barbed wire, cow country ethics were actually on the rustler's side; the origins of his occupation were respectable and entirely in tune with the early Western tradition that possession was ten-tenths of the law.

At the end of the Civil War when the Great Plains teemed with wild Longhorns cowmen regularly branded unmarked animals as their own. They were regarded as a natural resource, like the buffalo and the mustang. Rancher John James Haynes explained how he'd built a trap to catch strays. He'd confine them there without food or water until they were amenable enough to be driven to other pens. Few ranchers could bring themselves to cease practising the gentle art of mavericking.

Mavericks are named after Colonel Samuel A. Maverick, a lawyer from San Antonio, Texas. In 1847 he took over a herd of cattle as part payment of a debt, and had them delivered to his ranch on the Matagorda Peninsula on the Gulf coast. There they were in the charge of a Negro who worked for him. The Negro, however, failed to brand the herd, and for the next six years the cattle roamed the plain. Other ranchers who came across these unbranded animals referred to them as 'mavericks'.

Understandably, many head were stolen, and in 1853 Maverick decided to sell what was left of his herd. The buyer was Toutant de Beauregard of New Orleans; whenever his men found an unbranded animal they automatically claimed it as a 'maverick' and branded it as Beauregard's. The increase in the original herd was astonishing!

Mavericks were a constant source of friction. The ownership of a calf rested entirely on the fact that calves follow their mothers—so anyone who could separate the two before round-up time was likely to be able to keep the calf. One of the main reasons why round-ups were given official starting dates was to enable every man to have an equal chance at the mavericks. Eventually there were so many disputes that most areas ruled that all mavericks belonged to their cattlemen's associations.

This applied equally to their employees. It was only too easy for a man sent out to bring in mavericks to start a little brand of his own. A foreman, riding the range miles away from headquarters, would find a solitary maverick, and brand it. What with one thing and another, it would come out as his own brand, not the boss's. Pretty soon he'd have a few head, enough to enable him eventually to start his own ranch. With the enormous acreages involved, it wasn't difficult to keep his cattle grazing peacefully out of sight. Although many ranchers were tolerant about this kind of individual enterprise, others just wouldn't employ a man who had his own brand.

Between friends and neighbours, rustling was often looked on as something of a joke. If a man snitched the odd maverick here and there, and didn't get carried away, his neighbouring cattle barons were content to look the other way—and vice versa.

This cheerful attitude didn't apply to the man with no social or business connections: the lone cowboy without means, or the farmer. For them, there was a different set of rules. In Texas, John Leaverton, a lone rustler, was caught putting his brand on a calf belonging to a rich rancher at Adobe Walls. Unwisely, he fought—and was killed on the spot. In 1875, cowmen in Mason County, Texas, broke into jail and lynched three out of five rustlers held there (the sheriff rescued the other two).

This kind of rough justice was deeply rooted in the Western credo. Take the case of Isaac Hobart. A deserter from Robert E. Lee's Confederate army, a killer, robber and rapist, he eventually found his promised land, west of the Pecos River, and a new career—rustler. His name changed to Ike Smith, nobody cared what his business was, as long as he didn't involve anyone else. But they sometimes wondered how he managed to rear so many cattle on the Alkaline Salt Flats near his home. Ike had a good run until one of his neighbours, Old Man Dubose, discovered that 'Alkali Ike' was adapting his brand, and stealing his cattle. Dubose showed up with two of his hands and, without fuss, hanged Ike from his own rafters.

Hangings were sometimes called 'necktie parties': a hanging at Russell, Kansas

Then there was Pete Kitchen of southern Arizona, who discovered that a certain Mexican was stealing his horses. When the man stole one of his favourite mounts, Pete got in his buggy and drove after him. When he returned—alone—a few days later, everyone knew he'd caught the man. Finally, somebody asked what had happened. Pete explained that the man had suffered a mishap: 'I was leading him back on the stolen horse. Night come, and I had to rest. I says to myself then, "How can I rest and not let this rustler escape?" So I tied the man's hands behind him, tied a rope around his neck and put him astride the horse. Other end of the neck rope I tied to the limb of a tree, just keeping the slack of it. It wasn't hurting him none, so I laid down on a blanket near by and went to sleep.' 'What happened then, Mr Kitchen?' Pete replied: 'Why, come daylight, doggone if I hadn't forgot to hitch the horse, and it had wandered off grazing in the night! I had a right hard time catching it again.'

John X. Beidler participated in a vigilante hanging in Virginia City, Montana, in 1864. He adjusted the nooses when five men were hanged simultaneously from a beam before several thousand spectators. 'When you put the rope about that poor fellow's neck, didn't you feel for him?' a spectator asked Beidler. 'Yes,' replied the worthy Beidler, 'I felt for his left ear.'

Even when rustlers were brought to court, it wasn't always possible to secure a conviction. Sheriff J. A. Elliott, of Weld County, Colorado, arrested a man for having seven calves belonging to the Pony Cattle Company in his barn. Several witnesses came forward to testify, with straight faces, that it was common for calves to leave their mothers and break into barns. The man was acquitted. The sheriff, consoling himself in the lobby of a nearby hotel, observed that no other result could be expected when a cow thief was tried by a cow thief jury and a cow thief judge. When the judge heard of this comment he fined Elliott $25 for contempt of court.

In the early days, all a man needed to start his own brand was, so the saying went, 'a rope, a running iron, and the nerve to use it'. Unlike a legal branding tool, which had a set pattern, the running iron was in effect a metal poker that could be used to 'write' any brand at all on the side of a beast. The rustler was commonly known as a 'rewrite man'. He would either find a brand and register it with a clerk in some small county, or ignore formalities and use an unregistered 'slow' brand. Ideally, it had some characteristics in common with the brand of the local big ranch so that only minimal alterations had to be made. This method could be so effective that it was necessary to skin the animal to see from the inside whether the brand had been changed.

Other tricks included the 'cold' brand: a rustler who was employed on a ranch would place wet sacking between the animal's fur and the iron when branding for the owner. Only the fur was scorched with the brand mark—and this soon grew out, leaving the animal apparently ownerless. In the 1870s a law forbidding the use of running irons was passed—and even before this a man found in possession of one might find himself answering awkward questions in front of an impatient jury.

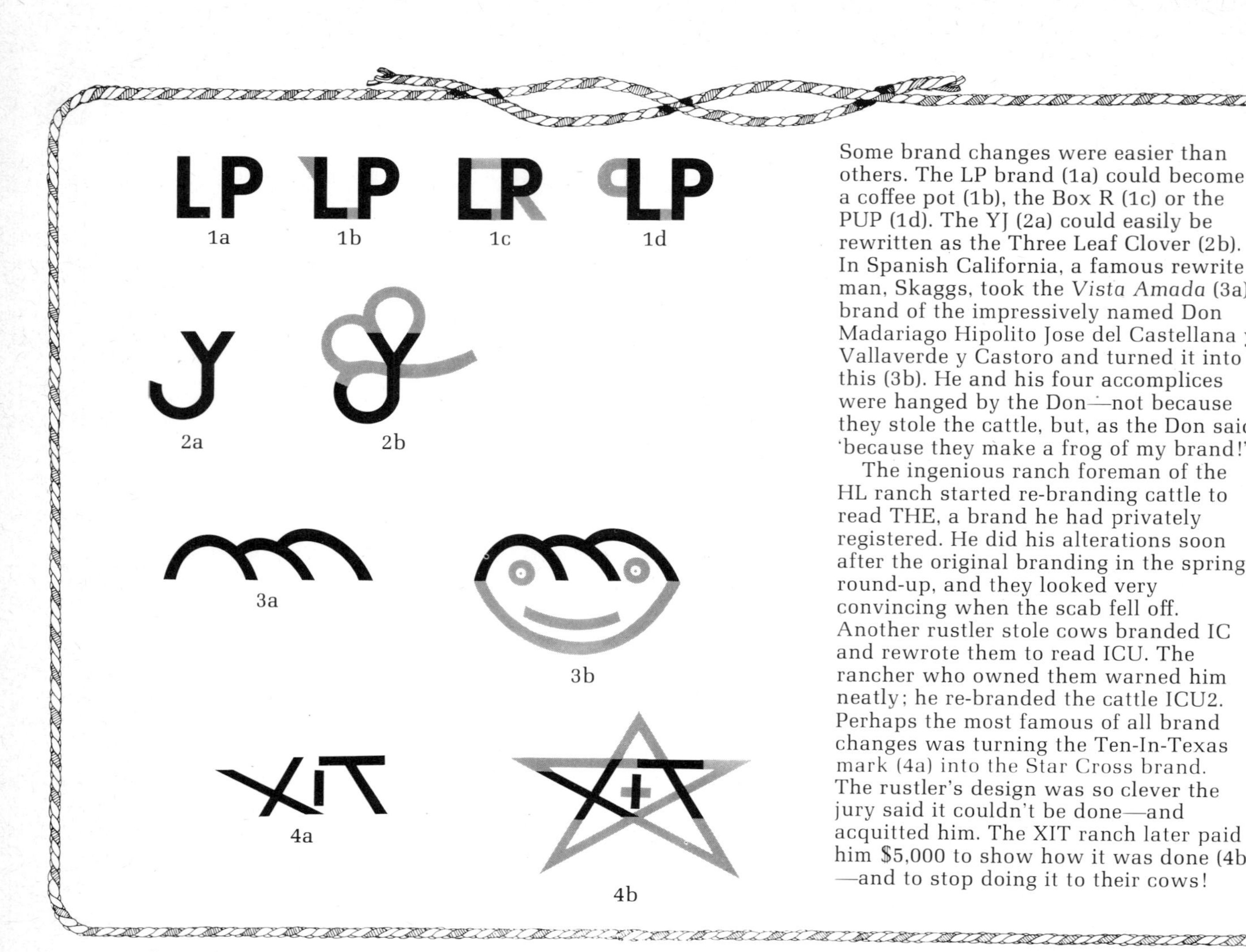

Some brand changes were easier than others. The LP brand (1a) could become a coffee pot (1b), the Box R (1c) or the PUP (1d). The YJ (2a) could easily be rewritten as the Three Leaf Clover (2b). In Spanish California, a famous rewrite man, Skaggs, took the *Vista Amada* (3a) brand of the impressively named Don Madariago Hipolito Jose del Castellana y Vallaverde y Castoro and turned it into this (3b). He and his four accomplices were hanged by the Don—not because they stole the cattle, but, as the Don said, 'because they make a frog of my brand!'

The ingenious ranch foreman of the HL ranch started re-branding cattle to read THE, a brand he had privately registered. He did his alterations soon after the original branding in the spring round-up, and they looked very convincing when the scab fell off. Another rustler stole cows branded IC and rewrote them to read ICU. The rancher who owned them warned him neatly; he re-branded the cattle ICU2. Perhaps the most famous of all brand changes was turning the Ten-In-Texas mark (4a) into the Star Cross brand. The rustler's design was so clever the jury said it couldn't be done—and acquitted him. The XIT ranch later paid him $5,000 to show how it was done (4b) —and to stop doing it to their cows!

Rustling became so widespread that there weren't enough mavericks available to keep its practitioners in business. So the rustlers created them by taking calves from their mothers before they were weaned. By nature, calves will follow their mothers anywhere. Various stratagems were used to create instant 'orphans'. Rustlers might 'sand' a calf's eyes: fill them with sand so that the animal couldn't see where it was going. Even more brutally, they sometimes cut the muscles that held the eyelids up. They healed eventually, but always drooped slightly—droop-eyed calves were immediately suspect. The most drastic method was to kill the mother.

The increasing authority of the cattlemen's associations, in the 1870s, marked the beginning of the end for 'respectable' rustlers. The associations introduced new rules for organizing the range. For example, the Wyoming and Montana associations pledged all their members not to employ men who had brands of their own. At the end of 1883 the Wyoming association ruled that all unbranded mavericks should be association property, to help pay expenses. In the same year the Texas association, alarmed at the spread of rustling, announced rewards of $250 for information leading to conviction, and started their own 'Scotland Yard' of the cattle country—the range inspectors.

Stuart's Stranglers were formed in 1884 when Granville Stuart, then leader of the Montana Stock Growers' Association, returned home to discover that his prize stallion and 35 steers had been stolen: Granville Stuart, 1883; photograph by L. A. Huffman

The Montana Stock Growers' Association employed men to check brands at the markets, ride the ranges and perform other essential tasks: 'Montana Manhunters'; photograph by L. A. Huffman

These range detectives watched at cattle pens, checked herds on the trail—and knew every brand in their districts. An inspector could tell at a glance if a brand had been changed, and knew enough about the men within a 100-mile radius to have a pretty shrewd idea whether or not they were adding unlawfully to their herds. In 1883, association inspectors recovered 501 head worth $12,500; in 1884, the total was 853 cattle (value: $21,325).

Rustling was no longer respectable, but it continued to flourish. The old tradition of the wide-open West was reinforced by a deep-rooted dislike of the big men. The great cattle barons and companies wanted to increase their (highly favourable) hold over the range. The little man felt he had the right to build up his own spread as others had done before him. Feeling against the big barons was so strong that, as in the past, rustlers were often acquitted. After one unsuccessful case the secretary of the Wyoming Stockmen's Association remarked plaintively: 'It seems to be popular nowadays to hamper the work of the Association . . . the judge and the jury, as well as the newspapers and the general public seemed combined to place the Association in the light of criminals.'

This conflict between large and small holders was aggravated when the big owners were absentee landlords, often faraway companies in England or Scotland. The case of the Rocking Chair Ranche Company, established in 1883, was typical. Principal shareholders were James Gordon, Earl of Aberdeen, and Edward Marjoribanks, Baron Tweedmouth. Its ranch was in the Texas Panhandle between the North and Salt Forks of the Red River, and was known locally as 'Little England'; how the two Scots noblemen felt about this name isn't recorded. Another sobriquet was 'Nobility Ranch'.

Whatever its name, the ranch was undoubtedly an unfortunate venture. The British owners called their ranchers 'cow servants'. When Archibald John Marjoribanks came over from Europe to set things in order, he insisted that the cowboys call him 'Sir' Archibald. The results were inevitable. The cowboys took to hiding out on the range, where they lay in wait for young Archibald. When he appeared they charged at him like Indians, firing off their pistols. His imported English thoroughbreds were dismissed as 'peckernecks'. And the rustlers had a field day.

Within no time at all, every neighbouring outfit was mavericking from the Rocking Chair. When the two main shareholders came over to investigate, their manager drove the same herd past them time and again. The reason for this deception became clear when the ill-fated enterprise was finally sold off. Out of an estimated 14,000 head, only 300 could be found—and they had to be tracked down by specially imported bloodhounds.

The associations' efforts were backed up by vigilante groups who took the law into their own hands. One of the most notorious, formed in Montana in the spring of 1884, was known to the local people as Stuart's Stranglers. Fourteen of the most close-mouthed cattlemen in the north-west, they met secretly at Granville Stuart's ranch and called themselves a vigilance committee. Their method was to track down their prey and summarily hang him, leaving a placard saying 'horse thief' or 'cattle thief' attached to his clothes. Everyone knew what was happening, but no one spoke of it. The *Mineral Argus* of Maiden, Montana, observed: 'Eastern Montana is rapidly reducing the number of horse thieves.' The vigilance committee became so well organized that it sometimes announced the happy events in advance.

Stuart's friends were so effective that by the end of the year, the Montana and Dakota ranges were free of stock-thieves. Nobody knows how many rustlers met premature ends, but estimates run as high as 75. Certainly, hundreds more fled to less dangerous regions. Some went to the 'Hole in the Wall' country of Wyoming.

In 1892 the established ranchers in Johnson County, Wyoming, reacted to the enormous rustling industry by importing 20 hot-shot Texas gunslingers. In April of that year, a small army of 40 cattle kings, their horses (and the gunslingers) entrained to Casper, then rode towards Buffalo. The rustlers, unperturbed, sent for reinforcements. Every disaffected cowboy for miles around was happy to lend a hand. A full-scale battle broke out, and only the arrival of the US 6th Cavalry ended the conflict.

As fencing spread in the 1870s and 80s the number of unbranded cattle declined, driving another nail in the old-fashioned rustler's coffin. People began to regard branding or killing a stray as a crime; mavericks should be left until round-up time, when they could be fairly divided among neighbours or, as in Wyoming, taken over by the stockmen's association to help pay expenses.

Townsfolk were often given prior notice of executions: invitation to a hanging in Helena, Montana. The men were eventually hanged on different days

— underneath its clouds of sin,
The heart of man retaineth yet
Gleams of its holy origin;
And half-quenched stars that never set,
Dim colors of its faded bow,
And early beauty, linger there,
And o'er its wasted desert blow
Faint breathings of its morning air,
O, never yet upon the scroll
Of the sin-stained, but priceless soul,
Hath Heaven inscribed "DESPAIR!"

Mr. Frank Adkins

You are invited to witness the execution of William Gay and William Biggersta
on Friday, December 20, 1895, at 10 o'clock A. M., at the Lewis and Clarke County Jail.

Respectfully,

Henry Jurgens

Sheriff of Lewis and Clarke County.

As the barbed wire unrolled, so did another Western conflict. Some ranchers objected because an animal that scratched itself on the wire was wide open to screw-worm and other infections. Smallholders just didn't like the open range being fenced in by the big boys; contrarily, the big stockholders disapproved when homesteaders erected fences that blocked the free movement of their great herds. The average cowman believed passionately that he was entitled to both the freedom of the plains and the right to protect his own property. With a fine disregard for consistency, he put barbed wire around his own range and cut his neighbour's fences.

These blows for individual freedom soon flared into fence-cutting wars. They started in Texas in the early 1880s, and spread rapidly to Montana and Arizona. In 1883 no less than $20 million worth of damage was done in Texas alone. (Cowman R. A. David built a four-strand fence around his 1,000-acre pasture; in just two days it was cut in 3,500 places.) It finally became an offence even to carry wire cutters. As W. S. James wrote, 'The advent of barbed wire in Texas brought with it a reign of lawlessness and terror such as has no parallel in the state's eventful history.' Any man who erected a fence was in danger of being shot at, and any man who cut it faced death.

Fence-cutting, like large-scale horse-stealing, is now just a chapter in the history of the West. But rustling is still a lucrative business—and motorized rustlers steal more steers than ever their forebears did. The modern cow thief is after meat rather than stock. He'll drive a pick-up truck to a suitable point, load a dozen fat steers, and take them to a convenient slaughterhouse. The invention of the deep-freeze inspired amateurs to try their hand; recently there was an epidemic of rustling half-carcasses for the family freezer.

The modern rustler's main problem is still the brand; he must dispose of the hides, etched with that tell-tale mark. One inventive solution is to burn them inside rubber motor-car tyres. The American establishment was slow to outlaw this last remnant of the old West. In 1937, and again in 1939, Congress passed a federal anti-rustling law. On both occasions President Roosevelt refused to sign it. Only in 1948 was rustling made a federal offence.

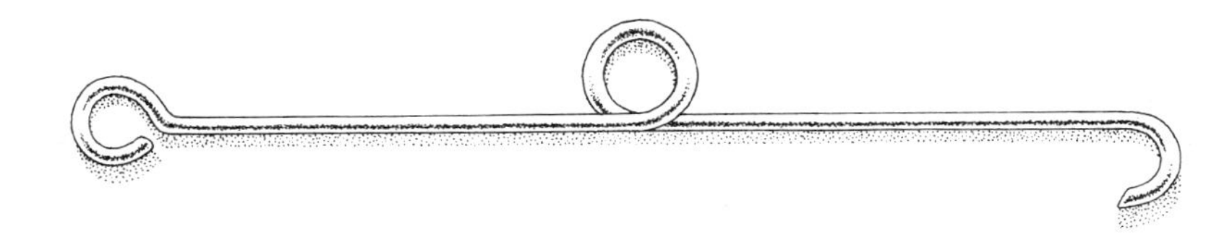

Myths and Legendmakers

'The real cowboy needed no romanticizing. He was a serious worker, with a respect for life. He was courageous; cowards were despised. He was reliable. And he was tough.'

To 19th-century Easterners, the land beyond the Missouri was the Great American Desert—savage, hostile, rough. A man who faced its many challenges was a hero. And so he was. Teddy Roosevelt, America's 26th president and a rancher in South Dakota, called the cowboy 'the grim pioneer of our race . . He lives in the lonely lands where mighty rivers twist in long reaches between the barren bluffs; where the prairies stretch out into billowy plains of waving grass, girt only by the blue horizon.' Another writer described him as 'more god than man', a being who rode horses that 'by comparison would make Pegasus limp with four clubbed feet' and tended 'mossy-horned cattle that could surpass the combined cerebrations of the Institute of Advanced Learning'.

This view of the cowboy as stereotyped hero existed almost from the day he first rode the range—and from the first it was far from the whole truth. Myths aside, the average cowboy was extraordinary in his self-reliance, chivalry and honesty. He was self-reliant because he had to be. He rode the empty West's immense distances, relied on his own judgement, depended on his own skills and courage, and fended for himself. He was chivalrous because he knew how hard life was for women who had to cope with harsh country, solitude and sheer physical hard work. What's more, women were rare and were valued accordingly. Above all, he was honest. The devil-may-care desperadoes of Western fiction and film are as different from the hard-working cowboy of fact as chalk is from cheese. Ninety-nine per cent of cowboys were law-abiding citizens. It was the remaining one per cent who inspired the hard-living, gun-toting cowboy image.

The real cowboy needed no romanticizing. He was a serious worker, with a respect for life. He was courageous; cowards were despised. He was reliable; he knew that at times (in a stampede, or crossing a flooded river) other people's lives depended on him. He was loyal to his friends and boss. And he was tough.

Rufus Zogbaum, a US Army artist, was one of the cowboy's earliest glamourizers: 'A Cowboy' by Zogbaum; from Harper's Monthly Magazine, *1885*

This nostalgic portrayal of the cowboy shows Remington in romantic mood: 'The Last Cavalier'

Pala Pala (Mexican for 'stick-foot') was a one-legged cowboy who forced himself to become a top bronc-buster. It took years of sweat and pain, but in the end he could outride most two-legged riders. Another, Si Dawson, ripped his hand clean off while roping a steer with a lariat. Undaunted, he rode with the reins in his teeth, and could still rope and tie down any steer on the range.

Artists were in the forefront of the popularizers, the men who glamourized—and misinterpreted—the West. Charles Russell was one of many who brought an undeniably romantic view of cowboy life into the homes of the East. Works by Rufus F. Zogbaum, an official artist attached to the US Army, were reproduced in Eastern magazines from 1885 onwards. Frederic Remington was more true to life, though even some of his pictures—like *In from the Night Herd* and *Indian Scouts*—glamourized the cowboy's hard daily routine.

Writers did even more to nurture the myth—they could (and did) make men into legends. Ned Buntline (real name Edward Judson) was one scribbler who made the West wilder than it was. He wrote the first dime novels (books that cost 10 cents each) about William Cody—whom he christened Buffalo Bill—in 1869. By 1933, nearly 1,700 books about the legendary Bill had appeared. Prentiss Ingraham was responsible for about 200 (he'd been press agent to Buffalo Bill for three months). Ingraham also idolized mountain man Kit Carson, and Billy the Kid—whom he immortalized as wielding 'the fastest gun in any man's hands'.

Owen Wister's *The Virginian: A Horseman of the Plains*, published in 1902, was the first popular cowboy novel (Remington was among its illustrators). Written by an Easterner—a Philadelphian—it told the tale of a Virginian in Montana, a man who could 'ride a horse, love a girl, tell a story and kill a Trampas.' It sold $1\frac{1}{2}$ million copies, and established the cowboy as the tall, lean, laconic hero of the world's imagination.

Eugene Manlove Rhodes made the cowboy about ten feet tall, and loaded him with guns, whisky and menace. But he himself had been a cowboy for 25 years, and his *Good Men and True*, published in 1910, also portrayed cowboys as they really were: tough and loyal. He blatantly regarded them as the equal of classic heroes when he wrote: 'If Ghengis Khan, Alexander the Great, Napoleon and a cowboy were put together there would be just four [equal] men in camp.' Rhodes got it wrong. The average cowboy was less savage than Ghengis Khan, less domineering than Napoleon, less brilliant than Alexander —but harder working and more selfless than all three.

Zane Grey followed hard on Wister's and Rhodes's heels and by 1912, when his *Riders of the Purple Sage* (total sale over $1\frac{3}{4}$ million) was published, the West was widely accepted as a land of heroes. The flood of myth swelled as the cowboy's heyday receded—and the distortions of one writer were incorporated by others. Although the record was set straight as early as 1903, when Andy Adams published his *Log of a Cowboy*, the tide couldn't be stemmed. Written from experience, and faithful to the facts of cowboy life, his book was rejected by a public who were eager for more purple prose and fewer prosaic truths. Today, *Log of a Cowboy* and others, like Ramon F. Adams's authoritative *Old-Time Cowhand*, are recognized as true portrayals of the cowboy as he really was.

Frederic Remington's first cowboy illustration was published in 1886. His pictures were more down-to-earth than most, but even he sometimes idealized the cowboy's tough life: 'In From the Night Herd' by Remington; from Harper's Weekly, *1886*

The Pony Express is one of the West's most enduring legends—yet it lasted only 79 weeks and was a resounding financial failure. It was an ambitious project: relays of horses and riders were to span the 1,966-mile course between the Missouri River and Sacramento, California, and carry mail faster than it had ever been carried before. The sponsoring firm, Russell, Majors and Waddell, spent $100,000 on 500 fast horses (mustangs, mostly from California) and 80 intrepid riders, and on building 190 way-stations at ten-mile intervals along the route, where the riders could change horses.

On 4 April 1860 the first westward ride took place. Young Billy Hamilton covered the first 20 miles in 59 minutes. The whole crossing took only $10\frac{1}{2}$ days; a stagecoach at that time took at least 22 days, the normal mail a month. But neither horses nor men could keep up the pace. The furious pounding was too much for both, and marauding Indians took their toll. What's more, payments from subscribers fell way below the cost of keeping up the service, and an expected government subsidy failed to materialize.

The death knell of the enterprise came on 22 October 1861 with the opening of the first transcontinental telegraph line. Two days later the Pony Express ended in honourable failure.

Pony Express symbol

Pony Express staging post

'Wild West' shows were another major factor in the making of the cowboy myth. Before films and television, they gave most city-dwellers their only chance to see the West in action. Their sharp-shooters, stagecoach-robberies and Indian 'raids' added fuel to the legendary fires of Western lawlessness and violence.

The first-ever Wild West show, in 1870, was a flop. Its creator was 'Wild Bill' Hickok—lawman, Indian scout, and legend in his own lifetime. The show was called *The Daring Buffalo Chase of the Plains*. For it, Wild Bill collected together three cowboy ropers, six buffalo, four Comanche Indians and a monkey, and took them by train to Niagara Falls. But there's more to running a circus than being a legend; the buffalo wouldn't perform, the bear hibernated, and box-office receipts dived. Worst of all, the Comanches threatened to scalp their boss if they weren't paid. So the buffaloes were sold to a butcher to pay the Indians' wages, and Wild Bill trekked back to Kansas to sign on for the less arduous task of cleaning out Hays City's outlaws.

Buffalo Bill Cody's show had a different story. It started in 1883 in North Platte, Nebraska, as *Old Glory Blow-Out* (to celebrate 4 July). Later it became *The Wild West Rocky Mountains and Prairie Exhibition*, then *Buffalo Bill's Wild West Show*. It was a roaring success, and Manhattan audiences thrilled as Buffalo Bill drove the Deadwood Coach, staged a hold-up, and contrived a buffalo chase inside the arena. (Back in the West, exhausted cowboys fought to control 2,000 stampeding Longhorns during a fierce storm at about the time New Yorkers were gaping at this showman's-eye view of their world.) Buffalo Bill created the first cowboy hero when, in 1884, he introduced Buck Taylor—a 6-foot 5-inch Texan cowpuncher—to audiences as 'the king of the cowboys'.

In 1887 he took his *Wild West Show* to Europe and dazzled audiences all over the continent. At a Royal Command Performance before Queen Victoria, four kings rode in the Deadwood Coach—and the Prince of Wales sat beside Cody, who drove the six horses. The Grand Duke of Russia rode Cody's horse in the buffalo chase. Annie Oakley, 'Little Sure Shot', shot the ash from the German Crown Prince's cigar (he later became Kaiser Wilhelm). The Sioux chief Sitting Bull was regarded with awe; he'd helped to rally the Sioux nation in the war that culminated in Little Bighorn in 1876.

While both Buffalo Bill and Wild Bill Hickok fostered their own legends, most cowboys (though not averse to a little nostalgic exaggeration) would have roared with laughter at the folklore that's grown around their way of life. Here are examples of some of the more persistent myths—and the truth behind each.

Cowboys and conversation didn't mix. True. They probably weren't as monosyllabic as Gary Cooper, but they didn't waste words.

When he was working, which was most of the time, the cowboy kept speech to a minimum; alongside a moving herd was no place for chatterboxes. He yelled at the cattle to get them going, sang to them to keep them moving—but used hand signals to communicate with his workmates. In the bunkhouse or around the campfire, he happily joined in the storytelling and banter—but his general comments were pithy and to the point. A cowboy who arrived at a ranch at three in the morning, only to be wakened at five by the breakfast bell, commented, 'A man sure can stay all night quick at this ranch.'

The men knew that a wry remark could defuse a quarrel. A man whose hat had just been shot off his head exclaimed: 'That's a helluva joke. How'd he know how much of my head was in that hat?' And when a roper continually missed his throws at a steer, another recommended that he put a stamp on the rope and send it to him by mail. Or when a greenhorn had been thrown five times by a bronc, a senior cowboy, looking at the marks in the dust, inquired laconically: 'What you doin', kid? Putting in a crop?'

When he felt like yarning, the cowboy was one of the world's great storytellers. His language was colourful and vigorous, and his tall tales grew taller as the night wore on. Filled with graphic observation —yet becoming steadily more fantastic—the tall tale was almost an art form. When a master started on a story, his audience settled down to listen with relish. If one of the men was a newcomer, the narrator would string him along with anecdotes about totally fictitious characters—like Rattlesnake Jake who claimed he was nursed on whisky, cut his teeth on a saw and played with rattlesnakes. If the tale was well told, the greenhorn often reported it as fact back home—thus adding to the West's myths.

Since their start in the 1870s Wild West shows have carried the cowboy image as far afield as China and Australia as well as Europe: Buffalo Bill's cowboys, photographed in 1893

Cowboys and alcohol were inseperable. False. Most cowboys drank less than the average commuter today. And, like a modern bar, the saloon was a meeting place as much as a drinking place, a social centre where the latest gossip circulated and town business was transacted. Cowboys could find out about jobs, and which were the best—or worst—outfits to work for. Most of them were 'regulars' and knew they had to behave themselves—or be barred from their favourite haunts. So most cowboys didn't brawl around the saloon until they were paralysed with drink. They certainly didn't insult every decent woman in earshot, shoot up the church bell, or smash every bottle in sight. Nor did the average cowboy stand at one end of the bar and send his glass (or bottle) skimming along its length.

Though alcohol was banned on drives even tired, dry trail hands didn't immediately make for the nearest saloon on their first night in a cow town. Their first thought was to pen their cattle, take a bath and then have a haircut. After that, their next priority was to discard their trail-worn clothes and buy themselves a new rig. Then, and only then, would a cowhand plant his foot on the rail of the bar counter and enjoy a yarn with the bartender and his fellow cowboys. The whisky was more likely to make him sentimental than inspire him to reach for his gun.

Admittedly, cowboys sometimes made fools of themselves, even nuisances. But town traders and saloon owners were only too happy to take their money. And, as one said, 'Let him whoop it up, he's payin' for it, ain't he?' So no one minded when he let off steam by firing his six-gun as he rode off down the main street. Only Eastern

The gun-toting cowboy who lived beyond the law is a potent Western myth. But most hands were law-abiding; the rustlers whose ruined corral is shown here are unlikely to have numbered a cowboy among their members

greenhorns automatically twinned gunfire and lawlessness.

Sometimes a hand rode his horse into a saloon out of sheer high spirits. One Easterner's drinking in a Western saloon was interrupted when two young cowpunchers rode in on their horses. He spluttered indignantly to the bartender. The barman glared at him. 'What the hell you doin' in here afoot, anyhow?' he demanded. Like many bartenders, he'd once been a cowboy.

And there were epic drinking sessions—though even some of these may have been apocryphal. For example, there is the story of the two cowboys who bought a saloon and immediately closed it. The townspeople assumed they were redecorating. After a few dry days they gathered anxiously outside—to be told that the cowboys had only bought the place so that they could enjoy some uninterrupted drinking. Then there was cattle baron Shanghai Pierce, who, when the mood took him, used to ride into town and dispense free drinks to all comers until supplies ran out. Eccentrically, the English-born rancher the Earl of Aylesford occasionally bought a saloon, and personally served free drinks for a day or two. When he tired of doing this, he handed the saloon back to its previous owner—free.

Western alcohol was often raw—as cowboys knew only too well. 'Red eye', 'coffin varnish' and 'tarantula juice' are just three of the names given to the less-seasoned rye and whisky. Ramon F. Adams tells of two hands riding a train. One opened a bottle and took a swig just before the train entered a tunnel. When the other grabbed for the bottle, the first yelled: 'Don't drink that, Shorty, it's made me blind as a snubbin' post.'

Alcohol and cattle herding don't mix, and drinking was—and still is—strictly an after-hours pastime for working cowboys: a modern sign advertises a bar

Cowboys could beat cardsharps hands down. False. They certainly enjoyed playing cards—or any other form of gambling—and probably played illicit poker in the bunkhouse or on the trail, against ranch and trail rules. But the cowboy was no expert. What's more, he hated transient professional gamblers, men who 'followed the annual cattle drives like vultures follow an army'.

But a cowboy was always prepared to chance his arm; if the velvet-jacketed card-sharp could make money, maybe he could too. Invariably he was fleeced by the professionals until, as Ramon F. Adams says, 'he could usually count his coin without taking it from his pocket . . . he wished now he had all the change the bartender forgot to give him back.'

Cowboy humour was rough and ready. True. Cowboys were dedicated practical jokers, and their pranks ('jobbing') were as boisterous and rough as the life they led: like loosening the saddle when a man was about to gallop away; saddle and rider would crash to the ground, while the horse took off.

Old hands were slow to accept a greenhorn, and practical jokes were as good an initiation rite as any. The new man could find himself sent on an unnecessary errand to a ranch at the bottom of a mountain that looked deceptively close-by. A horned toad might be

The cowboys' gift for graphic description is reflected in the names they gave to the many varieties of rye and whisky. 'Coffin varnish' and 'tarantula juice' are examples: two saloon interiors

DINING ROOM

T.S. LINDER
POST
CMRussell
1909

THE HOFFMAN
HOTEL
LICENSED GAMBLING
$1000
REWARD
FOR
KID CURRY

(Previous page) *Even when hands occasionally cut loose after hard months on the trail or range, there was more high spirits than malice in their actions: 'In Without Knocking' by Charles Russell; by courtesy of the Amon Carter Museum*

put in his bedroll, a cactus or lizard find its way into his boots. A favourite prank was to tie a sleeper down and shake a rattlesnake's tail in front of his eyes. If a greenhorn didn't take the jokes in good spirit he wasn't very popular. But once a man had been accepted, he was in—the bond between cowboys was as strong as that of any secret society.

Newcomers weren't the only victims of practical joking. A Montana ranch boss who was too straitlaced for his men's taste got his come-uppance one day in a Miles City hotel lobby. One of the cowboys who knew Calamity Jane persuaded her to throw herself suddenly onto the boss's lap, kiss him passionately, and ask him why he hadn't been to see her lately. During her performance, the cowboys stood by expressing moral shock, and tut-tutting. When Calamity finally let the man go he bolted from the hotel.

'The only good Indian is a dead Indian.' False. The constant warfare that plagued the frontier from the early days of the West (more than 1,000 battles took place between 1789 and 1898, not including small local skirmishes) left a legacy of mutual respect at best, distrust and

Relations between cowboys and Indians were generally good: a cowboy uses sign language to trade with an Indian

hostility at worst. But by 1875, the Indians of the Texas frontier and the borders of Kansas, Colorado and New Mexico were largely confined to reservations. When a drive passed through Indian Territory, the trail boss paid the toll (usually ten cents a head) without question. If he didn't—or if the cattle destroyed Indian crops—trouble might flare up. To cement relations with the Indians, many trail bosses offered them a few head of cattle as a gift.

Indians were welcome to live in the towns; and the lone rider in Indian country was more often received with hospitality than with a tomahawk—not that he wouldn't keep his rifle near to hand. The only time a cowboy pursued Indians deliberately was when a ranch's cattle were butchered. Always loyal to his employer, he wouldn't hesitate to volunteer for the revenge posse. Yet, in general, cowboys and Indians respected each other's skills and horsemanship. They shared the great wilderness, faced the same harsh demands of nature. Only the tenderfoot in the saloon sneered at 'painted savages'. The working cowboy knew better.

Cowboys were embryonic boxing champions. False. Those magnificent movie fist-fights that destroy saloons—but seldom break a jaw—were rare. When a cowboy got into a fight he much preferred to tap the barrel of his gun on his opponent's skull to put him out for the count. Nor did those 100-cowboy mêlées in which the staff of four ranches swing punches at each other ever happen in the real West. Cowboys had a great sense of fair play; they might intervene to stop a man being badly beaten up, but a scrap between two evenly-matched strangers was none of their business.

Cowboy equals gunfighter. False. Few cowboys enjoyed gunplay; they knew the wisdom of the old Western saying ' 'Nother man's life don't make no soft pillow at night.' Although most cowpunchers could kill a rattlesnake or coyote with one shot, they despised men who lived by the gun.

One explanation for the gunslinging myth is that Texans at one time packed guns as a matter of course to deal with anything from hostile Indians to charging wild cattle. When they arrived in Kansas at the end of a trail they wore a gun in a holster on their belt, like men today wear ties. This astonished the Kansans, who embroidered the myth of the gun-carrying Texan cowboy until many people would have sworn that all arguments were settled with a hail of bullets.

From about 1874, states passed laws banning the carrying of guns in town, and fielded marshals to enforce them. Cowboys—even Texan cowboys—had to leave their hardware with the sheriff before going into town. On the range, the cowboy usually kept his gun wrapped in his saddle blanket. If he did wear a gun it would only be one; he'd never dream of weighing himself down with two shooting irons, because they'd impede his work. The two-gun man was usually despised as a braggart—or a coward.

The cowpoke's favourite weapon was often a Colt ·45, or 0·45-inch calibre, single-action revolver (the Peacemaker)—with a plain cedar stock. Gleaming metal guns were for men who never left town. The sun reflected off the metal could be seen for miles around—a signal for hostile Indians or rustlers to give a wide berth.

Cardsharps were as unpopular with the cowboys as they were with saloon keepers, but this didn't stop hands from losing money to them: 'Bucking the Tiger', gambling in a Western saloon in the 1870s

When Samuel Colt invented his revolver (patented in the United States in 1836) he produced what W. P. Webb described as 'the first mechanical adaptation made by the American people as they emerged from the timber'. Rifles and pistols could take up to a minute to load—during which an Indian could loose off more than a dozen arrows. A man could load a revolver in less than half the time.

Colt's first six-chambered revolver was manufactured in about 1838, but it was 1873 before the Colt Peacemaker finally established the six-shooter as part of the American scene. Colt's first cartridge-loaded gun, the Peacemaker cost about $15. Its stock was wooden, the steel finish was blue, and it weighed 2 lb 5 oz; its barrel was $7\frac{1}{2}$ inches long. Legendary figures who used the Peacemaker included 'Wild Bill' Hickok, Sam Bass and Pat Garrett.

Colt revolvers were popular—'God created men: Colonel Colt made them equal', as the saying went—but they were by no means the only guns in the West. There were also names like Remington, Smith & Wesson and Deringer; and, of course, Winchester rifles. The first Winchester repeating rifle was manufactured in 1866; seven years later, in 1873, the Winchester .44–40, or Model '73, made the name Winchester synonymous with rifle.

The Colt was immortalized as 'the gun that won the West' **(Right)** *'The Fateful Colt' by William Harnett* **(Below right)** *The Colt Navy Model revolver, 1851* **(Below)** *An 1861 model Colt revolver*

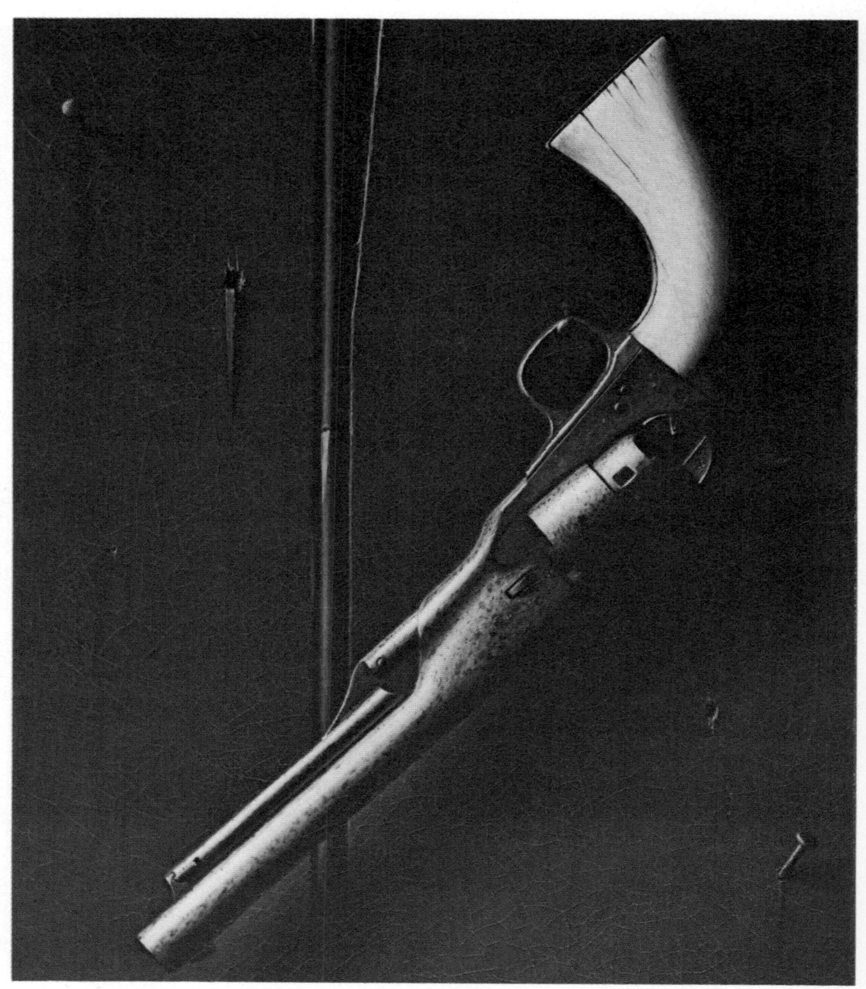

Traditionally, a cowboy never loaded more than five cartridges into the six chambers, and always kept the firing hammer down on the empty one. Shooting by mistake, and explaining 'I didn't know it was loaded,' didn't do a man's reputation any good. As the saying went, 'If it wouldn't do the job in five shots, it was time to get the hell out of there.' This first law of gun-toters wasn't always obeyed. Even Wyatt Earp, that legendary marshal, once left the hammer on a full chamber. The subsequent embarrassing accidental discharge, when the revolver slipped from its holster onto the floor, resulted in a 'lively stampede' from the saloon.

Two other gunslinger myths need debunking. The single-action gun couldn't be cocked fast enough to shoot with the continuous roar beloved of dime novels. And 'fan shooting'—holding the gun in one hand and hitting the hammer repeatedly with the heel of the other to cock it as quickly as possible—was impossible. The recoil couldn't be smothered, and the fanning jerked the gun out of line.

Only a few professional gunmen wore special holsters that allowed them to draw their guns quickly, and had the sights filed down on their hair-trigger hardware. For the cowboy, the gun was a piece of equipment, not a weapon—and certainly not a symbol. E. C. Abbott, a former cowboy, dismissed the many accounts of gunfights that appeared in the Eastern press as 'nearly all exaggeration'. He went on: 'I worked up here [in Kansas] from 1883 on, and I saw a lot of hard work on the range, but very little shooting. In fact, from '85 on, until it quit being a ranger, there never was but one shooting scrape and then nobody got killed; and over on the Judin and the Moccasin, which were the next ranges, they never had one.'

The real cowboy was law-abiding, hardworking, loyal and tough. His conditions of work made him seem romantic. It's even money that—the facts notwithstanding—he'll continue to be glorified and eulogized. The image of the range rider as totally good, totally bad—or a 'Robin Hood' who breaks the law to help others—is indestructible. Less than a century after its birth, the myth of the cowboy holds promise of continuing for a long run.

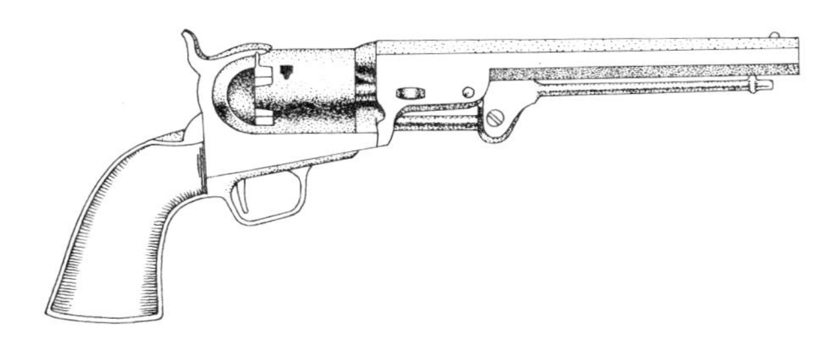

The West created a host of legendary characters in addition to the cowboy; some of them are featured on the pages that follow.

Belle Starr, 'Queen of the Bandits', had a varied career as prostitute, informant, horse-thief and fence. She was born Myra Belle Shirley in Missouri in 1848. Her first brush with violence was when Union troops killed her brother Ed in 1863, during the Civil War. In revenge Belle strapped on a pair of revolvers and joined the Confederate guerillas as an informant. In 1866 she became pregnant by Cole Younger, who rode with Jesse James. Shortly afterwards she left her child, Pearl Younger, with her parents, and went to Dallas, Texas, where she became a card-dealer, dance-hall singer and probably whore.

She married—or went through a form of marriage with—Jim Reed, a notorious horse-thief, and had a child by him. In 1873 three men and a woman dressed as a man stole $30,000 from the home of an Indian. Two of them were later identified as Jim Reed and, probably, Belle, who sometimes wore men's clothes. Jim was eventually killed near Paris, Texas, and Belle joined the Reed-Starr gang. She planned their robberies, acted as a fence and was suspiciously successful at getting them released after arrest.

She later married Sam Starr, son of an Indian. In 1882 they were caught stealing horses and given short prison sentences. When husband Starr was shot in a gunfight she married another horse-thief, Jim July. He was later suspected of arranging her death, by shooting, in 1889. Her daughter had this verse inscribed on her tombstone:

Shed not for her the bitter tear,
Nor give the heart to vain regret;
'Tis but the casket that lies here,
The gem that filled it sparkles yet.

Butch Cassidy was born George LeRoy Parker on a ranch at Circle Valley, Utah, in 1866. He was called 'Butch' because he once worked in a butcher's shop, and took the name Cassidy from Mike Cassidy, a cowboy who once worked for his father and later became a rustler and horse thief. Butch learnt Cassidy's illegal trade, and in 1894 he was arrested in Wyoming for horse-stealing and sentenced to two years in jail. He was pardoned before the term was up on condition that he didn't 'molest' the State ever again.

Butch Cassidy soon had his own gang—the Wild Bunch. Their hideout was a valley in northern Wyoming, the Hole in the Wall. They rustled cattle by splitting them into small groups; if challenged, they said they were rounding up strays. They also robbed stagecoaches, express trains and banks. In 1901 they blew up a train on the Northern Pacific railroad and made off with $40,500 in bills so new that they weren't even signed. They forged the signatures—badly—providing the Pinkerton National Detective Agency, who were trailing them, with a useful clue. In 1902 Pinkerton's issued a handbill offering a $4,000 reward for Butch Cassidy.

He, Henry Longabaugh ('the Sundance Kid') and pretty Etta Place started to live openly together under assumed names. They were even photographed for a joke—but the photo helped Pinkerton's to trace them. The trio moved to Bolivia in South America, where the Sundance Kid died in a battle with the Bolivian cavalry. Butch Cassidy returned to the United States, where, some old-timers maintain, he spent the rest of his days as a peaceable cowboy.

Wyatt Earp, legendary lawman, was more impressive in fable than in fact. His chequered career included stints as a railroad labourer, stage-coach driver and buffalo hunter before he became deputy marshal in Wichita, Kansas in 1875—for a year.

He left Wichita after being involved in a street brawl. (The city commission had to withold his pay to get the money he'd collected in fines). After another year as assistant marshal in Dodge City, Earp turned gunman and joined the Deadwood Gold Rush. In 1879 he arrived in Tombstone, Arizona where he was employed as a guard by the Oriental, the town's biggest gambling house. In 1881 Virgil Earp was made marshal at Tombstone—and took on his brothers Wyatt and Morgan as deputies, together with John H. (Doc) Holliday, a one-time dentist now handier with a six-shooter than with a drill.

In October of that year the Earps tried to arrest suspected rustlers from Sulphur Springs Valley—an action that led to the now-famous gunfight at the OK Corral. The Earps pulled guns, three suspects were killed, and Virgil and Morgan were wounded. A court freed the brothers but the judge censured Marshal Virgil Earp for calling on Wyatt and Holliday to help arrest the men. In December 1881 Virgil, no longer marshal, was shot and crippled. In March 1882 Morgan was shot and killed while playing billiards. Wyatt was the luckiest of the three brothers: he died in his bed in Los Angeles, in 1929.

Tom Smith, marshal of Abilene, was a true Western hero—a lawman who really did establish law and order. His first action after being made marshal in 1870 was to ban carrying firearms in the town. Contemptuous visitors had—literally—shot holes in the notices that proclaimed the ban, but Smith soon established the law's supremacy with his fists: on his first Saturday night Big Hank challenged Smith to run him out of town and the marshal felled him with a single blow to the jaw. Soon afterwards Smith, unarmed, knocked out another gun-carrying braggart in the local saloon. Abilene became comparatively law-abiding—and Smith's pay was raised from $150 a month (plus $2 per conviction) to $225 a month. In the fall of that year he was appointed deputy US marshal for Abilene's federal judicial district.

He died in November 1870 when he rode out of town to Chapman Creek to help the local sheriff re-arrest a farmer, Andrew McConnell, who'd killed his neighbour, and Moses Miles whose evidence had earlier resulted in McConnell's acquittal on a plea of self-defence. A fight started, and Tom Smith was winning; but Miles struck him with his gun, knocked him out, then nearly severed his head from his body with an axe.

Smith was given a magnificent funeral, and a monument later proclaimed him 'a fearless hero of frontier days who . . established the supremacy of law.'

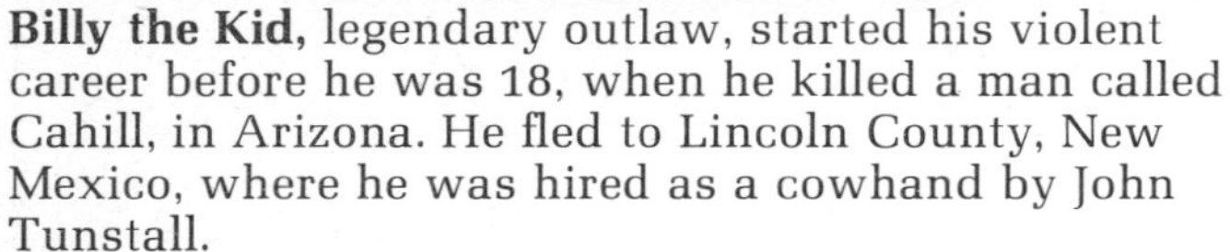

Billy the Kid, legendary outlaw, started his violent career before he was 18, when he killed a man called Cahill, in Arizona. He fled to Lincoln County, New Mexico, where he was hired as a cowhand by John Tunstall.

Shortly after Billy joined him Tunstall was killed by a posse in the first violence of the Lincoln County War. Billy set out to revenge his boss and, with others, gunned down the sheriff and his deputy in broad daylight in Lincoln. He was indicted for this killing (and the killing of another man) but his trial was delayed for a year. Before he could be tried, a new sheriff was elected and set out to arrest him. The Kid escaped in the darkness, and became an outlaw, wanted for several murders.

In 1880 Governor Wallace offered $500 reward to any one who'd deliver Billy to Pat Garett, the newly-elected sheriff of Lincoln County. Garett besieged Billy in a stone hut and starved him into surrendering. After a trial in the Spanish-speaking town of Mesilla, he was sentenced to be hanged. While Garett was away, Billy killed his two guards and escaped. To reinstate his reputation, Garett traced Billy to his hide-out at Fort Sumner, and shot him dead.

Billy the Kid's reputation spread far and wide. According to legend, he'd killed 21 men by the time he was 21. More factually, most authorities agree that only three deaths can definitely be attributed to his hands.

Wild Bill Hickok, Indian fighter, scout, gunslinger, showman and marshal, was the son of a clergyman. A marksman by the age of 14, he developed his shooting skill until he could split a bullet on the edge of a dime at 20 paces. His reputation was built on the McCanles gunfight, where he claimed to have killed, singlehanded, a band of nine or ten outlaws. The truth? Hickok, with two accomplices, killed three men without much of a fight.

Wild Bill created his own myth. Six feet tall, with shoulder-length hair and a drooping moustache he usually wore buckskins—or 'steamboat gambler' outfits: a frock coat worn with check trousers and an embroidered silk waistcoat was an example. He wore cowboy boots with patent leather tops and packed a pair of pistols even when he was asleep. When Henry Stanley of the *New York Herald* (and of 'Dr Livingstone, I presume' fame) asked him how many men he'd killed he told him, 'considerably over a hundred'.

After a brief and unsuccessful flirtation with show business he took on the role of lawman, as marshal of Hays City and, for about eight months in 1871, of Abilene (a town which had been cleaned up by Tom Smith). He spent most of his time drinking and gambling and shot his own deputy by mistake. Hickok eventually took to carrying a sawn-off shotgun and a bowie knife as well as pistols. After Abilene his career included another stint as marshal of Hays City and a tour of the country with Buffalo Bill's theatrical company. In August 1876 he was shot in the back of the head while playing poker in a Deadwood saloon. His killer was a stranger called Jack McCall whose only motive seemed to be that he wanted to kill a famous gunman.

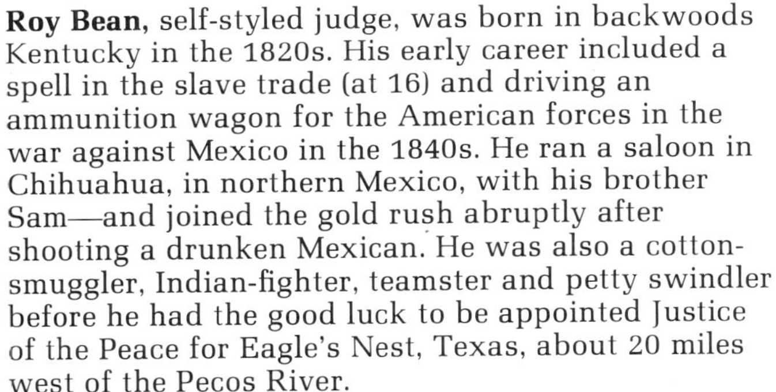

Roy Bean, self-styled judge, was born in backwoods Kentucky in the 1820s. His early career included a spell in the slave trade (at 16) and driving an ammunition wagon for the American forces in the war against Mexico in the 1840s. He ran a saloon in Chihuahua, in northern Mexico, with his brother Sam—and joined the gold rush abruptly after shooting a drunken Mexican. He was also a cotton-smuggler, Indian-fighter, teamster and petty swindler before he had the good luck to be appointed Justice of the Peace for Eagle's Nest, Texas, about 20 miles west of the Pecos River.

He moved the court to Vinegarroon (called after a local variety of scorpion) and dispensed justice in his saloon, the 'Jersey Lilly' (named—and mis-spelled—after Lily Langtry, whom he adored). He renamed the town Langtry and the actress sent him a pair of silver-plated six-guns in gratitude.

The judge ran his court along strictly businesslike lines. When a man was brought in dead after falling from a high bridge, Bean found $40 and a six-gun on his body. He fined the corpse $40 for carrying a concealed weapon. On another occasion an Irishman was accused of killing a Chinese. The Irishman was accompanied by a group of tough and violent friends who put it to Bean that the wrong decision could lead to his bar being wrecked. The judge thumbed through his law book and gave his verdict: 'I'm damned if I can see any law against killing a Chinaman.'

The judge wasn't above a spot of horseplay. On one occasion, when a corpse had been found in a nearby canyon, the judge said, 'I know all about that corpse. I rule that this hombre met his death by being shot by a person unknown who was a damn good shot.' Bean stayed in office, with only one two-year break, until 1903, when he died of pneumonia after a binge in San Antonio. His justice was rough, but it worked.

The Code of the West

'One of the most fundamental rules of the code was that a man's word was his bond, whether this involved small favours or deals worth thousands of dollars. Nor would one man abuse another's trust.'

In the early days of the range, there was no organized society or formal system of laws. So the men who made the West made their own. This 'code of the West' was based on loyalty and co-operation—the keys to survival in a land where men came from many different backgrounds.
The rules of the code were few and simple; to an outsider they often seemed excessively harsh. Any major violation of the code was punished severely, usually by death or ostracism. The latter could be as serious a penalty as the former. A man on his own had virtually no chance of surviving in the West, and was forced to pack his bedroll and start a new life elsewhere. Although legislated law slowly became established throughout the frontier, it often had little bearing on range life. Cattlemen had no scruples about ignoring the 'law of the East' whenever it suited them. By contrast, the unwritten laws of the code were rigorously respected and upheld.

One of the most fundamental rules of the code was that a man's word was his bond, whether this involved small favours or business deals worth thousands of dollars. Nor would one man ever abuse another's trust, especially if the other person was at a disadvantage. Honesty was the cornerstone of a cowboy's sense of honour. Its influence on everyday life could be surprising, even for the West; the foreman of the N Bar ranch, it is said, once fired a hand because he rode out of Miles City, Montana, without paying his bill to a local prostitute.

Out on the range, a man could leave money lying freely around a bunkhouse without the least fear of it being stolen. That doors were left unbolted when ranchers were away from their homes—locks were virtually unknown in the early years—was a measure of the trust people had in one another, and their respect for personal belongings.

The code was more than a set of rules. It encouraged men to adopt 'ideal' forms of conduct. Loyalty to friends—who could always be

ESTRAYS.

TAKEN UP—Came into my enclosure in the fall of 1892, one grey horse branded 5 on left thigh. Owner can have same by calling on C E Taylor, Hudson, Colorado.

TAKEN UP—On or about December 10th, 1893, at Y L Atkins' ten miles north-east of Colorado Springs, one buckskin horse, small white spot in forehead, brown stripe down back, bad scar on left hind leg, branded H on left hind shoulder, weight about 800 pounds The owner can have same by proving stock and paying bill. For information concerning this horse apply to R B Cothern, Colorado Springs, Colorado Lock Box 911.

TAKEN UP—At my ranch, six miles northwest of Trinidad, Colo., on October 1st 1893, one bay mare, about eight years old, heavy with foal, will weigh eleven or twelve hundred, branded V on left thigh, white star in forehead, no other brands or flesh marks, gentle to work Owner can have same by paying pasturage and feed bill up to time of claiming animal W S Lee, Trinidad, Colorado.

TAKEN UP—December 22nd, 1893, one red muley cow and one dark brown heifer, both branded with lay down heart on right hip C B Lawsha, Boulder, Colo.

TAKEN UP—Red steer five years old branded m on left hip and on left side, left ear cropped and under slope right ear Said animal has been on this place fourteen months Samuel Reynolds, Zilar, Colorado.

TAKEN UP—One bay mare six years old brand thus on left hip weight about 900 pounds on ranch one mile south of Broadway electric on Stark Bros Ranch JOHN CHRISTIAN, Littleton, Colorado.

Honesty was fundamental to the code of the West: advertisements inserted in Field and Farm, *1894, by ranchers who had picked up strays*

counted on in times of trouble—was one. It was unforgivable treachery for a man to double-cross a friend. The code was also humane. If a person was in trouble, it was a man's duty to help him—friend, stranger or enemy.

The high standards of personal integrity that the men of the West set themselves were expressed in many ways; the most remarkable was their almost legendary hospitality. It sprang from the great bond of fellowship that united people who lived in isolated ranch communities for months on end, surrounded only by an endless sea of prairie and scattered herds of cattle. E. N. Dick described how, in the range country, 'A man could ride his horse across the prairie for days hunting stray cattle or horses and never be asked to pay for his board and lodging and his horse's provender.' Luxuries were rare in the average ranch home, yet any passing traveller—friend or stranger—was welcome to share a meal and to bed down for the night. No payment was expected—and most hosts were downright insulted if it was offered. An inhospitable man was loathed by his neighbours.

If playing host was one ritual, being a proper guest was another. A visitor always observed various formalities. It was discourteous to come right up and knock on the door without first shouting the familiar greeting, 'Hello the house!' Riders stayed on their horses to give the household a chance to look them over from a distance. They dismounted only after they had been invited to come inside. A man packing a pistol always dismounted in full view of his host to dispel any suspicion of hostility. Similarly, when a rider neared a camp, or another person whose back was turned, he always shouted to make his presence known well before getting within gun range.

The men of the West put their trust in their fellows' sense of honour: a scene in a cowboy camp: the men in this photograph may have known each other for only a few weeks—or days—but they'd never suspect each other of dishonesty

As the number of Plains people increased, some ranchers received a regular flow of visitors. In her autobiography, Nannie Alderson recalls that at one point travellers came to her ranch at least weekly —a real flood by range standards. Yet all of them 'came and stayed exactly as they pleased; we obeyed the law of Western hospitality and took in all comers, whoever they might be . . . None of the stockmen ever charged; that was their custom and their pride.' If a traveller showed up while the owner was out, he was welcome to take what food he needed—provided he cleaned up afterwards and cut more firewood to replace what had been used. This tradition of hospitality was so much a part of Western life that it was seldom violated.

Every guest was treated equally, whatever his or her station in life. When a sheriff, his deputy and an important local cattleman showed up at the Alderson ranch escorting a prisoner who had been arrested for illegally butchering steers, Mrs Alderson unhesitatingly invited all four inside for a meal. She later recalled, 'Perhaps because of our previous acquaintance, the poor fellow was so embarrassed at the removal of handcuffs while he ate, that I could hardly keep the tears from falling into his coffee while I poured it. One of the men said later that no one could have told from the treatment they received which was the cattle king and which the man under arrest.'

Frontier hospitality was strengthened by the hardships of Plains life. People were forced to depend on each other. Food, tools, clothing —anything a family owned—were shared with friends and neighbours. People were also generous with money. If a man fell sick and couldn't afford to buy medicine, everyone chipped in to make sure he didn't go without.

Hospitality in the West was a magnificent, open-hearted expression of concern for the welfare of one's fellow man. It would be natural to suppose that Westerners were equally concerned about the private and business lives of the people they so willingly invited into their homes. Nothing could be further from the truth. An enormous respect for privacy existed alongside this tradition of hospitality and friendliness. The West operated on a 'live-and-let-live' principle. It was acceptable to treat a stranger in an open, unassuming and friendly fashion and to be interested in him—up to a point. But a man also had to know when to keep his mouth shut and attend to his own business without 'horning in'. As Ramon F. Adams remarked, 'A person's past belonged to 'im alone, and should remain a closed book if he wanted it so.'

Many men came to the frontier to escape a life that had become too difficult back East. Some came to avoid debts or entanglements with the law. Others wanted to carve out a new living for themselves. Whatever the reason, it was a serious breach of privacy to ask a man what he'd done before coming to the frontier. As one cowhand wisely observed, 'Minding one's own business is the best life insurance.'

This respect for privacy was highlighted by the cowboy's complete disregard for names. Many men were known to their employers and their fellows only by a nickname, or their surname. Jim Culver, who worked for the Lang Ranch in Dakota was typical of many hired hands. He arrived one day from out of the blue and soon showed

Relationships between cowboys were easygoing and friendly. At the same time, men respected each other's privacy, and it was rare for a hand to ask a newcomer to his outfit what he'd done before (Right) *Men of the N-N ranch; photograph by Dan Dutro, 1890* (Below right) *Matador cowboys*

N—N

himself to be an energetic worker with lots of initiative. Two years later, when he was killed in an accident (his horse side-flopped), all anyone knew of his past was, 'He said his name was Jim Culver.'

The conflicting rules of hospitality and anonymity explain the characteristic way cowboys greeted strangers. If two riders saw each other on the open range, they were always expected to pass within speaking distance. Not to do so was either a deliberate insult or an open admission of wrongdoing. The two men approached slowly, taking care not to startle each other, or the horses, with any sudden, possibly hostile move. This was especially important if either wore a gun. If one man dismounted to talk, so did the other. The conversation might range from a polite discussion of the weather to talk about work and their outfits. But unless further information was volunteered, neither asked personal questions. This restraint contrasted strongly with the continuous friendly banter, storytelling and jokes among cowboys who knew each other well. But even here, among friends, it was taboo to mention certain areas of a man's life.

Mounted cowboys face each other and reflect, perhaps unconsciously, the 'man to man' tradition of the Western code: cowboys on an Oklahoma ranch, about 1910

Women and the code The code inspired extraordinarily chivalrous behaviour toward women in even the roughest men. They were treated with the sort of reverence and courtesy normally only associated with the knights of old. Among themselves men swore, talked coarsely, and behaved roughly and crudely. Yet in the company of women, a near-miraculous transformation took place—and they fell over themselves to be respectful and polite.

A 'real' lady (as opposed to a 'soiled dove') was always held in the greatest esteem. She was never insulted or embarrassed. 'No matter how drunk or hilarious frontiersmen became,' said E. N. Dick, 'they showed every respect for a virtuous woman. It was almost entirely unknown for a young woman to become an unmarried mother.' Ranch owners' or managers' wives were treated with the most elaborate politeness. Women left alone for long periods on isolated ranches while their menfolk rode the range had little to fear; every cowboy considered himself a champion of womankind. A man who dared mistreat a woman was treated as a social pariah

Cowboys divided women into 'real ladies' and 'soiled doves'. A good woman's name was never mentioned in a saloon or gambling den: young girl, photographed in Arizona

Nearly every newcomer to the West commented on this chivalry. And Nannie Alderson, who spent years as a ranch wife, never ceased to wonder at 'the boys' good manners—for few of them had any advantages, and some could not read or write.' She never worried if she was left alone on the ranch with one of the hands. 'This was a commonplace of the times . . . So complete was the faith of Western men in the chivalry of their fellows, that one time when the boys all had to be away at once, they thought nothing of letting a perfect stranger, who had ridden in to look for a job, stay and look after me and my small baby.'

Insults to women were rare—and were harshly punished. Yellowstone City, Montana, passed by-laws that made hanging mandatory for 'murder, thieving or for insulting a woman'. A man who forgot himself in the presence of a lady (at least, one who wasn't his wife) was lucky if he escaped with only a beating. It took a quick mind to get away with rudeness. Stan Hoig tells of the cowboy who had too much to drink and insulted a girl who refused to dance with him. He soon found her furious brother towering over him, demanding an apology. 'The brother was big and the cowboy wasn't that drunk. He promised to make an apology. "I take it all back," he told the girl when he found her. "You don't need to go to the devil after all. Your brother 'n me has made other arrangements." '

The greatest single reason for women's status was easily identified: their scarcity. Often men outnumbered them ten to one. This imbalance also gave marriages an extra-firm foundation—particularly necessary in the West, where separation and divorce were relatively easy to come by. Women were also treasured because they represented the finer side of life. They were the teachers, the driving force behind social activities, and a constant reminder of the more comfortable, civilized lives so many men had left behind in the East.

This romantic view of women had practical results. The first woman to arrive on a ranch triggered a sweeping transformation. Typically, when neighbours who had two attractive young daughters moved near Granville Stuart's ranch on the Montana frontier, the men's manners and dress improved overnight. 'Every man in camp has shaved and changed his shirt,' wrote Stuart. 'We are trying to behave like civilized men.' When Mrs Lang arrived on her husband's ranch, swearing almost disappeared, grooming improved, Sundays were observed for the first time—and the men's diet was rounded out with milk, butter and vegetables.

Yet, in spite of their determination to be the gallant champions of women, the cowboys' natural selves sometimes still showed through. Stan Hoig tells how a newly-wed cowboy came to town with his wife to find the local paper full of kidnapping stories. Before leaving on his errands, he locked his worried bride into their hotel room where she would be safe, then crossed the street for a quick drink in the saloon. He was soon caught up in a friendly poker game, and totally forgot all his worldly cares—until he suddenly jumped up exclaiming, 'If there's anything left of me in fifteen minutes boys . . . I'll be back. But I done left Eda May locked up in a room for twenty-four hours an' I ain't neither fed nor watered her!'

A bedroll often carried all a cowboy's possessions—and it was a serious breach of etiquette to leave it unrolled: a modern cowboy packs his bedroll before starting work on a round-up

Hired hands and bosses In pointed contrast to the deference shown to women, relationships among the men were easygoing and totally uninhibited. The rugged life of the range bred a strong sense of comradeship, even clannishness. Their loyalty to the 'their' ranch was almost feudal. 'Once a cowhand had throwed his bedroll into the wagon,' wrote Ramon F. Adams, '. . . and turned his private hoss into the remuda of an outfit, he'd pledged his allegiance and loyalty.' Hired hands were usually identified by the brand of the rancher who employed them. A cowboy was a 'Bar W man' as long as he worked there. (An allegiance that was always transferred to the next spread he rode for.)

Intensely proud of their calling, cowboys willingly shared the hardships and responsibilities of running a ranch. They'd perform almost any task, with only one condition: it had to be done from the back of a horse. They stoically endured the hardships and the long hours spent in the saddle watching over the herd. They accepted that the welfare of the cattle was more important than their own comfort or safety. Their hard life only reinforced their image of themselves as the 'supermen' of the range. As an old frontier saying quite accurately observed, cowboys, as a breed of men, were 'too proud to cut hay, but not wild enough to eat it.'

For all their loyalty, pride and willingness to work, cowboys weren't exactly the most tractable of employees. They believed they were their bosses' equals and refused to show false respect. Any

Western cooks, like cowboys, gave respect only where it was due. They were as cantankerous with their bosses as they were with the hands: chuckwagon cook preparing a meal

good boss knew that cowboys resented being ordered around. A hint was more effective than a command. Whether a boss was the owner or only the foreman, his style of leadership had to be acceptable to the men. A hard, autocratic man never got the best out of his employees. A boss had to be 'one of the boys' to gain their friendship and respect, and had to be prepared to do any of the jobs he asked his men to do. He was expected to give them credit for good work, and allow them to exercise their professional skills and responsibilities.

If the men disagreed with their boss, they were quick to say so, and they argued their case as experts who knew exactly what they were talking about. As John Dobie noted, 'When any man who draws wages or a salary gets so good that he can tell his employer to go to hell, he has realized the dream of independence in every hired man.'

If cowboys could be cantankerous, chuckwagon cooks could be impossible. Notorious for being short-tempered and autocratic, their word was law within a lariat-throw radius of the wagon—for men and for bosses. Bill Simms, cook for the Chiricahaus Cattle Company (the Triple C) in New Mexico, hated it when the men dipped into his cookpots with anything other than the serving spoons he set out. When he caught one of the Triple C owners one day spearing stewed dried apples with his eating fork, Simms turned on him in a high fury: 'You go to town, I guess, and eat around them fine cafés and talk to society folks and laugh about the manners of poor ignorant cowboys. By God, any cowboy that ever straddled a Triple C horse has got more manners than you show . . . Nobody round here wants to eat out of a pot after you've licked your fork and pronged into it. Damn such manners I say.' To further emphasize his indignation, Simms picked up the pot of apples and threw them out on the ground—beyond the 60-foot radius of his kitchen. Owner Boyce didn't say a word. An observer wrote: 'He backed down like a little boy caught stealing jam, and after that was strictly on his manners when around the chuckwagon run by Bill Simms.'

Ranch and range discipline Cowboys were often rough and boisterous, but they were also disciplined. Although some owners posted sets of regulations, they were exceptions. Most ranch rules directly reflected the Western code, and were so widely accepted that it wasn't necessary to list them. The most important dealt with the proper treatment and care of horses. No outfit tolerated abuse of its riding stock. Beating a horse over the head, or spurring it in the shoulder where the muscles could be damaged, were grounds for instant dismissal. Every cowboy jealously cared for 'his' string of horses. (Though they were owned by the ranch, they were his special pride, and it was a serious breach of etiquette to ride another man's horse without his permission.)

Range rules were mainly based on common sense. Men never unsaddled their horses within a hundred yards of a bedded herd; the least noise could set off a stampede. Night herders always made sure they knew where their replacements slept—otherwise they might waken the wrong man and disturb his much-needed sleep. It was also prudent to wake a sleeping man by whispering his name rather than by shaking him. Nerves were often frayed after a hard day, and an unexpected touch on the shoulder could make a man explode into wakefulness, instinctively brandishing a gun or knife. Rules strictly outlawed drinking. A drunk cowboy was a danger to himself and the other men; rowdiness could start a stampede.

Ranchers who didn't know the unwritten laws of the West sometimes tried to lay down their own regulations. One of the strictest sets of rules was created by 'Bar-B-Q' Campbell, manager of the XIT ranch. (It was owned by four men who 'didn't know a cow from a horse', bankers and politicians who acquired the land in a property deal.) Campbell framed 23 strict rules that included no gambling, no drinking and no guns or other weapons on the three-million-acre ranch. Cowboys weren't allowed to keep private horses, nor to race ranch horses or use them to chase mustangs. They were also forbidden to kill stray cattle or mavericks for beef.

Campbell's rules extended to visitors as well as people who worked on the ranch. Passing travellers who could conceivably be described as 'loafers, deadbeats, tramps, gamblers or disreputable persons' weren't permitted to stay, or be given or sold grain or provisions.

These regulations contravened all accepted codes and practices and were regarded with 'hilarious contempt' by his men. It may be that the regulations made for bad working relations: certainly, the XIT was never a success. Although it was huge—some 200 miles long and an average of 27 miles wide—the XIT did badly from the start; it never made a profit and was liquidated in 1901. Ironically, property values had soared by then, and the XIT, sold as 'parcels', made more money than it ever had from cattle.

Bosses were chosen for the way they could handle men and cattle, and their sense of fairness: detail from Edward Borein's illustration of a trail boss

A man who violated a ranch's rules in a big way was soon back on the trail, looking for work. No hired hand was indispensable if he was a threat to the herd and his fellow cowhands, and there was never a shortage of men wanting to become cowboys.

Guns and gunfights Most cowboys were law-abiding; to them guns were cumbersome pieces of equipment which they preferred to do without. The code of the West forbade shooting an unarmed man, so it made sense not to pack a pistol. Branch Isbell, an old Texas trail driver, explained that he 'never buckled on a six-shooter anywhere. I figure my life has been saved several times by not having one handy. No gunman ever bothered a man without a gun, and a man without a gun shore wasn't going to bother a man with one—if he had any sense. I never felt undressed or out of place without a gun.'

The brave young bloods who did pack pistols accepted the code's established rules. A man whose personal sense of honour had been threatened was justified in taking a shot at the man who'd insulted him. To gun down an unarmed man, or a person who didn't know he was being hunted, was beyond the pale.

The cowboy image The cowboy's status was based on his being a man with a horse. Mounted, he was an aristocrat with no equal in the West. On foot, he was reduced to the same despised level as the overalled farmer or staid storekeeper. This was one reason why cowboys were so notoriously reluctant to walk even the shortest distances. For these men, the ultimate humiliation was to be ordered to turn in their horses after being fired, and be forced to leave a ranch on foot.

Cowboys deliberately cultivated their hard-riding, hard-living, 'superman' image. To most people, chasing steers at all hours of the day and night, in fair weather and foul, risking life and limb, was a crazy way to earn a living. But to men who'd committed themselves to the life, these hardships had an altogether different significance. They were the basis of the myth of the cowboy—the supermale who could take the worst the range had to offer, and always come through smiling, honest, good-humoured, and riding tall in the saddle.

Other Cowboys, Other Times

'Even when separated by half a world, the tough men who ride herd share a deep affinity that arises from their common tradition of freedom under the open skies.'

The American cowboy, far from being unique, is the inheritor of a tradition that stretches back over 1,000 years and spans the globe from the steppes of Mongolia to South America's pampas. Mongolian *arats*, Hungarian *csikosok*, French *gardians*, the *vaqueros* of the Iberian peninsula, the *gauchos* and Mexican *charros* all share a way of life with the Americans. Riding on horseback, they tend and control cattle.

Details vary: not all herders deal only with cattle; some also tend sheep and horses. And objectives differ: the *gardians* breed bulls essentially for fighting; the Australians and Canadians, like the Americans, are geared to produce beef for the world's markets. But the similarities are far greater than their differences. All these men show pride in their work, professionalism in doing it well, endurance in the face of the elements (often against improbable odds), and steadfastness in maintaining a great tradition. These other cowboys of other times deserve just as much attention as the much more widely popularized cowboys of the American West.

Arats of Mongolia

Man first began to ride herd over 6,000 years ago. Anthropologists believed the first cows were tended on the undulating steppes of eastern Asia, in what we call Mongolia. In this 600,000 square miles of mountain, desert and vast grasslands, sandwiched between China and Russia, nomadic Mongolian herdsmen (*arats*) today control millions of head of cattle and sheep just as their ancestors cared for smaller herds thousands of years ago.

The land, once free to all comers, is now owned by the state, but the *arat* himself hasn't changed much over the centuries. Short, stocky, bandy-legged and with black hair, slanted eyes, high cheekbones and a yellowish skin burned brown by the fierce and extreme climate, he looks much as his forefathers the Huns did when they were, for centuries, the scourge of Europe. These Mongol warriors swept on their small, shaggy horses in hordes to the very doors of Rome. A contemporary Roman soldier wrote: 'They even sleep in the saddle, along the horse's neck; they are on the move ceaselessly. Men of small build, they appear gigantic in the saddle.' Another wrote of the 'rivers of blood' brought by their leader Attila in the 5th century.

Eight centuries later, Ghengis Khan, recruiting among the neighbouring tribes of Cossacks and Turkestans, forged these intemperate herdsmen into another great tide of death. A 13th-century historian called them 'a terrible people of Satan . . . who flowed like diabolic waves across eastern Europe, like a flight of locusts that wreaked terrible devastation, ravaging it with fire and with baths of blood.' More than half the world paid homage to the banners of Ghengis Khan and it took a rider months to gallop across his empire.

Today's Mongol herdsmen are descendants of the warriors of Ghengis Khan: Mongolian arat

Wrestling is an age-old Mongolian sport, one of the Three Manly Sports: competitors perform at a traditional festival

Today about two-thirds of the $1\frac{1}{4}$ million population of Mongolia work with livestock: cattle, sheep, horses, and also goats, reindeer and yak. Two-thirds of the country is good grazing land, and with an estimated livestock population of 20 million, the area has a higher proportion of stock to herdsmen than any other part of the world.

Like that of all cowboys, the *arats'* working life is governed by the seasons. In spring they take their herds to mountain slopes sheltered from the bitter north winds and melting snows of the grasslands. In summer they wend their way down to the fertile river valleys where the cattle fatten on lush grasses. This is when sheep-shearing starts and newly-born calves are tended. In July they prepare their supplies of *ayrag* or *kumiss*, a virulent cocktail made from the fermented milk of mares and sometimes called the 'secret of Ghengis Khan'. In autumn the cattle are driven to the windier regions where they can find relief from the swarms of stinging insects that plague them. And in winter the stock is moved back to the sheltered valleys, where they survive the cruel weather in crude wooden shelters.

The *arats* were completely nomadic until 50 years ago, and their traditional home was a *yurt*. This dome-shaped hut, made from latticed branches covered with strips of felt, was easily transportable. Today the *yurt* is usually a permanent home, and *arats* live in transportable reed huts when out on the range. Smaller animals like goats

Arat's huts once travelled with their nomadic owners. Today they're usually permanent homes: hut or yurt

and sheep traditionally join the family in the warm if foetid interior of the *yurt*, where piles of rough furs serve as beds. The centrepiece is often an altar. In the past it was hung with religious images, but today these are likely to be replaced by family photographs. A skin bag of *ayrag* often hangs behind the square wooden door.

Historically, the main Mongolian meal was *manj*, an unappetizing concoction of shavings from tea 'bricks' boiled with milk, grain and butter, and eaten with hunks of mutton. Today these tea bricks are used mainly as currency in trading, and a typical *arat* meal consists of unsalted mutton, thick broth and tea. Range riders used to put freshly killed beef under their saddles, where it was pounded down until it was tender enough to eat raw; that's the origin of *steak tartare*.

Arat food has improved over the centuries, but change for change's sake has no part in their way of life. They still prefer to wear traditional dress: a *deli*, or long tunic-like coat (silk for fancy dress, wool for winter), bound at the waist by a broad belt of brightly coloured silk. Trousers are tucked into knee-length leather boots with pointed, turned-back toes.

Hunting is one of the main relaxations in a region where wolves abound, especially in winter and spring in and around the Gobi desert. Guns are regarded as the sissy's way. Like their ancestors, the *arats* use whips which they aim between the wolf's eyes as he attacks them. Falcons and eagles are trained for two years to swoop down on and kill the fur-bearing animals that provide the herdsmen with hats, coats and furniture for their *yurts*. Less agressive forms of relaxation include *shatar* (chess) and story-telling; Mongolian lore is rich in tales of early heroes.

The highspot of the year is the Great Naadain Festival of the Three Manly Sports (wrestling, archery and horse-racing). This is celebrated every national day, 11 July, in all *aymags* (small villages) and *somons* (communities). The wrestlers, in tight-fitting costumes called *dzodog shudags*, perform a ritual dance before competing for titles like *Titan*, *Lion*, *Elephant* and *Falcon*. The winner of three bouts becomes *Parkham Avraga* (*Invincible Tartar*) for the day. For the archery contests the competitors use the same traditional bow, reinforced with horn, that they used to terrorize Europe centuries ago. They fire at a leather-covered target to become *Merghen* (*Supermarksman*). Outstanding archers are given the title *Miraculous Archer* or *Most Scrupulous Archer*.

Horse-racing is performed by seven- to twelve-year-old boys and girls over an adult-sized course of 20 miles across country. Because the riders are so young and lack adult skill and control, the result of the race depends mainly on the horse's endurance. During the Mongolian New Year in January and February, national horse races for competitors of all ages are held, a custom that stretches back to the earliest days of history.

Over the centuries, the Mongolians' influence spread throughout Europe. Often this was a direct result of military invasion, but there was also a more subtle mingling as the *arats* joined with other nomadic tribes in an ever-widening search for new pastures.

Csikosok of the Hungarian Plain

About a thousand years ago, a group of nomadic herdsmen ended their westward wanderings at the foot of the Carpathian hills, in what is now Hungary. They chose the region well—a great plain of grassland, lakes, small hills and groves of trees, where cattle, horses and sheep could graze. Today herdsmen live on the *puszta* much as their forefathers did.

The *csikosok* (breeders of young horses; singular, *csikos*) are tall, dark, lean men who spend nine months of the year in the saddle, moving herds from pasture to pasture. Direct descendants of the Hungarian Magyars, they preserve the nomadic tradition in this part of Europe. As well as the Hungarian red-spotted cattle, the *csikosok* breed the ancient type their ancestors brought from the steppes of central Asia. Grey, heavily built, with forked horns, these tough beasts are found only on the *puszta*. Their *ratzka* sheep are also unique. Hardy, with twisted horns, they graze alongside Merinos introduced only two centuries ago.

Hungarian herdsmen are the descendants of westward-moving nomads: Hungarian csikos

The climate of the *puszta* is harsh. In spring strong winds blow constantly across the plain. In summer the scorching sun bakes the earth into choking dust. Autumn rains churn the tracks into thick mud, which the winter frost first freezes into deep ruts then buries under deep snow. Blizzards sweep down from the mountains to obliterate herdsmen's tracks and bury the stock in deep drifts.

During the three months of late winter and early spring, the *csikos* stays at home with his family in their small, roughly made hut. This is when he mends saddles, cuts new reins, breaks in young horses at the local corral—and rests from his exertions. For the rest of the year, when he's riding the range, his shelter is often a primitive clay and straw hut which he shares with the shepherds (and the shepherd dogs that accompany them everywhere). In the past the *csikos* ate game or wildfowl, washed down with mare's milk. Today he prefers meat goulash and red Hungarian wine.

Although his diet has changed, he still follows the old, hard traditions of the cowboy. He lives through long winter nights on horseback, huddled in a thick, warm coat, and chokes through swirling dust clouds under the summer sun. Summer or winter, he is constantly on guard against the lynx and bears that threaten his stock. His working clothes are a blue shirt, billowing trousers tucked into knee-high, supple leather boots, and a wide-brimmed black hat tilted over his forehead and held in place with a chin strap. In winter he wears either a thick sheepskin coat, or one made from white felt with red and yellow embroidery. This reaches the ground and is slit down the sides. On festivals and holidays, the *csikos* wears fringed leather trousers, a red embroidered coat and a black felt sombrero.

In the past the *csikosok* were devout Roman Catholics. For centuries they erected small statues of saints at dusty crossroads far out in the *puszta* to bless them as they rode past. Remote and rare water wells, prone to dry up in summer, were also consecrated.

Like the American cowboy, the csikos *spends much of his time on the range: a herder prepares supper in his clay and straw shelter*

Because of their dashing horsemanship and bravado, the *csikosok* were eagerly sought after as mercenaries during Europe's many wars, and Napoleon valued them as cavalry in his campaigns. They've

Csikosok *today carry on the tradition of horsemanship and courage that once numbered them among Europe's most popular mercenaries: Hungarian festival sport*

bequeathed two words to our military vocabulary: the *csikos* custom of fighting in 20-man detachments gave us *hussar*, from the Hungarian *husz* (twenty). And *shako*, for a cavalryman's tall hat, is a corruption of *csikos*. Today the *csikosok* use the same saddles that they used during their military greatness. Made of wood, they are tied with leather thongs and covered with sheepskin. But the *csikos* is used to riding bareback.

The *puszta* cowboys always lived by a strict code of honour. Duels over women were commonplace, though the weapons weren't: a 45-foot-long lasso can easily strangle an opponent. Today the *csikos* fierceness is sublimated in folktales that tell of war and conquest, and giants, witches and evil spirits that attack his cattle.

Gardians of the Camargue

Far eastwards and south from the Hungarian plain, just 50 miles west of the great French sea port of Marseilles—but a thousand years and miles away in spirit—lies the Camargue, 300 square miles of flat marshland, swamp and plain. The small population of 10,000 and the uninterrupted stretches of pasture give a tremendous sense of space and solitude. Flamingoes and wildfowl wheel in the boundless skies, and herds of white horses and black bulls roam at will. It is a most unlikely setting for an ancient cowboy community.

This is the homeland of the *gardians*, a close-knit community of cattle- and horse-breeders. Their origins are uncertain, but their traditions go back to Roman times. Julius Caesar replenished his cavalry with Camargue horses in the 1st century AD, and the area was named after a Roman senator, Annius Camar, who was proconsul of this region.

The gardian's homeland—marshes, plains and swamps—is only 50 miles from Marseilles

In many ways time has stood still in this part of France: a young girl wears traditional Camargue costume

Tides of invaders have swept across this curious corner of Europe. All left their mark. The Romans, following the Phoenicians, were themselves followed centuries later by Attila the Hun at the head of the Mongol hordes. Even today the *gardians* use a supplementary rein similar to the Mongols'—the *mourraioun*. It lets the rider lead without pulling the horse's mouth, and this increases the animal's agility. Nomadic Saracen and Moorish horsemen who followed the Mongols also left their mark. The iron head that tips the 7-foot pole the Camargue cowboys use to control their cattle is of ancient Saracen design: a half-moon set between two sharp iron horns.

Today, as in the past, the *gardians* are a race apart, the 'aristocrats' of the Camargue. Their lives are devoted to tending the herds of horses and cattle, and their art has been passed from father to son since time immemorial. Even their diet remains traditional—sausages made from horsemeat, goat cheese (cows are never milked; their only role is to breed bulls), fish from the plentiful streams, and lots of the strong local spirit *pastis*. A regional speciality is *aioli*, a dish of snails, octopus, boiled fish, hard-boiled eggs, potatoes, carrots and sometimes other vegetables such as cauliflower, cooked with herbs and served with garlic-flavoured mayonnaise.

There are about 80 main *manades* (ranches), owned by *manadiers*. These proud men are the region's top breeders, and between them 30 *manadiers* control a total of 1,500 horses. Fifty ranches are devoted to bull-breeding, and each has between 200 and 300 head. Some present-day *gardians* live in bunkhouses on the *manades*, others in reed huts or *cabanas*, while a minority live in small boats moored in the region's marshy creeks. But most of these French cowboys live in small clay houses with thatched roofs. Traditionally they face south-west, away from the prevailing north-easterly mistral, which blows down the Rhone valley.

Descended from ancient, Asiatic stock, these black bulls are revered by the gardians

The working *gardian* wears a brightly coloured shirt, a broad-brimmed hat, skin-tight trousers and leather or rubber boots. On feast days—each village celebrates two or three every year—their plumage is brighter: moleskin trousers, black velvet jackets, short Spanish-style boots, and blue, flower-patterned shirts. Horses and bulls both graze free. They're raised wild, and the *gardians* check the calves occasionally until the round-up and branding days of early spring. Cows also roam wild, and live naturally through the cold winters and hot windy summers of the Camargue.

The off-white Camargue horses are unique. Small compared with the American cutting horse, they stand about 12·2 hands (50 inches) high, and their endurance and strength are legend. They can reach high speeds even over short distances, and are able to turn on the proverbial dime with the skill of a crack polo pony. Allowed to run free for centuries, they're inherently wild and unruly. But when saddled they display an innate instinct for herding the black bulls.

Small, active and agile, the bulls come from ancient Asiatic stock. The people revere them: when a champion dies, it is buried standing up as a mark of respect. The annual round-up and branding—the *ferrade*—is a great fiesta. Calves, cut out from the herd, are driven to the branders who seize their horns as they gallop past. To the accompaniment of traditional songs, the animals are branded with the ancient heraldic or family emblems of the *manadiers*. *Pastis* is drunk by the potful during the festival.

The *gardian's* way of life can be distilled down to one moment: when man and bull face each other in the bullring. From April through to October more than 1,000 contests are held in arenas throughout the region, the best-known being the Roman arena at Nîmes. Unlike Spanish bullfighting, the Camargue version is bloodless. The object is to glorify the bull, not to destroy it, and the audience divides its cheers impartially between bull and bullfighter (*rajeteur*). The bulls' wild way of life makes them fierce opponents at these *courses libres*, even though their horns are capped. Broken legs, crushed ribs and even deaths of bullfighters have been recorded after this always hazardous event.

When fight day dawns, the *manadier* and his *gardians* cut the six biggest bulls from the herd and drive them at a gallop through the streets of the town to the arena. The *rajeteur's* object is to snatch a red cockade from the bull's forehead, using a kind of steel comb. In 'fighting' the bull, all he's allowed to do is slap the animal and pull its tail. The contest lasts for 15 minutes, after which, if the bull retains his cockade, the band strikes up the 'Toreador's March' from the opera *Carmen* and the bull's breeder takes a bow. If the *rajeteur* succeeds in snatching the cockade, he wins points—and money—for his performance. At the end of the day the champion bull and winning *rajeteur* both receive gold cockades.

Off-white Camargue horses are renowned the world over for their alertness, dexterity and sturdiness

For centuries, the people of the Camargue have prided themselves on their way of life. In 1512 *L'Antique Confrerie des Guardians de Taureaux et de Cheveaux de Camargues* was formed to look after the welfare of *gardians'* families. A more recent development in 1904 was the *Nacioun Gardiano*, a professional advisory body. And 50 years ago games popular in the Middle Ages were reintroduced to link the 20th-century *gardian* even more strongly with his past. In one of these, the *jeu du bouquet*, men on horseback try to retrieve a bouquet or scarf that one player has received from the girl of his choice. In another, a *gardian* rides bareback at full tilt and switches to another horse in mid-gallop.

Vaqueros of Andalucia

The dashing, chivalrous Spanish *vaquero* emerged when Spain became one nation in the late 15th century. Like the *gardian*, he herds cattle—and breeds bulls for the bullring.

The Moorish proverb, 'The horse, the woman and the rose are God's most beautiful creations' fired the Spanish imagination, and nowhere more so than in Andalucia. This southern region (whose capital was Seville) is renowned for its fast, strong, handsome horses and fierce fighting bulls. The horses are more than 15 hands (5 feet) high; the great black Miura bulls of Andalucia, with needle-sharp horns, are star attractions in the bullrings. The breed dates back to 1842, and a bullfighting superstition holds that a Miura bull's neck is like an accordion—it can stretch out to twice its length to catch an unwary opponent.

Bullfighting is a high-point in the vaqueros' *year: bulls are led down a village street to the arena*

More than half of Spain's 150-plus major breeding ranches, or *ganaderias*, are in Andalucia, and every breeder keeps a register of the exact pedigree of his bulls and horses. Although former cattle runs are today being turned into crop-growing land by the government, the cowboy tradition lives on. The Andalucians are lively, good-humoured individualists whose Spanish blood is mixed with Moorish, gypsy and Jewish strains; their distinctive dialect includes many words of Moorish origin.

The skills of the *vaqueros* are passed from father to son, as they are among the *gardians*. The cowboy's life is hard; he spends many weeks on the scorched range, far from his home (a primitive stone house close to the breeder's ranch), and is poorly paid. He lives on horseback, and even rests in the saddle by crossing his legs over the horse's neck. When he's injured he cleans the wound with harsh red wine from the leather bottle, or *bota*, he carries with him. Alive to his herd's every mood, he keeps the *bravos*, or fighting bulls, separate from the others and tends their injuries when they fight each other. (The *bravos* are so aggressive that each animal has its own trough.) A *vaquero* never makes a pet of a bull calf: the animal's aggression towards man must remain intact.

In autumn the *vaqueros* drive their charges from the grasslands to the slopes of the Sierra Nevada mountain range, south of Granada. Here they feed the bulls a precise mixture of salt, oats and barley mixed with straw. This formula strengthens the bull and is said to imbue it with vigour.

Bravery trials are held to divide bullocks destined for the glory of the arena from those that will end up as beef. The young bulls are herded together, and two *vaqueros*, each wielding a long, blunt lance, cut them one by one out of the herd. One *vaquero* rides after the young calf to prevent it turning. The other prods it in the rump and turns it over, or up-ends it by jerking its tail. If the bullock charges the *vaqueros*, he is sure of a place in the bullring. If it runs away, the abattoir is its destination. In the past, only five-year-old bulls were sent to the ring. Today they are considered ready at four years or even younger.

The Andalucian bullfight dates back to the 'chivalrous' *corrida* of the Middle Ages when Spanish nobles first fought bulls from horseback. In those days the *caballero* used a lance or sword and wore armour, but this protection was abandoned in the 16th century. Today the Andalucian *rejoneador* (a *matador* on horseback) uses the same sword and darts as the *matador*. *Afficionados* believe that fighting bulls from horseback is the epitomy of man and horse moving in unison. The horse has an innate instinct for bullfighting, and even a flick of the bull's ear is enough to alert it to the beast's next move. Traditionally, the last bull is always killed as the sun is about to set.

The *vaqueros* and the bulls of Andalucia both made their mark in the New World. The *vaquero* bequeathed his name, and skills, to the Mexican—and eventually the American—cowboy. And the Longhorns of North America can trace their descent back to 16th-century Andalucian cattle.

Gauchos of South America

If cowboys are all seen as romantic figures, the *gaucho* is the Rudolf Valentino of them all. The very word conjures up a picture of dashing steeds, swirling cloaks, and brilliant feats of derring-do unparalleled in the annals of cowboy history.

The early *gauchos* were the casual offspring of Spanish settlers and Indian and Negro women. Half-castes, they were often illegitimate. During the 17th and 18th centuries they wandered the 750,000 square miles of dry, dusty pampas, from the far north of Argentina and Uruguay to the tip of Patagonia. The Spanish settlers at first regarded them as vagabonds, thieves, unwashed gamblers and ne'er-do-wells. They reserved special contempt for the white outcasts, *criollos*, who joined their ranks. These *gauchos vagabondos* were useful casual labour on the *vaquerías*, the primitive cattle ranches, and were superb horsemen and herdsmen. But come pay day, they went on their way—so much so that their nomadic habits earned them the title 'the arabs of America'.

Over the years, a growing number of *gauchos* decided they liked the life of cattlemen, and were licensed to work on the great private *estancias* (estates) of the rich Spaniards. These *gauchos libretos* took great pride in their skill with stock. By the late 18th century the pampas were alive with vast herds of wild cattle and horses, descended from the stock brought by the conquistadores. The *estancias* grew and their *gaucho* populations grew with them. It was at this time that the word *gaucho* became synonymous with *cowboy* and gauchos became part of the South American ranching scene.

The 18th-century *gaucho* was something of a dandy. An eyewitness described him as wearing a cloth jacket embellished with silver buttons, trousers slit up to the knee, silver spurs with enormous rowels on colt-leather boots, a straw hat and coloured scarf, a belt, or *rastra*, covered with silver coins, and a fierce 14-inch knife stuck in his boot. To cap it all he wore a poncho coloured with broad stripes and lined in green, red or blue.

Gauchos finally won complete public approval in the early 19th century, during the struggle for independence from Spain. Organized into *montoneras*, or armed bands, they fought brilliantly against the Spanish army. On small, agile horses, armed with machetes, *boleadoras* and long, knife-tipped lances, they won every battle with flair and audacity. One despairing Spanish general wrote: 'We shall never be able to beat these extraordinary horsemen.' (Their guerrilla tactics were a model for the Mexican revolutionary Pancho Villa a century later.) As a token of national pride, the fighting *gauchos* wore red ponchos in striking and colourful contrast to the royal blue uniforms worn by Spanish soldiers.

'No man is so sincere, free and independent,' an English merchant wrote in 1817. Another writer declared that, though wary and fierce, 'the gauchos are elegant, chivalrous and free-handed, loyal and often very handsome.' But he added, 'There is a sense about them of not being tamed.' Never again did the Spaniards call them vagabonds. They were honoured men in the reborn Argentina and still have great symbolic force today.

Early gauchos rode horses descended from the animals brought to South America by the conquistadores: a modern rodeo horse wearing traditional silver bridle

Like his 18th-century predecessor, a modern gaucho in traditional dress is an impressive and colourful figure: Argentinian gaucho

The working *gaucho* lived in cramped, low-roofed mud huts—but decorated their belts with silver coins. They made do with broken-down furniture, yet their boots and saddles were the finest available. Men of great personal pride, they presented their best front to the world. It was customary for a *gaucho* to have riding horses all of the same colour—roan, chestnut or piebald. (Some *estancias* even boasted herds of colour-matched cattle.) A *gaucho* baby started to learn his trade in the cradle. His first toy was a string lasso, and he could ride when he was four. At eight he was able to help the men on local round-ups. Later he mastered the *boleadoras* and learnt how to track and hunt ostrich, puma and jaguar.

The *gaucho* ate well: beef or mutton, roasted or stewed with spices, potatoes and beans, washed down by the invariable maté—tea made from the leaves of a Paraguayan tree. Many years ago this refreshing drink was denounced to the Inquisition in Lima, Peru, on the grounds that it made the *gaucho* lazy. Anyone found drinking it was threatened with excommunication. Today the habit is stronger than ever. The modern *gaucho* starts his day with three or four matés and a piece of *galleta* (hard biscuit), and brews up whenever he has a chance. The unvarying ritual is for a group to drink from the same gourd, sucking the tea through a small tube, or *bombilla*.

A gaucho's home may be cramped and poor but his clothes will be the finest available: gaucho *wearing a belt decorated with silver coins*

As a hunter the *gaucho* had few equals. With his long knife he could impale a snake's eye at 20 feet. With his lasso he could noose a rock at 60 feet. But he really came into his own with his *boleadoras*, with its two or three leather-wrapped stone balls, attached by leather straps. The *gaucho* swirled them around his head then threw the weapon around his prey's legs over distances of up to 100 feet. The modern *gaucho* still practises this skill.

Traditional firefighting methods were inventive and effective. When the pampas thistles caught fire during the long dry spell, the *gauchos* killed a couple of sheep, attached the bodies to their horses, and dragged them through the thistles to make a primitive firebreak—a method not unlike that used in the American West. They then beat out the flames with horse blankets.

Few true descendants of the early *gauchos* survive. Those that do are found only in remote pockets in the Sierras and the Chaco forest regions of the far northern pampas, and in the windswept isolation of Patagonia. But the modern ranch worker is proud to bear the name and follow the old ways. The pampas is now partly fenced into huge paddocks, and living quarters are more comfortable. But ten-foot-high thistles still tear at a rider's legs and face, the burrows dug by the *viscacha* (a large rodent) still test horse and rider, and the pampas itself is still frighteningly vast and hostile.

Today's craftsmen still carry on the traditional skills: a modern Argentinian silversmith works on a pair of spurs

It's little wonder that feast days are eagerly looked forward to, and enjoyed. The *fiesta a carne con cuero* is celebrated when the *patrón*, the owner of the *estancia*, makes a good sale. A whole steer is roasted in its hide, and lambs and sucking pigs are grilled over red-hot ashes. The men put on their black capes with bright tassels, black sombreros, coloured silk scarves, vivid blue, red or green shirts, and billowing trousers tucked into embroidered leather top boots—and the old *gaucho* songs and dances come alive again.

After vast platters of meat and equal amounts of beer and wine have been consumed, there is a short break for a siesta. Horse-racing —*cuadreras*—follow, when plenty of money changes hands. As the day cools ballads (*payadas*) are sung and tales (*estilos*) told while the guitars throb. Occasionally two men start a singing duel (a *criollo*, the name given to white *gauchos*) and try to insult each other in song. This has been known to end up in a real duel to the death with knives instead of words.

During a big fiesta a space is cleared for the *sortija*. Riders armed only with a pencil or twig try to spear a small ring suspended from a bar while galloping at full speed. The older men play *taba*, pitching a cow's kneecap, and others pit their skills at *truco*, a card game that demands real cunning and roguery. Or a game of *pato* may be staged. Two teams of galloping *gauchos* try to take a hard ball, attached to rope handles, into each other's side of the field. It's a rough and dangerous sport—a sort of lethal polo. The older, traditional version was even more vivid. The ball was a live duck wrapped in a hide sheath; when the game was over the now dead duck was eaten by the bruised and bloody competitors. President Perón declared *pato* a national sport—one more sign of the respect and admiration the Argentinians have for their version of the cowboy.

Tea is brewed up at intervals throughout the day: a gaucho sucks maté through a bombilla

Vaqueros and Charros of Mexico

In 1519 Gregorio de Villalobos set sail from Cadiz for the New World with seven Andalucian calves—six heifers and a bull—in the hold. This was the start of the great herds that now roam over the sandy wastes of Mexico's northern *mesas* (plateaux), and the beginning of Mexico's cowboy culture.

The conquistadores were lesser nobles, *hidalgos*, who built their ranches, or *haciendas*, on Mexican land granted by their king, Charles V. These were precise replicas of the houses they had left in Andalucia and Navarre, with courtyards unfolding behind light stone façades. Normally the first courtyard, or *patio*, was the focus for the large high-ceilinged living rooms. An archway led to the second patio, which housed the kitchens and store rooms. From here another archway led to the third patio where the saddle-horses, mules and wagons were kept. Most of the *haciendas* were destroyed during the War of Independence between 1810 and 1821, but were later rebuilt in faithful imitation of the originals.

The Andalucian stock brought in by the Spaniards settled in well with the native wild cattle, despite poor grazing, searing summer heat, frequent dust storms and marauding mountain lions (puma) and jaguars. Over the years the herds grew, and more and more labour was needed to tend them. The Mexican Indians, and the ever-growing throng of half-castes (the Spaniards settled in with enthusiasm) proved to be natural horsemen. Guided by the Spanish ranchers, they soon mastered the wide repertoire of riding skills that the conquistadores had brought with them. The Franciscan missions also did much to spread Mexican cowboy skills. The friars' influence stretched as far north as San Francisco, California, and as far east as San Antonio, Texas. They, too, trained the local Mexican Indians in the skills they needed to tend the herds of cattle and sheep.

By 1750, the local cowboy, the *vaquero*, was a professional cattleman. He had mastered all that the conquistadores and the monks could teach him, and had developed his own skills and tools. His influence—and name—spread north into what are now Texas, Arizona and New Mexico.

The *vaquero* was always poor. Even after the War of Independence, when the Mexican government encouraged ranching, opened new cattle markets, and gave grants to induce American cattlemen to settle in Mexico, his salary averaged a paltry $14 a month. He was a gambler, womanizer and fighter. His life on the *mesas* was hard and lonely. He lived in crude, lean-to shelters of sticks and rawhide, and ate buck, jack rabbit or wild turkey (shot with bow and arrow), and corn mash. In the towns he haunted the saloons, and drank *pulqué* made from the agave plant. He was so addicted to this drink that he invented a Goddess of Pulqué. She had 400 children, mysteriously called rabbit children, and drunkenness was measured on the 'rabbit scale'. A man who was ten rabbits overboard was barely high; if he reached 200 rabbits he was spectacularly drunk.

In 1910, the *vaqueros* flared into discontent under two leaders, Pancho Villa and Emiliano Zapata. Villa was a *hacienda* foreman who led the *vaqueros* against the government forces. Zapata, a small rancher, became a legendary guerrilla leader.

Mexicans wear colourful charros *costumes and practise traditional skills at their modern 'games'*

The *charros* were another, superior, breed of Mexican cowboy. As the ranchers' acres spread, they formed troops of mounted retainers, disciplined cavalrymen who raised the art of horsemanship to new heights. The *charro* was a devil-may-care dandy whose cult inspired the Mexican ideal of *machismo*, or maleness. Too fond of women, he gambled to excess, rode hell-for-leather, could 'speak' to horses, and was master of sword and pistol.

He never cut his hair, but parted it in the centre and tied it back in a single long plait. He shaved once a week, and grew long side-burns. He bound his head with a black silk kerchief, topped by a sombrero. Originally a low-crowned, broad-brimmed hat, this gradually evolved into a hat shaped like a steeple. His bell-shaped trousers fitted tightly at thigh and calf and were made of chamois leather, as was his short bolero jacket, embroidered with intricate designs in white leather braid. In cold weather he shrouded himself in a vividly coloured cloak; though larger than life, he recognized life's hardships.

Mexican *charros* toured Europe and North America in the late 19th century. Some joined Buffalo Bill's *Wild West Show*, while others competed with all-comers in cowboy skills—and generally won. These skills, *charreria*, are very much alive today, a Mexican heritage practised by thousands of devotees. The big ranches hold weekly rodeos. At these the young *rancheros*, today's cowboys, can

The charros' *wives, daughters and girlfriends also wear the old-style costumes, for parades and riding events at* charro *fiestas*

sharpen their skills in competition. 'Weekend' cowboys—doctors, lawyers, shopkeepers and others—show their skill on Sunday mornings when, in *charros* costume, they muster at Chapultepec Castle, and other places in Mexico City, to compete in events like lassooing and bull-tailing that are still part of daily *hacienda* life.

This enthusiasm for the cowboy isn't surprising. Mexico influenced the first American cowboys; indeed, almost a third were Mexicans. Even branding, that regular entry in the cowboy's annual diary, originated in Mexico. Conquistador Hernando Cortés burnt a G (for *guerra*, or war) on the cheeks of his Indian slaves to signify they were his property by conquest. And he branded his cattle with a triple cross for Father, Son and Holy Ghost. It is from these cattle that the North American cowboy culture spread; first throughout Mexico, then across the borders to the United States and thence to Canada.

In modern Mexico the old skills are acquired by a wide variety of enthusiasts from doctors to machinists: a demonstration of roping

Cowboys of Canada

Canadians have been ranchers since 1874, when herds were driven up from the United States. In those early days, ranches were vast—100,000 acres and more—and frequent gun-battles broke out between the encroaching cattlemen and the farmers who had already settled the land. The early ranchers included gentlemen-adventurers and noble black sheep from Europe.

Canada's mountainous geography limits ranching to a small region, the Western Plains, and the long bitter winters mean that fewer cattle are reared than in the United States, Australia or Argentina. Australia, for instance, has a third of Canada's grazing land, but supports 30 per cent more stock. Southern Alberta, southwest Saskatchewan and the southern interior of British Columbia raise about $2\frac{1}{2}$ million head. Southern Alberta provides the most pasture. Over this entire region the growing season is short and hot; the cold and snows of winter last for almost six months.

Although there are one or two immense ranches with up to $1\frac{1}{4}$ million acres of grazing, and some spreads of 70,000 acres, the average ranch today is only about 10,000 to 15,000 acres. The rancher generally owns the nucleus of the land and leases extra grazing from the land authority. A 15,000-acre Plains ranch supports year-round grazing for 350 to 400 head. But every rancher depends on a good hay crop to tide him over if there is a really savage winter.

The Canadian cowboy is a hill cowboy, and spends most of his saddle life riding his sure-footed quarter horse up and down the slopes that abut the pasture lands. In late April, after the calves are born, he drives the cattle from their winter grazing close to the ranch up to the lower hill grasslands. As the snow melts the cattle advance upslope to higher pastures. In late September, when the frosts begin to bite, he leads his stock down again to the open grassland near the ranch. These are tasks no jeep can ever do. He takes a strong pride in his small community. The basic skills of rope and branding iron are like the American cowboys', but his legends, folk tales and heroes are his own.

The average ranch consists of the owner's house, a log-built bunkhouse for single men, cabins for married hands, one or two outbuildings for tools, and a few crude corrals. A flock of sheep may graze nearby. A small ranch employs only one or two hands, but a large one needs a dozen or more, including a foreman, cook and carpenter. Reveille in the bunkhouse is at 5.30 am, and the hands ride out at 7 after a big breakfast. Most of their days are spent riding herd, and horse and rider may cover as much as 50 miles in a single summer's day.

The Calgary Stampede is the highspot of the Canadian cowboy's year, when ranching folk compare prices, swop tall tales and booze it up with former saddle partners. It dates from 1912, and has been a regular annual event since 1919. It's the cowboy carnival supreme, with day after day of bronc-busting, bull-riding, roping and branding. The more scholarly ranch hands may spend their time looking at the cattle and horses, but the rodeo arena is the main attraction for the people who attend the stampede every year.

Canadian cowboys spend most of their working lives riding the mountain slopes that edge onto their pastures: two riders are almost dwarfed by the surrounding scenery

Stockmen of Australia

On the other side of the world, the lean, laconic Australian stockman rides the largest, most inhospitable land that ever saw stirrups and lasso. Cattle country in Australia covers about two-thirds of its total land, much of it unsettled desert with summer heat of up to 140°F (60°C). The principal cattle areas are in the Northern Territory of over half a million square miles, west and north-west Queensland, and the vast area of Western Australia, which includes three deserts and one-third of the total land mass. These three areas merge in the centre of the continent, forming the great 'outback'.

Intense sunlight, crystal air, stone-littered plains, sandstone hills, orange earth and dry river-beds mark much of the Western area. North-west Queensland has a small amount of tropical vegetation, and a few hills. The Northern Territory is grassy table land, with porcupine grass and gum trees (eucalyptus). Almost everywhere, rainfall is scant, and artesian wells bring water from deep underground.

The cattle and sheep stations (ranches) of Australia are the largest in the world: in essence, small towns set in an unvarying wilderness so inhospitable that each animal needs several acres to graze. The stations are self-contained, and essential stores are bought every 6 or 12 months. For example, Alexandra station in Queensland is almost as big as Belgium, covering 11,200 square miles; Victoria River Downs station in the Northern Territory covers 5,494 square miles and has over 80,000 head of cattle.

A typical ranch has an airstrip, a large bunkhouse for as many as 50 unmarried stockmen, smaller houses for stockmen with families, a house for the overseer (foreman), and one for the manager known as 'the Big House'. Each is normally long, low, made of wood and has a corrugated iron roof to trap rainwater. Adjacent stone buildings generally house a general store, post office, butcher, baker and the all-important blacksmith, as well as sheds for tools, harnesses, cattle feed and the ranch's generators. Most of the stockmen are locally-born Aborigines, and know virtually every creek, stone and lizard within a hundred square miles. Their wives help with the cleaning and other odd jobs around the station. The foreman, the manager, and usually the cook are, in most cases, white Australians.

Ranching started in Australia after the 1851 gold rush, when the western territories were settled. The government eventually granted long leases to anyone who could stock five head of cattle, or 25 sheep, per square mile. This started a land rush and, little by little, the great stations grew. In those bygone days the problem was finding men willing to work in such parched land where lack of fencing meant that hands had to ride long distances and stay away from the main homestead for weeks on end. By 1873 the picture had changed for the better. Prices for cattle and sheep rose, and the cowmen were able to build fences and corrals. The introduction of refrigerated ships in the 1880s enabled meat to be exported, giving stock-raising another boost. But life was always tough in the outback—between 1894 and 1903, for instance, drought reduced 7,000,000 cattle to 2,500,000 and 21,500,000 sheep to 7,000,000.

Australian cowboys work the world's toughest cattle country

The late 19th century heralded the arrival of Australia's first cowboy hero—the boundary rider. He lived a solitary and hard life, patrolling on horseback the hundreds of miles of fences that enclosed the huge cattle 'paddocks', doing running repairs, tending to sick stock, taking parched animals to water. All this he did with just his horse and perhaps a dog to keep him company through long days of scorching sun, caking wind and choking dust storms, and never another human being to talk to. Care of the cattle was all-important to the boundary rider; his skill determined whether they lived, or died of thirst to be picked clean by packs of dingoes (wild dogs). At night he pitched a canvas tent, or made a shelter from boughs and leaves, brewed his tea, ate hard-tack biscuit and, if lucky, some meat, then fell asleep exhausted before yet another pre-dawn saddle-up. Today, the boundary rider's work is often done by jeep and helicopter.

Most Australian stockmen are Aborigines: a ranch hand takes time out for relaxation

Today, cattle complete their journey to the railhead in giant motor trailers or 'road trains'

When the time approaches for the fattened cattle to be driven to market, the station goes into top gear for the round-up, or *mustering*. Fifteen to 20 stockmen ride out in the cool of the dawn (always accompanied by a 'tucker' wagon—the Australian version of the chuckwagon) shouting and whistling, and driving before them a posse of spare horses, generally four for each man. The head stockman assigns a separate area for each day's round-up, and the best riders canter ahead to search out the cattle. As each group is found, three or four men are sent to round them up until all the small herds in the area being worked have been brought together in one big group or *mob*. At sun's height all the stockmen, except for a few cattle guards, rest. Then the more experienced men, working in pairs, start checking the cattle for the unbranded calves, which are driven to the branding teams. Each animal is set free to roam once it has been branded. This rounding-up and branding continues for many weeks until the entire station has been covered.

Matching the boundary rider in popular esteem has always been the breed of overlanders, or trailmen, who drove the market-ready cattle to the nearest railhead. In Australia, trailing is called *droving*, and droving time is known as 'the turn'. In groups of seven (boss, drover, four stockmen, cook and horse trailer), the stockmen ride out for several weeks, roaming the range to muster all the saleable cattle, usually the five- to six-year-olds. Today, light aircraft may be used to locate the herds, but it is still a tough job. The stockmen herd the steers into mobs of 1,200 to 1,500 head during the hot days while the horse trailer goes ahead to prepare the night's camp.

When the mustering is complete, 'overlanding' begins. In the past this was a hot, dusty and exhausting process which could take weeks, or even months—cattle cover only 8 to 12 miles a day, sheep about half that distance. The men camp overnight at prepared spots near water-holes. At the railhead, the cattle would often have to be fattened up after losing weight during the long journey. One of Australia's most famous droving feats was in 1905, when trail boss Walter Rose and his stockmen brought 4,000 head across the outback during a drought. Conditions were so bad that 800 head died, all but two men deserted, and the drive took 17 months.

Today, droving covers much shorter distances, thanks to the network of roads that enable giant motor trailers to haul the cattle to the railhead, a trip of never more than two days. The proportion of cattle sold, however, is at best 20 per cent annually, with an average of about 8 per cent, compared with the United States annual average sale of 30 per cent.

Back on the station, the men drink beer, sing and gamble—often betting simply on a toss of a coin, in a peculiarly Australian game known as two-up. And they argue. Arguing is taken seriously in the outback, and a state-wide competition is organized to find the champion arguer. Tall-tale telling is another diversion. One of the hands' favourite stories is of the man from Marble Bar, Australia's hottest spot, where the average summer temperature is 93°F (34°C); when he died he went inevitably to Hell—and asked for an overcoat. It's just a variation on a favourite saying of the American cowboy—a sign, perhaps, that even when separated by half a world, the tough men who ride herd share a deep affinity arising from their common tradition of freedom under the open skies.

Drovers are the modern Australian equivalent of the American trail drivers: a drover cooks a meal over an open fire in the outback

Practical Skills

'Cowhands lavished endless care on their saddles, bridles and ropes. This was more than just vanity. Unexpected dangers were part of the job; and it was essential for equipment to be totally reliable.'

Cowboys took a pride in their way of life, and this was reflected in their equipment and clothing, as well as in the way they behaved. Factory workers and other wage-earners might regard the tools of their trade as impersonal belongings of the boss; to the cowboy his equipment was an extension of the skills by which he lived. And his clothing, virtually a uniform, identified him as a 'knight of the Plains'. (It wasn't far-fetched of Mark Twain to dress his Connecticut Yankee in cowboy clothes when he sent him to challenge the iron-clad champions of King Arthur's court; the cowboy was a fitting inheritor of the romantic knight tradition.)

Cowhands lavished endless care on their saddles, bridles and ropes. This was more than just vanity. Unexpected dangers were part of the job, and it was essential for equipment to be totally reliable. A well-made pair of boots was vital for a firm grip on the stirrups while roping a plunging steer. A man's life, or his comrade's, could depend on a rope holding at the crucial moment.

Cowboys were also fiercely proud of the skill with which they carried out their duties. A top cowhand stood out from his comrades by the style with which he rode and roped—and by his knowledge of cattle habits, brands, and the range where he lived his working life.

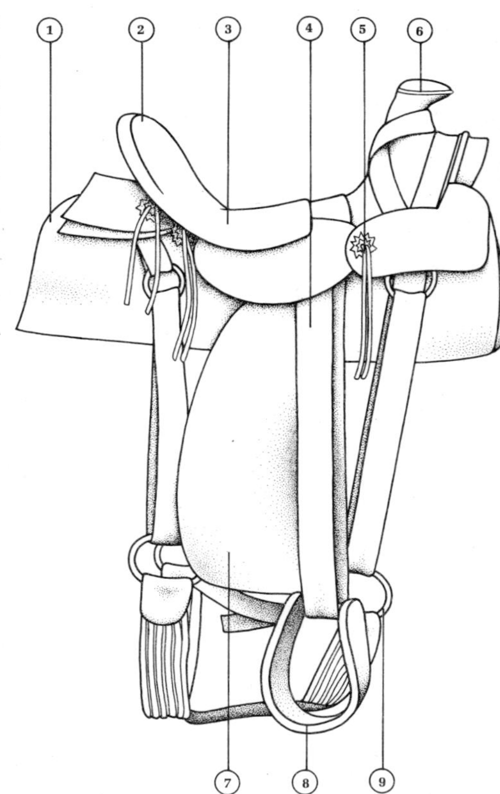

1 Skirt 2 Cantle 3 Seat 4 Stirrup leather 5 Latch strings 6 Horn 7 Fender 8 Stirrup 9 Cinch ring

Saddles and Bridles

A cowboy's saddle was his most prized possession, a symbol of his way of life. The horse he rode often belonged to the ranch; his saddle was always his own. A puncher might pawn his guns, his horse—even his clothes if necessary, but to part with his saddle was a real wrench. To say of a man that he'd 'sold his saddle' was to say that he'd fallen as low as a cowboy could fall. A cowhand's saddle was his work bench, his pride and his throne. Without it he felt degraded. It was often lavishly and lovingly decorated, for it was in this seat, on top of a running, twisting, jumping, bucking 900-lb horse that a cowboy's work was done. It was the most expensive single piece of equipment a cowboy possessed; no one thought it incongruous for a man to ride a hundred-dollar saddle on a ten-dollar horse.

The cowboy saddle was directly descended from the Spanish conquistadores' war saddles—heavy, ornate seats with high, straight pommels and bizarre forward-curving cantles (back-rests) that wedged the rider so firmly in place that he was more likely to be snapped in half than be unseated. The Mexican *vaqueros* added a horn to the pommel so that a rope could be fastened to it, and lowered and flattened the cantle to make mounting and dismounting easier. The horn on a typical Mexican saddle (nicknamed the 'dinner plate') was so broad that a game of cards could be played on it.

The 'skeleton rig' was an early—and aptly named—Western-style saddle. It consisted only of a tiny seat, a girth (or *cinch*) and the straps that held a pair of wide ox-bow stirrups. The classic Western saddle came into its own after the Civil War. Beautifully crafted, it was designed for hard riding—and to withstand the strain of roping 1,500-lb steers running at full speed. It was comfortable; it had to be, considering that cowboys often spent the entire day, and sometimes half the night, in their saddles. It was deep-seated so that a rider could doze while his horse walked. It was also big enough for the rider to attach his canteen, waterproof slicker, various tools and personal belongings by leather strings. A saddle also had to be comfortable for the horse. Hours of hard going carrying a heavy saddle, a rider and all his gear could wear a horse's back painfully raw if the saddle fitted poorly. Men were fired from their jobs for 'beefsteaking' their mounts.

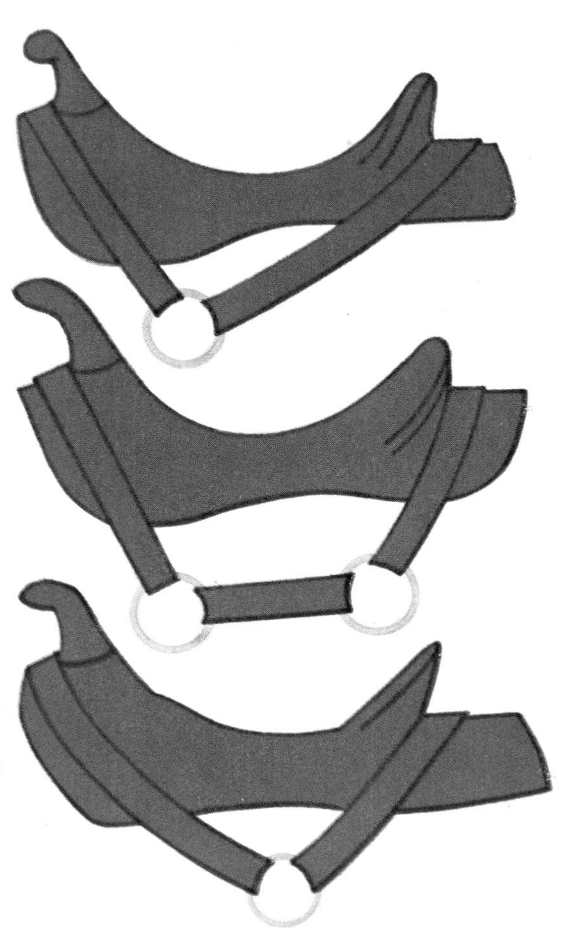

Varieties of rigging: Spanish (top), *an early type; double cinch* (centre), *the strongest and most secure; Centrefire* (above), *common in Nevada in the 1880s and 1890s*

A well-built, comfortable saddle was a cowboy's most important piece of equipment (Left) *Heavy-duty Porter Saddle No. 78 from Abilene Texas. Diagram* (far left) *shows its high cantle double-cinch rigging and ox-bow stirrups. Long stirrup leathers allow the cowboy to ride 'standing up.' He could sleep in the saddle by throwing one leg over the horn—the strongest part. To anchor himself securely he dug his spur into the thick leather beneath the horn*

The *tree* is a saddle's wooden foundation. Saddles were identified by their tree (California, Visalia, White River) or the name of their makers (Taylor, Nelson, Porter, Ellenburg). The Ellenburg was one of the best saddles made, and became the standard competition saddle for large rodeos. The tree consisted of the fork, to which the saddle horn was connected, the cantle and two side-pieces connecting the fork and cantle. The two side-pieces also formed the frame-work for the seat. The parts were fastened together with glue and heavy screws, and the tree was bound with wet, green rawhide that shrank as it dried and held the entire frame tightly together.

A *strainer*, a strip of galvanized iron, covered the space between the side bars. It ensured that the seat didn't sink under a man's weight, and also strengthened the saddle as a whole. A soft, thick layer of leather was laid over the strainer. The size of the seat depended on whether the rider preferred a tight-fitting or roomy saddle. The horn was the working end of the saddle. Cowboys always tied or turned one end of the lariat around it to prevent the rope being jerked out of their hands when they were roping.

The saddle's fork swelled behind the horn so that the rider could sit securely in the seat. Saddles with large swells and high cantles were called 'form-fitters'. Cantles were designed to cowboys' specific requirements. Cowhands in flat country preferred low cantles for easy mounting and dismounting. In hill country, high-cantle saddles were popular—they were more comfortable to ride in rugged sloping terrain.

Saddle skirts varied in shape. 'California' skirts were short and rounded; they were comparatively light, but allowed the saddle blanket to slip and bunch up. 'Texas' skirts were long and square, covered more of the horse's back and increased the saddle's weight to as much as 40 lb. Skirts were often stamped with fancy designs which were both attractive and useful—they increased the friction between a rider's leg and the leather, and helped him stay mounted.

Broad straps—the *rigging*—connected the tree to the saddle rings and the saddle to the horse. A one-cinch (single-girth) saddle was *single-rigged*; a two-cinch one was *double-rigged* or *double-fire*. A single cinch placed under the centre of the saddle was a *centre-fire* or *California rig*; a forward-placed cinch a *rim-fire* or *Spanish rig*. Owners of double-rigged saddles always claimed that rim-fire saddles were 'meat and hide hungry' because they shifted on a horse's back. (To confuse matters, the term *full-rigged* has nothing to do with the number of straps that held a saddle in place, but describes a tree entirely covered with leather.) A blanket, often of Navaho wool, which was colourful, durable and sweat-absorbent, was always placed under the saddle for protection. But a single blanket was the maximum—more than one made the animal sweat even more than usual and made its back even more sensitive to chafing.

Western stirrups, whether wooden or metal, were always adjusted low, for 'long-legged' riding. 'Ox-bows'—early, wide, wooden stirrups—were heavy and clumsy, but were also strong enough to prevent a man's foot being crushed if a horse fell sideways. Later stirrups were narrower and lighter.

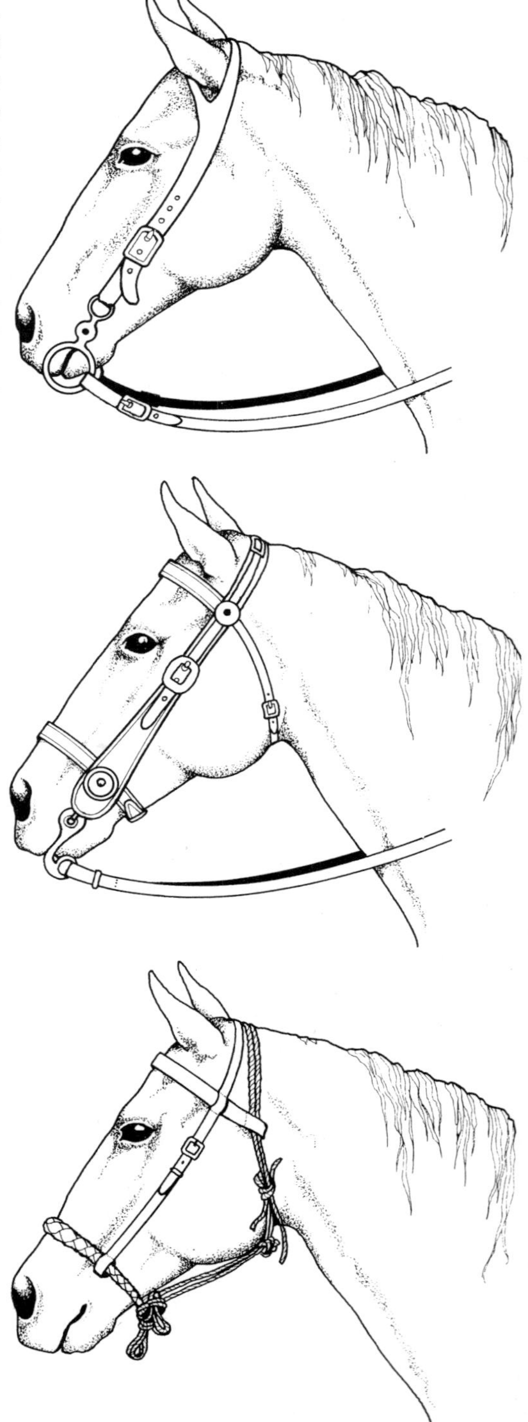

Type of bridle: split-ear (top), *the trail driver's favourite; standard bridle* (centre), *a slightly later model; hackamore* (above), *used for training newly broken-in horses*

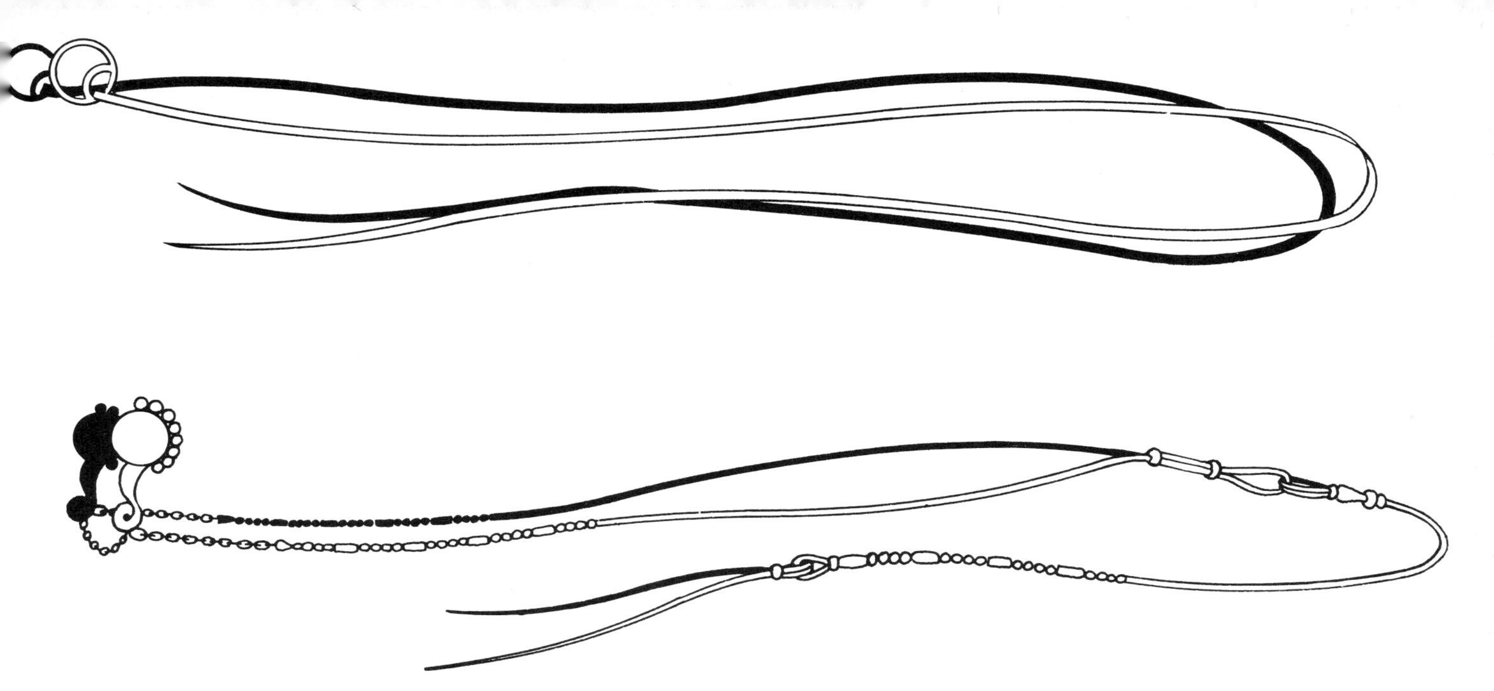

Decorative *California* reins (above) and split or *Texas* reins (top)

A horse's headgear consisted of a bridle, bit and reins. Bridles were open-face (split-ear) or a standard design that included a nose-band, brow-band and throat latch. The *hackamore* was used west of the Rockies to break and train cow ponies. Instead of a bit, it had a nose-band that rested on the sensitive crest of the horse's nasal bones and was held in place behind the lower jaw by a plaited rawhide rope. A soft leather cheekband passed behind the ears and held the hackamore over the head. It was an ideal bridle: it could be left in place when the animal ate and drank, and didn't have to be wrestled into the mouth every morning. And because it made a bit unnecessary, there was no danger of cutting the horse's mouth and tongue to ribbons—which could happen with some of the crueller bits.

The simplest bit was the straight or slightly curved *bar*, a round metal rod with bridle rings at the outer ends to which the reins were fastened. The *snaffle* bit's mouth-bar was in two sections connected by a centre hinge that pinched the tongue when pressure was applied to the reins. *Curb* bits were the most widely used; an upward slanting curb, or *port*, in the middle of the mouthpiece could bruise the horse's mouth brutally if the reins were jerked roughly. However, once a horse was trained, all the rider had to do to guide it in the right direction was lay the reins along one or other side of its neck. Bits were intended to hint at pain rather than actually hurt.

Nevertheless, there were bits that made no concession at all to an animal's comfort and could easily ruin a horse's mouth. The *spade* bit was an example. A broad three- to four-inch screwdriver-like projection from the mouthpiece bent backward at the end and pressed painfully against the tender roof of the mouth when the reins were pulled. *Ring* bits or 'chilenos' had metal loops that encircled the horse's lower jaw and a variety of painful gadgets that fitted into its mouth. These savage bits could break a horse's jaw, and most cowboys would have nothing to do with them. They were almost never seen in cow country.

Reins were made of leather, rawhide or a braided horsehair rope known as a *mecate* or *McCarty*. Most cowboys used open reins about seven feet long. 'California' reins were tied together at the end. Although a *romal* (flexible whip) was sometimes worked into the latter as an extension, knowledgeable use of the long end of the reins was usually enough to move most horses along.

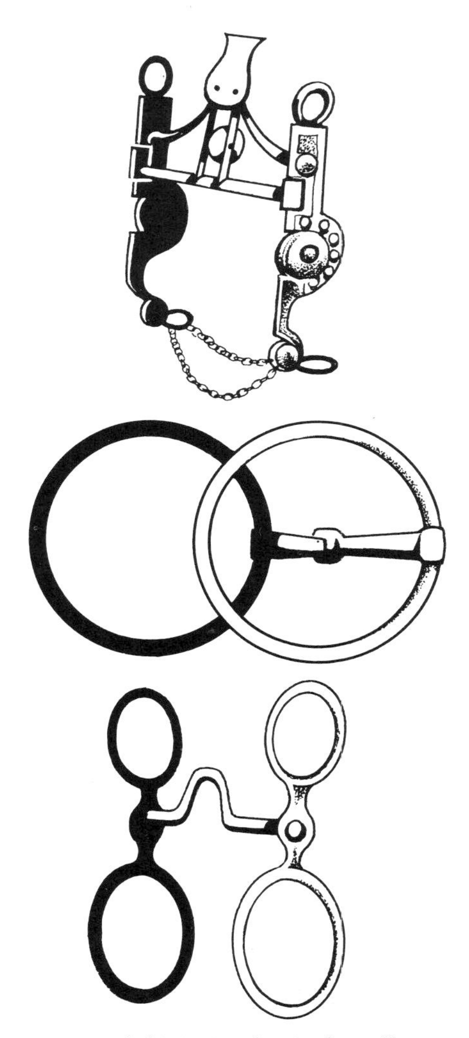

An ornate spade bit (top) *and a simple snaffle* (centre). *The curb* (above) *was the most widely used: like most bits it was only intended to hint at pain*

Clothing and Equipment

From his battered ten-gallon hat to the jangling spurs on his boots, a cowboy's clothing was totally functional. Heavy-duty, close-fitting clothes that protected the body but in no way hampered movement were essential. Levi Strauss of San Francisco set the universal range style in the 1850s, when he produced his first pair of durable, tapered, low-waisted trousers. The early models were made from canvas but he soon switched to more pliable denim—and the 'wonderful pants of Levi's' became a cowboy institution.

Cowboys wore tough and sweat-absorbent heavy flannel or wool shirts. Over these came leather or cloth waistcoats; these had much-needed extra pockets for tobacco, cigarette papers, matches, a short pencil and a tally book for keeping track of brands, and money. Bulky coats restricted movement and tended to catch on the saddle horn, so jackets—essential in heavy brush where a man's shirt could literally be torn from his back—were short and made from canvas or tough denim.

Every cowboy carried a tightly rolled yellow oilskin slicker behind the high cantle of his saddle. In wet weather, these tent-like garments entirely covered man and saddle. Although they protected him from the rain, they had two major disadvantages: they handicapped a rider's movements, and their constant rustle and crackle, combined with their bright flapping edges, could make horses 'spooky'.

Many early cowhands adopted the age-old practice of mounted men and wore gauntlets; made from buckskin, they didn't become stiff after being wet. Gloves protected hands and wrists from rope burns, the heat of smoking branding irons, and slashing brush and thorn. Smaller, wrist-length gloves, as worn by rodeo riders, became popular at the turn of the century.

According to J. Frank Dobie, 'the bandana deserves to be called the flag of the cow country.' Made of dark silk, or red or blue cotton cloth, and draped loosely over the chest and tied in a knot behind the neck, bandanas weren't just decorative accessories. To protect the neck from the blazing sun, they merely had to be reversed back to front; pulled up over the mouth and nose, they filtered out the choking dust when branding or riding drag on a herd of cows. In winter they protected a man's face from driving sleet and snow, or were wrapped over his ears to prevent frostbite. A man could stay cool-headed—literally—in summer by wetting his bandana and putting it under his hat. Bandanas were also used as towels, handkerchiefs, blindfolds for jumpy horses, makeshift hobbles, slings, bandages and holders for hot branding irons.

Hats were portable umbrellas. They were also used as drinking cups (for men and horses), and as buckets and wash bowls. A cowboy could fan a small fire to roaring life with his hat, or signal to other men from a distance. In winter, with the sides of the brim pulled down, a hat made an excellent ear-warmer. A cowboy's hat often revealed his origins. In the south-west, for instance, hats were wide-brimmed for shade and coolness. The Mexican *vaquero* influence could also be seen here: many men sported large, saucer-shaped sombreros, or even the huge, floppy straw hats worn by

A cowboy's hat helped to keep him cool in summer, warm in winter; and hat bands were used to hold cigarettes or tobacco and rolling papers From top: *ten-gallon hat; Montana peak; Texas hat; Stetson*

Mexican *peons*. In the windswept north-west, cowboys preferred high-crowned hats with brims that wouldn't be whipped away by a gust of wind. There were also innumerable local variations in the way crowns were creased and the angles at which brims were set.

In the early years, men wore a variety of headgear from home-made contraptions to fashionable (and unsuitable) town hats from the East. In the 1860s, when Philadelphia hatmaker John B. Stetson began to produce a high-quality, durable model called 'Boss of the Plains' he found a ready market. By 1880 his high-crowned hat with its four-inch brim was so popular that the name 'Stetson' was virtually synonymous with 'hat'. Any cowboy would have readily agreed with the old-timer who drawled: 'Ya can beat a John B. plumb to death, but danged if ya can make 'er unravel.'

About 20 years later in the south-west, it was replaced by a monster hat with a seven-inch-high sugarloaf crown, and a four-inch brim. The 'Big Four' was nicknamed the 'four-quart' hat, but the Western habit of exaggeration soon multiplied its capacity tenfold: by the 1920s it was universally known as the 'ten-gallon' hat.

Chaps, from the Spanish *chaparreras*, developed in the *brasado* country of Mexico, where thick clusters of prickly pear cactus, mesquite and thorn scrub could rip a man's trousers and legs to shreds. In the early 16th century they were heavy, apron-like pieces of cowhide, *armitas*, tied around the waist. They could be pushed forward

Chaps protected a cowboy's legs and trousers against scratches, rope burns—and the horns of angry steers (Below) *Angora chaps, worn on the cold northern ranges, first appeared in 1886* (Below left) *Batwings were the first chaps a cowboy could put on without first having to take off his spurs*

to shield a horse's forequarters or pulled back up over a rider's legs. 'Shotgun' chaps, the earliest tailored style, were seatless leggings joined together by a belt. Shotguns protected a rider's legs from rope burns, scrapes, and bites from aggressive horses far more effectively than the old armitas.

'Batwings', a later style, first appeared in the eastern Colorado Rockies. Wide, flapping wings on the outside of the leg gave some protection to a horse's flank. In the mid-1880s, California cowpunchers added a showy touch to chaps by covering the front with angora goat skins. These soon became popular, especially on the northern Plains, where they provided protection against the cold.

The first true 'cowboy' boots were the result of a lucky collaboration in 1878 between an unknown cowhand and bootmaker H. J. Justin of Spanish Fort, Texas. This new boot had a notably narrow toe that slipped easily into the stirrups. Its strong, high arch made for comfortable riding, and its high, narrow, forward-canted heel allowed the rider to grip his stirrups for extra support while roping without the risk that his feet would slide through them. This new style spread like wildfire. By the early 1880s it was the hallmark of a cowboy.

When a cowhand bought a new pair of boots, it has been said, 'Price was no object. Quality was the main consideration. They might squeak like they was made of goosequills, but he wasn't worryin' as long as they fit close and cost 'im plenty.' Trousers were tucked into the boots, which came up to the knees to prevent dirt kicked up by the horse from falling inside. High boots also protected

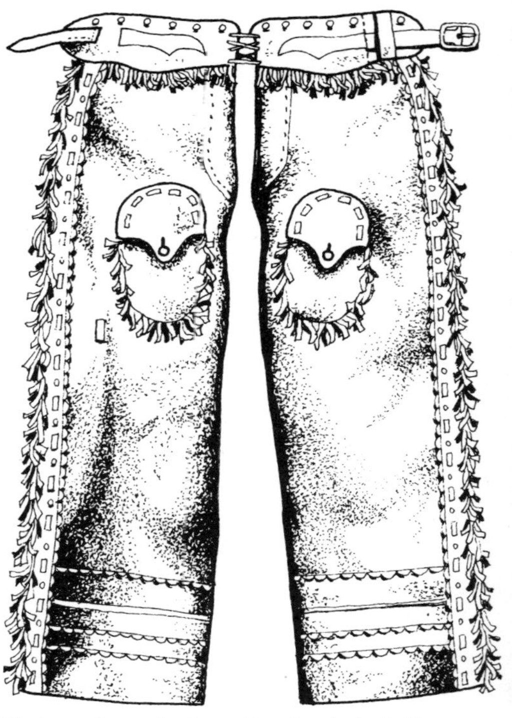

Shotgun chaps, the first tailored style, look like a double-barrelled shotgun—hence their name

Mule ear boots, an early model (right); *style popular in about 1900* (centre); *Pee-Wee boots* (below)

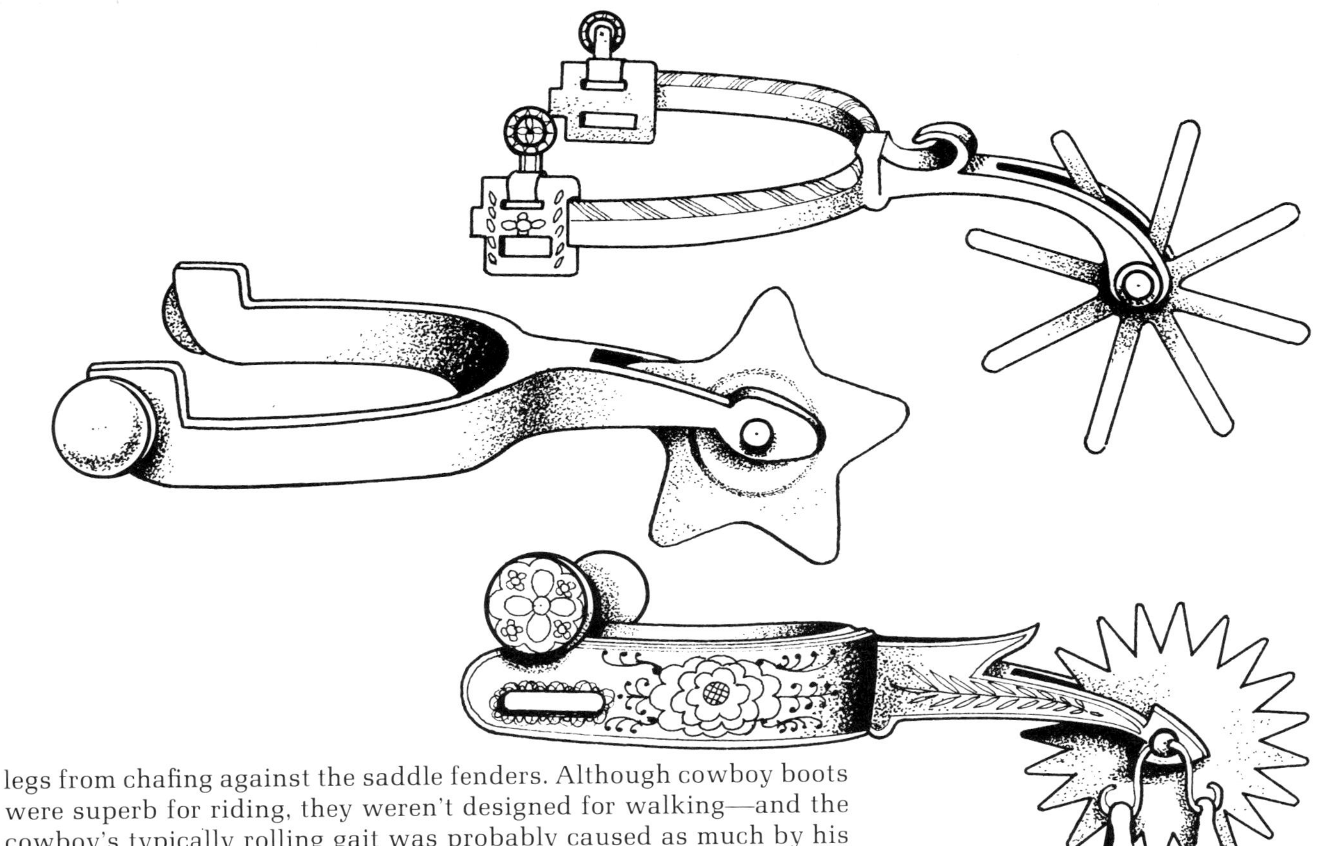

legs from chafing against the saddle fenders. Although cowboy boots were superb for riding, they weren't designed for walking—and the cowboy's typically rolling gait was probably caused as much by his tottering on high heels as by his attempts to swagger manfully along. They were later replaced by short 'peewee' boots.

A cowboy spurred his horse on by rolling the rowel up and down the animal's belly: early Mexican spur (top); blunt working spur (centre)—the type a hand used on his favourite horse; dress spur (above) with tear-drop jangles—their pleasant jingle soothed the cattle and also alerted them to a cowboy's approach

Spurs were first introduced to the Americas by the conquistadores, who strapped 12-inch baroque creations, with long drooping shanks and wicked-looking rowels, to their boots. Later, cowboys often wore spurs with pleasantly tinkling pear-shaped danglers attached to the axle of the rowel.

Cowboy spurs always reflected this Spanish influence, especially in California, where long trailing spurs remained fashionable. It was difficult to walk with them, so they were always removed after dismounting. The shorter shank spur of eastern Mexico was popular in Texas, and because it rode relatively high on the heel a man could walk with his spurs on. It's not surprising that this style became a favourite in Texas; it had always been the mark of the Southern gentleman to wear spurs at all times—and after the Civil War many such men drifted to the Lone Star State. Cowboys usually filed down the rowel points because sharp ones made horses nervous. Spurs were intended not to punish an animal but to encourage it to follow its rider's wishes.

Cowboys always travelled light. Anything they couldn't wear, or carry on their saddles, was stored in their bedrolls and carried in a wagon during round-ups and on the trail. A bedroll consisted of a huge waterproof tarpaulin, 7 by 18 feet, a couple of heavy quilts or *soogans*, and one or two blankets for extra warmth and padding. If it rained during the night, all a man had to do to stay dry was pull up the flaps of the tarpaulin and snap them shut. A 'warsack' inside the bedroll held cowboys' savings and personal belongings—including an extra change of clothes, and possibly a good shirt and suit for special occasions. During bad weather they took hats, boots, ropes and spurs to bed with them—even their horse's bridle came inside when the mercury dropped, so that the bit wouldn't freeze the animal's tongue in the morning.

Ropes and Roping

Roping was the most difficult of all cowboy skills, but one of the most important, for a cowboy's professional reputation depended on his proficiency with a rope. Few men became real experts—but any self-respecting roper was expected to make accurate 50- to 60-foot throws. Cowboys constantly practised with their lariats, trying out fancy casts and exotic tricks. Cattle apart, they were prepared to rope anything from a prairie dog to a bear, and nothing gave them more delight than dropping a loop over another puncher.

Ropes were the most important tool in the cattle business. Without them it was impossible to catch even the smallest steer. In the early days, lariats (from the Spanish for rope—*la reata*) were made from long rawhide pieces, cut from the best selected hides, cured, and braided; finished ropes were stretched to get rid of kinks and test their tension. Thin and light, they could be much longer than other ropes because they were so easy to throw. But they were expensive and were difficult to use in rain or snow.

Cheap fibre ropes made from hemp or tough grasses were the alternatives. Hemp was as strong and durable as rawhide, and much cheaper. By the mid-1860s, it was popular throughout the West. The most common fibre ropes were manila and maguey (the latter was corrupted to 'McGay' by cowboys). Maguey was made from the fibres of the agave, or century plant; very hard, it held a wide loop and could be thrown with great speed. However, it was stiff and difficult to handle in wet weather. Manila rope was exceptionally smooth,

A 50- or 60-foot throw was child's play to a skilled roper: cowboy in Texas ropes a calf by the hind legs

strong—and cheap. It could be used for light calf-roping work or for the heavier tasks of busting steers, depending on the thickness to which it was braided. Another bonus was that it could easily be waterproofed with tallow or paraffin.

A rope's length was determined by its composition and the use to which it was put. Easy-to-throw rawhide ropes were up to 80 feet long; general-purpose fibre ropes averaged about 40 feet. In California, where cowboys wrapped several turns of rope around the horn, held the loose end coiled in one hand, and threw with the other, lariats up to 60 feet in length were common. In Texas, where ropes were tied to the saddle horn, about 30 feet was the norm; the rider had to get close to a steer before he roped it, but, once caught, the animal could be quickly 'dumped' to the ground. At branding time, calf-ropers used 25-foot lariats with which they gently snared calves by the heels then towed them over to the fire.

Ropes weren't used only for roping. During round-ups they were strung up at night to make corrals. They were used to stake out horses, and to fasten loads to pack saddles. Hitched to a saddle horn, they were used to haul firewood or to pull mired cattle and stranded wagons out of bogs and potholes. A skilled cowhand often used his rope as a whip to hurry cattle along on the trail; he could even wield it to kill a rattlesnake. And of course, as one eye-witness put it, 'a rope was sometimes used to mete out justice in the absence of judge and jury. The result was a spectacular warning to other hoss-thieves and cattle-rustlers.'

Rope was made from flax, hemp or hide: Braided leather (top); *Maguey fibre* (centre), *a very strong rope; twisted hemp*

Branding

Ever since man has kept herds, he's branded his animals. Branding is the most efficient, fastest way to identify the thousands of steers owned by a big cattle ranch. It establishes a cattleman's right of possession, and it also identifies the animals for as long as they live: 'A brand is something that won't come off in the wash.'

In the days of the open range, cattle roamed enormous distances. The ability to identify, at a glance, the brands of every ranch in a district was a skill as highly valued as roping and riding. It was a hallmark of the truly professional cowhand. The booming range cattle industry gave rise to an incredible profusion of brands. In Texas alone there were over 20,000 different marks. To prevent different ranchers using the same mark, every owner was legally bound to register his brand with the county in which his ranch was located.

Cattle were usually branded on the left hip or shoulder. If an animal changed hands it was given a 'vent brand' that cancelled the original owner's mark and acknowledged the sale. This was a bar cancelling out the old brand, or a repetition of the original brand. The new owner's mark was also burned into the hide. In Texas, cattle were also branded with a county mark (a group of letters placed on the left side of the neck) that identified the county of the ranch they belonged to. County brands helped to deter cattle rustlers, who either had to register steers in the county in which they'd stolen them, or had to laboriously alter the brand on the neck.

Many of the herds driven north on the long drives were made up of cattle from more than one ranch, so a trail animal was identified by a road brand on its left side, behind the shoulder. A steer that had passed through several owners before being trailed north to Kansas could end up with its entire hide cluttered with brand marks. As a common range expression put it, such animals were 'burnt till they looked like a brand book'.

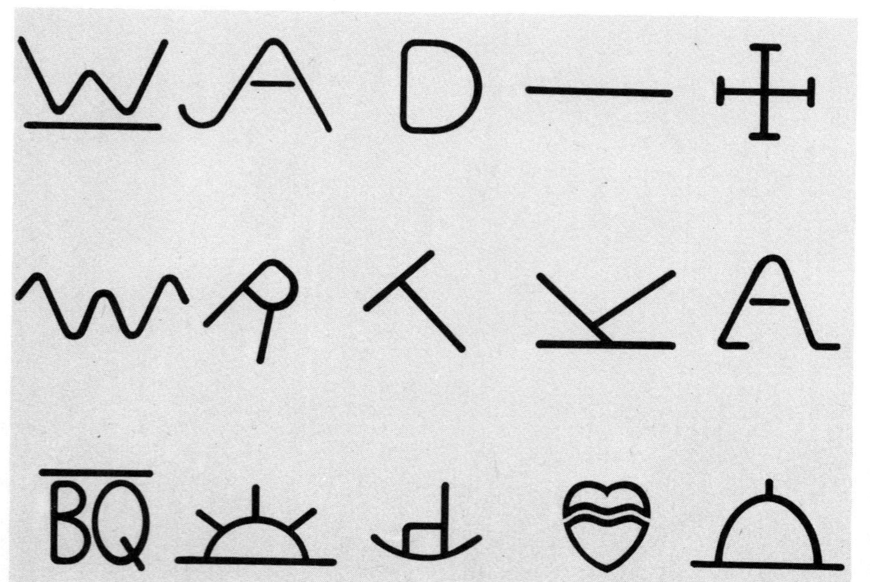

(Top) Cattle baron brands: Pierre Wibaux; the J A ranch; 'Shanghai' Pierce; John Chisum; Theodore Roosevelt
(Centre) Cattle country humour: Running W, Tilting R; Tumbling T; Lazy K; Walking A
(Left) Graphic descriptions: Barbecue; Sunrise, Rocking Chair, Broken Heart; Dinner Bell

In the days of the long drives north, an animal could reach its destination with a hide covered in brand marks. Today cattle are unlikely to stray far from home pastures: herding cattle to the branding fire

The Broken Heart branding iron. The brand itself is shown on the opposite page

Cattle were also given earmarks. These enabled cowboys to identify them easily, even in winter when their coats were thick and long. Like brands, they had to be registered with the county to be legally valid. Other methods of marking cattle included cuts in the pendulous skin under a cow's throat; these left hanging flaps of hide, *dewlaps*. *Wattles* were strips of skin cut on the neck and jaw; marks on an animal's nose were called *buds*.

Before the stamp iron was invented, branding was carried out with any piece of iron that would burn a distinct mark on the hide. The *running iron* was an early branding tool. A long metal rod, curved at one end, this simple implement could be used to produce amazingly complex brand designs. In later years, stamp irons were widely used and running irons became the rustler's trademark.

Calf-branding took place in springtime. Cows and calves were driven into a corral, and cowboys lassoed the young animals out of the herd, noting the brand and earmark of each one's mother. The struggling calves were dragged over to the branding fire, where *flankers* wrestled them to the ground and held them still for branding and earmarking. One eye-witness recalled that calves 'usually ... bore the knife without a sound, but the sizzlin' iron caused a doleful

Brands could be difficult to read when cattle were herded together, so cows were also given ear marks like this one

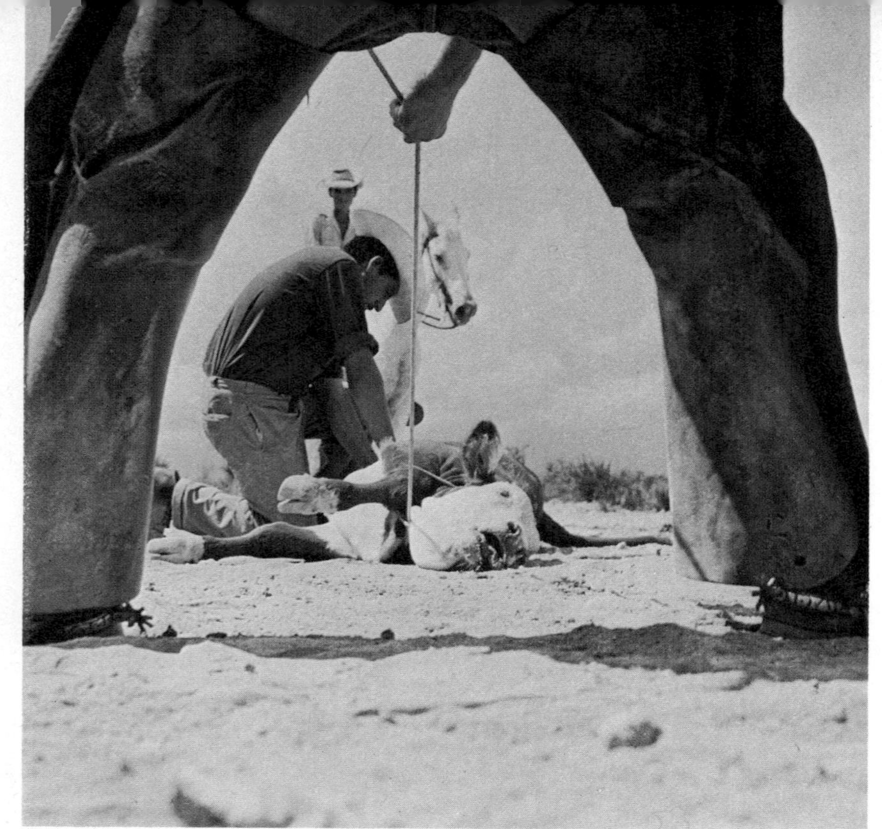

Branding was the main object of early round-ups. Today animals are also castrated and given shots against disease: a calf stretched out for treatment on a Texas ranch

wail of agony and fear. When released, the calf struggled to its clumsy legs and trotted off to seek its mother and sympathy.'

The rules for 'brand-calling' were well defined. Brands were always read from top to bottom, from outside to inside, and from left to right. However, not all brands read exactly as they appeared. In Wyoming, a revolving H brand was known locally as the 'damfino' in memory of the cowboy who, when asked to identify the brand, failed to recognize the mark and replied, 'Damn if I know.' In Texas, Shanghai Pierce's Big D brand was universally known as 'The Sea Lion'. Pierce had imported the first Brahman cattle into Texas. He sold some of them to another rancher whose spread lay along the Gulf coast. When this unfortunate man tried to corral the Brahmans, they avoided his men by wading out into the coastal shallows that extended more than a mile from shore. The rancher wrote to Pierce in desperation demanding he send help to round up 'them damn sea lions. They're in the ocean and on their way back to India, and I ain't going to pay a damn cent for 'em.' From then on Pierce acquired the reputation as the man who herded sea lions, and the name came to be associated with his brandmark.

Chuckwagon Cooking

'Most cooks produced a surprisingly varied menu. The staple ingredients were flour, beef, bacon, frijole or pinto beans, coffee, syrup and dried fruit—plus salt, sugar and soda.'

On the trail, or out on the range, the chuckwagon and its presiding genius, the cook, were the centre of the cowboys' existence. Like an army, they marched on their stomachs, and nothing did more for their morale than a well-appointed chuckwagon and an inventive and hardworking cook.

The wagon was the ingenious idea of master cattleman Charles Goodnight, who took the first mobile kitchen on the trail in June 1886. It soon became a fixture of life away from the ranch—a home-from-home to cowboys, and a far cry from the early days when each man was responsible for his own food and cooking.

The man known as 'dough-roller', 'grub-wrangler', 'biscuit-shooter'—or simply 'cookie'—could be a Northerner or a Southerner, Mexican, Negro, or Chinese. Generally older than the trail hands, more often than not he was a cowboy who'd been injured, like Ramon Hornette, a famous old cookie, who remarked that, 'Right back there thirty years this February the ninth a wild steer hooked me. Hooked me good and tore up my knee. Thirty years I've been havin' cowboys bring their plates back for more. Keeps morale up.' Sometimes hired —and paid—four weeks in advance, he was the highest-paid hand after the trail boss, and earned $15 to $25 a month more than the cowboys.

The respect accorded him was considerable, and this exclusivity bred a certain crankiness among trail cooks. There was rarely one who didn't make the most of his position, and play up his tetchiness. Every cook had rules, like the one who hung on his chuckwagon a sign that read, 'If you can't wash dishes, don't eat.' The 'wreck-pan' for dirty dishes was a feature of all trail camps.

Cowboys complied with cookie's rules because they never knew when they might need his help. The prospect of self-catering was a threat in itself, but cookie was more than just a provider of food. His first-aid box was frequently in demand for injuries, minor and—sometimes—major. He kept a variety of patent medicines such as

Cooks today use practically the same utensils as their 19th-century predecessors: a round-up cook prepares a meal

pills, salts and quinine. He was also the man to go to for rawhide to mend saddle straps, rope, horseshoe nails, hammer, ammunition, needle and thread. He had to stock up with anything a cowboy might need during weeks, and sometimes months, on the range. The cook was also dentist, vet, barber, banker, stakeholder for wagers, confessor, expert wagon-driver, and, on occasions, undertaker.

He may have been cranky, but he had difficulties few cooks would tolerate today: bad weather, flying sand, smoke in the eyes—and the regular appearance, three times a day, of a hungry horde of tough men. Split-second timing was crucial—empty stomachs often caused ill temper. Every cook had to know how to build a good fire—and that depended on what fuel was available. When wood ran out, he used buffalo- or cattle-dung 'chips' that gave a good heat. They smelled foul, but at least the pungent odour kept mosquitoes away.

When he arrived at the night's camping site, hopefully by a stream, he unharnessed and settled his team of oxen or horses. He dug a short trench, built a fire in it, set up his pot rack, ground the coffee, and put on the two-gallon coffee pot. Then he let down the chuckbox front, which formed his worktable, and set to work making bread. His menus were his invention, and for measuring he used his experience. The formula for feeding every working cowboy was food that 'stuck to the ribs', and coffee so strong 'a horseshoe wouldn't sink in it'. The standard recipe for coffee was a handful of coffee to a cup of water; cowboys believed there was no such thing as coffee that was too strong—only weak people. One cookie, Bill Jones, remarked, 'It seems that a lot of people never realize how little water it takes to make good coffee.' The cowboy drank it straight and black.

Although one old-timer held that 'cookin' duties consisted mostly of the ability to fry sowbelly, and cook beans so they wouldn't rattle on the plate, make passable sourdoughs, with an occasional cobbler of dried fruit, and strong coffee', most cooks produced a surprisingly varied menu. The staple ingredients were flour, beef, bacon, *frijole* or *pinto* beans, coffee, syrup and dried fruit—plus salt, sugar, and soda.

There was no yeast to make bread dough rise, so a magical substance, 'sourdough starter', was cherished by cooks. Before he left the ranch, cookie put three or four quarts of flour, a dash of salt, and enough warm water to make a moist mixture, into a large jar or keg twice the size of the combined ingredients. Then he added sugar, molasses, or mashed potatoes, to hasten fermentation. He let the ingredients ferment for a day or two, then made his first batch of sourdough bread—leaving a bit of the mixture—the 'sourdough starter'—in a jar. Too much heat—or cold—killed it. On cold nights cookie took the jar to bed with him.

The skill of cooking sourdough bread in a Dutch oven was to put it on the fire and pile plenty of coals on top so that the bread rolls (known as biscuits), came out with a deep brown crust above and below—and a deliciously soft, spongy inside.

Beef was always slaughtered at sundown, and was usually a stray; 'No man ever liked the taste of his own beef,' it was said. The carcass was chopped down the middle and hung overnight from a tree or on the side of the wagon. Next morning it was wrapped in a

1 *Tool box*

2 *Driver's seat*

3 *Wagon bed (bulk goods, bed rolls, guns and ammunition*

4 *Coffee grinder*

5 *Provisions*

6 *Coffee pot*

7 *Hinged table*

8 *Oil lamp*

9 *Sourdough keg*

10 *Kindling*

11 *Water barrel*

12 *Ropes*

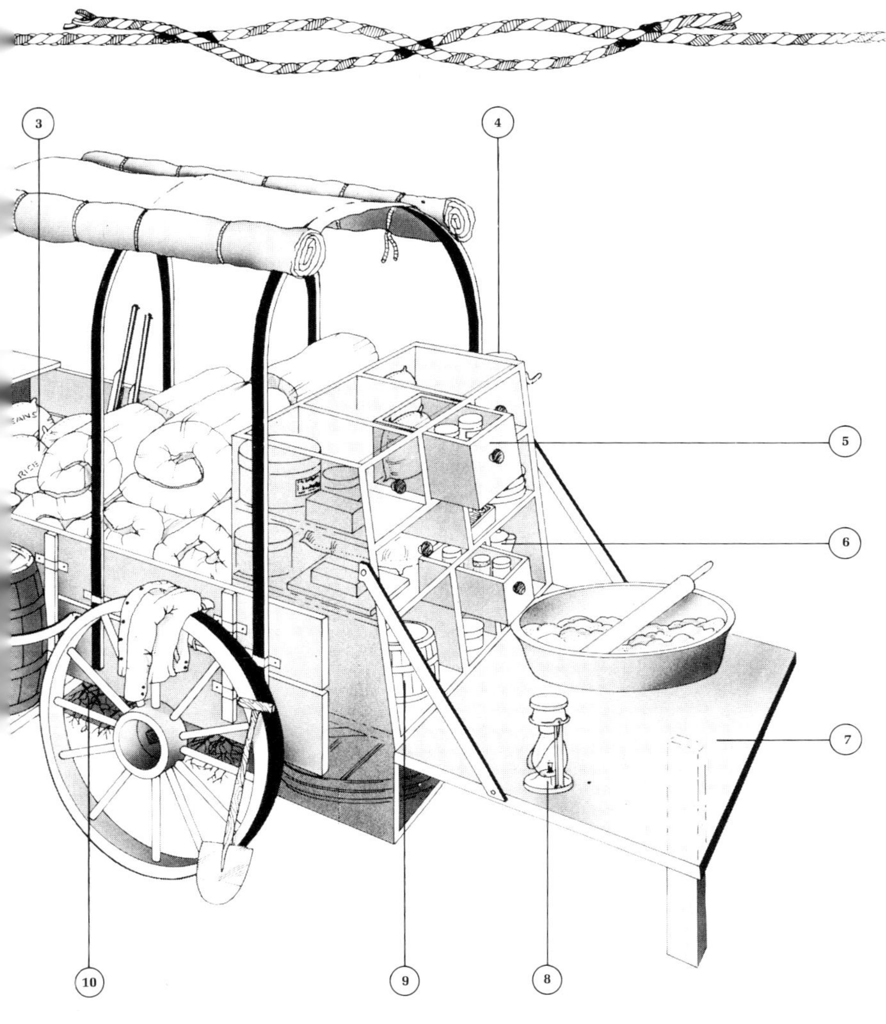

All chuckwagons, including the one shown here, were based on Charles Goodnight's original invention.

His was adapted from a wagon used in the Civil War. He rebuilt it with Osage orangewood, which the Indians used in order to give their bows their tremendous strength. He replaced the wooden axles with iron. At the back of the wagon was the chuckbox. About four feet high (the width of the wagon), it was divided into shelves and compartments, and looked like an enormous bureau desk. The sloping hinged front let down to make a work table, supported by a sturdy wooden leg, through which wagon rods passed to hold it firmly in place. (If the wagon rods were unscrewed, the box could be lifted out and nailed to a wall.)

Provisions were stored in tight-fitting tins that fitted perfectly into the various-sized compartments, so that was no risk that they would fall over and spill when the wagon jolted and shook. The Dutch oven, skillet, coffee pot, kettle, pot rack and other pans were all stored in the wide bottom shelf. The coffee grinder was usually fixed outside, as were the water barrels. Bedrolls, extra clothing, bulk stores in sacks and cookie's bed were all stored behind the chuckbox. A cowhide for carrying wood and buffalo 'chips' hung under the bed. An axe, hammer and spade were kept in a box underneath the driver's seat.

tarpaulin for protection from the heat and stored in the chuckwagon. The cook's bedding was also put round it for extra insulation; if it wasn't eaten that day, it could be hung out again at night to chill.

Like most Englishmen—but unlike modern Americans, who generally prefer their meat rare—cowboys liked their steak well done. If there was a suspicion that the meat might be tough, cookie pounded it with a hammer. 'Son-of-a-bitch' stew was a favourite dish, and every cook had his own version. In cowboy parlance: 'Put in everything except the hide, horns, and holler.' As one cook said, 'We don't usually make it at all; it just sort of accumulates.' The longer it cooked, the better it was: 'If you can tell what's in it you know it ain't made right.'

The sourdough bread, meat and well-seasoned baked beans were often followed by stewed dried apples, peaches or apricots accompanied by a jar of syrup. Milk and butter were rarities on the trail, unless by chance the herd included a cow with a calf. Even then it was unobtainable unless a cowboy was prepared to risk injury and wrestle with her for a cup or two of milk. He usually gave it up as a bad job. Occasionally there were tinned tomatoes or corn, potatoes, or wild onions. Rice was sometimes served; called 'moonshine', it wasn't highly regarded as food fit for tough cowboys. Raisins were sometimes added to the rice to make 'spotted pup'.

Depending on the region and season, the menu was enlivened with a variety of animals, birds, fish, vegetables and fruit, caught or collected from the wild. Quail, prairie chickens, geese, turkeys, blue grouse, deer, elk, antelope, buffalo, skunk, hog, rabbit, bear, brook and speckled trout were all there for the taking. Squash, potatoes, turnips, beetroot, and cabbage were found in Kansas, carrots and

The chuckwagon was the focal point of a cowboy camp and, after the trail boss, the cook was the highest paid man in the outfit

cabbage in Nebraska. Ohio produced pumpkin, squash, potatoes, beans, melons and corn. A Utah speciality was potatoes baked in the fire. In New Mexico there were red roots and pig weed for salad. Chilis were commonplace and popular; one man claimed, 'Forty-one years round a ranch and chili peppers, and I ain't had no bad cold.' Pies were filled with wild fruit: blackberries, dewberries, plums, grapes, pecans and walnuts.

The recipes that follow illustrate some of the changes that can be rung on the traditional cowboy diet of beef, beans and flour. A few traditional dishes are also included.

Brazos River Fish Fry—Serves 4

2 tablespoons flour
1 teaspoon each salt, pepper and chili seasoning powder
4 trout, mackerel or herring
2 eggs, beaten
4 oz (100 gm) oatmeal
Oil for frying

Season flour with salt, pepper and chili powder. Clean and bone fish. Coat with seasoned flour. Dip first in eggs and then in oatmeal. Fry in hot oil about 10 minutes, turning twice.

Planked Fish

1 trout, mackerel or herring per person
2 rashers streaky bacon per person
Melted butter or oil for basting

Remove head and tail of fish. Split open at belly and gut. Place flesh side down on work surface. Flatten out. Turn over and remove backbone and main rib bones, keeping skin intact.

Choose a thick, non-resinous board or log, 12 to 15 inches wide and 36 inches long. Cover one side with foil. Build a fire in front of rock or hill to reflect heat. Place fish, skin side down, on foil. Drive a wooden nail (or stake) through each end of the fish and lay bacon strips across in 4 or 5 places, depending on the size of the fish. Stand planked fish at a 75-degree angle in front of the fire with a piece of foil at the bottom to catch drippings. Cook 30 minutes, basting with butter or oil, until fish flakes. Eat off the board.

Barbecued Beef Ribs

Allowing at least ½ lb (200 gm) per person, select a wing or top rib of beef, well marbled with fat. Trim off excess fat. Spit roast on the diagonal for the best balance, allowing about 15 minutes per 1 lb (½ kilo) for medium rare or longer for cooked-through meat. If using a meat thermometer, roast until temperature registers 125°F (52°C). Remember meat will cook as long as 20 minutes after removal from the fire. Let meat rest before carving so juices can settle. This is very delicious barbecued over an open fire. If you cook this joint in the oven allow plenty of head room as it rises while being cooked. Allow 15 minutes per 1 lb (½ kilo) plus 15 minutes over at a temperature of 350°F (175°C) or Gas 4 for medium rare beef; 5 minutes longer per lb (½ kilo) for cooked-through beef.

Accompany with Black Night Barbecue Sauce (see next recipe) and jacket potatoes.

Black Night Barbecue Sauce—Serves about 8 to 10

½ pint (250 ml) strong black coffee
½ pint (250 ml) Worcestershire sauce
½ pint (250 ml) ready prepared tomato soup
4 oz (100 gm) butter
Juice of 1 large lemon
1 tablespoon sugar
1 dessertspoon salt

Combine ingredients. Simmer, uncovered, for 30 minutes, stirring occasionally. Serve with beef or ribs.

Beef and Tomato Chili—Serves 6 to 8

2 lb (1 kilo) raw minced beef
1 large onion, peeled and chopped
2 cloves garlic, peeled and chopped
2 tablespoons dripping
½ teaspoon ground oregano
½ teaspoon cumin seed
1 tablespoon purple-red chili seasoning powder
1 × 14 oz (375 gm) can tomatoes
Tabasco sauce
½ pint (250 ml) water
Salt

Brown meat, onions and garlic in the hot dripping in a casserole. Add all the remaining ingredients. Bring to boil. Cover. Simmer one hour. Skim off any excess fat. Serve with rice or jacket potatoes.

'Chicken Fried' Steak—Serves 6

2 lb (1 kilo) rump steak
2 oz (50 gm) flour
1 teaspoon salt
½ teaspoon pepper
1 tablespoon butter or oil

Trim fat from steak. Render down slowly in frying pan and add more dripping if necessary to fry steak. Cut meat into 6 pieces. Pound or beat until thin. Cover with flour. Season with salt and pepper. Fry meat 5 minutes on each side or less if you like it underdone.

Pan Fried Steak—Serves 2

1 lb (½ kilo) rump or sirloin steak
2 oz (50 gm) butter
Salt
Black pepper
½ teaspoon flour
½ teaspoon paprika pepper
¼ pint (125 ml) double cream
1 tablespoon lemon juice

Cook steak in butter in a heavy frying pan, browning quickly at medium heat. Remove and keep warm. Reduce heat then add dry ingredients. Finally stir in cream followed by lemon juice. Cook, stirring, till liquid bubbles, then pour over steak. Cut into 2 pieces.

Salt Fried Steak—Serves 4

1 teaspoon garlic salt
½ teaspoon ground pepper
1 tablespoon dry mustard
4 pieces of fillet steak, 1 inch thick
2 oz (50 gm) butter

Mix salt, pepper and mustard together and rub into steak. Heat frying pan, add butter and quickly cook steaks till brown. The meat should be nicely underdone in the centre.

Salt Steak—Serves 3 to 4

Sirloin steak, 3 inches thick and weighing about 1½ lb or ¾ kilo
2 cloves garlic, peeled and crushed
Pepper
1 lb (½ kilo) coarse salt
Water to mix

Remove excess fat from steak. Rub both sides with garlic and pepper. Mix salt and enough water to make a thick paste. Press half the salt mix onto top of steak. To cook over hot coals, place salt side down for 12 to 15 minutes. Cover other side with salt mix, turn and repeat. To grill, cook salt side 15 minutes, remove salt, turn, cover the other side with salt mix and repeat. To serve, remove salt crust from steak, place on a warm dish and cover with 'Lone Star' Steak Sauce. (See next recipe.) Slice meat and garnish with triangles of fried bread.

'Lone Star' Steak Sauce—Serves 3 to 4

4 oz (100 gm) butter
Juice of 1 large lemon
1 tablespoon Worcestershire sauce
1 clove garlic, peeled and crushed
½ teaspoon black pepper
¼ teaspoon dry mustard
2 drops tabasco
Pinch of salt

Combine all ingredients. Heat until butter melts and sauce bubbles. Juices from the grill pan or frying pan may be added if desired. Serve with Salt Steak.

Chili Bean Sandwich—Serves 8

1 large onion, peeled and chopped
1½ lb (¾ kilo) raw minced beef
1 tablespoon oil
1 can condensed tomato soup
¼ pint (125 ml) water
½ pint (250 ml) beef stock
1 teaspoon purple-red chili seasoning powder
¼ teaspoon cumin seed
Salt to taste
2 oz (50 gm) Cheddar cheese, cubed
2 × 14 oz (each about 375 gm) cans red kidney beans, drained
½ oz (12 gm) butter
Salt and pepper

Brown onion and beef in oil, fork-stirring to break up mince. Drain off excess fat. Stir in soup, water, stock, chili powder, cumin seed and salt. Simmer, uncovered, one hour. Stir occasionally, then add cheese. Cover. Simmer 10 minutes until cheese melts. Fry drained beans in butter about 5 minutes, turning often. Season. Spoon over fried tortillas or fried bread. Top with chili mixture and spoons of soured cream. Serve with a salad.

Dutch Oven Pot Roast—Serves 6

1 tablespoon dripping
3 lb (1½ kilos) topside or aitchbone of beef
6 tablespoons bottled barbecue sauce
6 tablespoons dry cider
8 medium peeled carrots, cut into 2-inch pieces
6 medium peeled potatoes, cut in dice
2 large onions, peeled and sliced

Melt dripping in casserole. Add meat. Brown on all sides over medium heat. Reduce heat. Add the barbecue sauce and cider. Cover. Simmer over low heat or in oven at 325°F (160°C) or Gas 3 for 3 hours. Add carrots, potatoes and onions 1½ hours before the end of the cooking.

Game Bird 'Saddle Mountain' Style—Serves 2

1 pheasant
2 tablespoons Worcestershire sauce
2 tablespoons black treacle
1 clove garlic, peeled and crushed
Salt and pepper

Pluck, clean and split bird. Skewer halves on two green twigs for easy turning if you intend to barbecue them. Mix Worcestershire sauce, treacle, garlic and seasoning together. Brush mix over bird. Wrap in foil. Grill over low fire about 20 to 30 minutes each side, depending on size of bird. Alternatively, cook in a medium oven set to 350°F (175°C) or Gas 4, ¾ to 1 hour. Remove foil before the end of cooking to allow the skin to crispen.

If using grouse or partridge, allow 1 per person and follow above instructions.

Son-of-a-Gun Stew—Serves 6

$\frac{1}{4}$ lb (100 gm) salted belly of pork, cut into slivers
1 oz (25 gm) dripping
1 lb (450 gm) chuck steak, cut into cubes
$\frac{3}{4}$ lb (325 gm) calves' or lambs' hearts
1 large carrot, peeled and sliced
2 medium onions, peeled and sliced
2 tablespoons flour
Black pepper, salt
12 fl oz (325 ml) tomato juice or can of tomatoes
12 fl oz (325 ml) beef stock
2 cloves of garlic, peeled and crushed
1 bay leaf
1 lb (450 gm) calves' sweetbreads
1 lb (450 gm) calves' brains

In a large casserole, lightly brown pork belly. Remove from pan and leave on one side. Add dripping to pan. Heat until hot. Add beef and brown quickly. Wash hearts, remove membrane and excess fat, cube and add to beef with carrot and onion. Sprinkle with flour, salt and pepper. Allow to brown, stirring meat and vegetables together. Pour on tomato juice and beef stock. Add garlic and bay leaf. Cover and bring to boil. Lower heat. Simmer for 2 hours, stirring occasionally. Simmer sweetbreads in boiling salted water 35 minutes. Drain and slip off thin membrane under cold water. Remove gristle and cut up. Soak brains in salted water 15 minutes. Remove dark veins and cut up. Check beef and skim off excess fat. If the sauce is too thin, turn up heat and cook rapidly for a few minutes. Lower heat. Add sweetbreads and brains. Heat thoroughly.

Son-of-a-Gun Stew
(A slightly more basic version from the old cowboy days)
4 oz (100 gm) fat
1 heart
1 tongue
Butcher's steak
1 spleen
1 liver
1 marrow gut (about 3 feet long)
Water
Brains
Sweetbreads

Melt fat. Cut heart into small pieces. Skin and cube tongue and add with heart to the fat and let them cook as they are the toughest ingredients. Cut up the rest of the meats, being sparing with the liver as it has a bitter taste. Cut the marrow gut into inch long rings and cover the lot with water. Add slowly to the stew, stirring all the time. Clean the brains and sweetbreads and cook separately then add to the stew. Season to taste. Cover with water and cook slowly for a long time. Marrow gut is not in fact gut but a long connective tube between the two stomachs of the young cud-chewing animals. It is only good when the cow is still nursing, being tender and full of a substance which looks like marrow and this gives the stew a delicious flavour.

'Texas Red' Chili—Serves 6

2 oz (50 gm) suet, finely chopped
3 lb ($1\frac{1}{2}$ kilo) chuck steak, cut into $\frac{1}{2}$-inch cubes
3 tablespoons purple-red chili seasoning powder
1 dessertspoon ground oregano
1 dessertspoon cumin seed
1 dessertspoon salt
1 dessertspoon cayenne
2 cloves garlic, peeled and crushed
1 dessertspoon tabasco
2 tablespoons flour
3 pints ($1\frac{1}{2}$ litres) water or beef stock

In a large casserole, fry suet until crisp; then add steak cubes and brown. Add seasonings, flour and water. Bring to boil, stirring. Reduce heat, cover and simmer $1\frac{1}{2}$ hours. Skim off fat and simmer further 30 minutes stirring occasionally. Serve with beans or sourdough bread. Dumplings (see next recipe) also go well with this.

Dumplings

Snip off small pieces of freshly-made scone dough and drop them into beef. Cook, covered, about 7 to 10 minutes; dumplings should puff up to 3 to 4 times their original size. If preferred, roll scone dough into 12 to 16 round dumplings. For the amount of 'Texas Red' Chili given above, use about 6 oz (150 gm) flour for making the scone mixture.

Venison Barbecue—Serves 5 to 6

2 oz (50 gm) salted belly of pork, sliced
3 lb ($1\frac{1}{2}$ kilo) haunch or loin of venison
$\frac{1}{2}$ pint (250 ml) tomato juice
$\frac{1}{2}$ tablespoon salt
1 medium onion, peeled and finely grated
3 tablespoons Worcestershire sauce
1 tablespoon tarragon vinegar
$\frac{1}{2}$ tablespoon purple-red chili seasoning powder
2 teaspoons prepared mild mustard

Fry slices of pork belly in heavy pan until fat runs. Add venison. Fry all over, turning frequently, until brown. Combine rest of ingredients in a saucepan. Bring to boil, stirring occasionally. Place meat in roasting tin and coat with sauce. Roast $1\frac{1}{2}$ to 2 hours in moderate oven set to 350°F (175°C) or Gas 4. Baste occasionally.

Beef and beans were staple ingredients in the cowboy's diet. Chili bean soup is a delicious mixture of the two, hotted up with chili powder and seasoned with spices

Utensils were heavy and strong, and big enough to hold enough food for 10 or 12 men. The main items were a two- or three-gallon coffee pot and kettle, a Dutch oven, skillet, and pot rack.

The Dutch oven was a cast-iron pan with a tight-fitting flanged lid; it was used for all baking, as well as for making the famed 'son-of-a-bitch' stew. The food to be baked was put in the preheated pan, which was then placed on red-hot embers; more embers were piled on the lid.

The skillet was a long-handled cast-iron pan with a lid. It was used to cook potatoes, bacon, steak and flapjacks; quail and other game was deep-fried in the skillet.

The pot rack consisted of two iron stakes with a rod across the top; pans hung from hooks. Iron bars were sometimes laid across the fire trench to support the pots. Cookie's utensils also included butchers' knives; an old bottle to roll the dough; knives, forks and spoons; tin plates and mugs for the cowboys; a jar or keg for the sourdough; a deep tin plate for fruit pies; miscellaneous jars and bowls; a jug for syrup; a stone jar or tin pail full of dried fruit; and a large pan for heating water and washing dishes.

Modern round-up cook

Vegetables (Mainly Beans)

Red Bean Soup—Serves 4 to 6

4 oz (100 gm) haricot beans
1 medium-sized onion, peeled and sliced
2 medium-sized potatoes, peeled and sliced
1 oz (25 gm) butter
1 dessertspoon salad oil
1 clove garlic, peeled and chopped
½ lb (200 gm) tomatoes, skinned
2 pints (1¼ litres) stock
Salt and pepper to taste
4 oz (100 gm) streaky bacon, chopped
1 tablespoon chopped parsley

Soak beans overnight. Drain and rinse. Slice onion and potato. Cook slowly in butter and oil without colouring. Add the beans, garlic, tomatoes and stock. Season. Cover pan. Slowly bring to boil. Simmer until beans are very tender, about 1½ to 2 hours. Pass through sieve. Dice bacon, fry until crisp and scatter, with parsley, over top of each portion of soup.

Chili Bean Soup—Serves 8 to 10

1 lb (½ kg) raw minced beef
1 medium-sized green pepper, de-seeded and chopped
1 medium-sized onion, peeled and chopped
1 clove garlic, peeled and crushed
2 tablespoons oil
2 × 14 oz (each about 375 gm) cans of tomatoes
1 tablespoon purple-red chili seasoning powder
1 teaspoon salt
¼ teaspoon ground oregano
¼ teaspoon cumin seed
3 drops tabasco
2 pints (1¼ litres) hot stock
2 × 14 oz (each about 375 gm) cans red kidney beans

Cook beef, green pepper, onion and garlic in oil until beef is slightly brown. Fork-stir frequently to break up meat. Add all ingredients except beans. Simmer covered for 45 minutes, stirring occasionally. Stir in undrained beans. Simmer 15 minutes.

Bean Salad—Serves 4–6

1 × 14 oz (375 gm) can red kidney beans, drained
1 large onion, peeled and chopped
¼ pint (125 ml) salad oil
6 tablespoons cider vinegar
1 dessertspoon sugar
1 teaspoon mustard
1 teaspoon lemon juice
Salt
Pepper

Place beans and onion in large bowl. Beat oil with vinegar and remaining ingredients. Pour over beans and onion and mix well. Chill. Chopped parsley or chives may be added to taste.

Cowpoke Beans—Serves 5 to 6

1 lb (½ kilo) haricot beans, soaked overnight
1 pint (525 ml) water
½ lb (225 gm) salted belly of pork, cubed
½ teaspoon cayenne pepper
1 medium onion, peeled and chopped
1 clove garlic, peeled and crushed
1 × 5 oz (125 gm) can tomato puree
1 tablespoon purple-red chili seasoning powder
½ teaspoon cumin seed
½ teaspoon marjoram
Salt

Drain beans and put with water into casserole. Bring to boil. Lower heat. Cover. Simmer one hour. Stir in remaining ingredients. Continue to simmer another hour or until beans are tender. Stir occasionally to prevent sticking. Add more water if mixture seems on the dry side.

Honey Bean Bake—Serves 6

1 lb (½ kilo) haricot beans, soaked overnight
½ lb (200 gm) diced bacon
1 medium onion, peeled and sliced
12 oz (300 gm) honey
½ teaspoon dry mustard
½ teaspoon ginger
Salt

Drain beans. Cook in water until skins burst; about one hour. Drain and reserve liquid. Place half the bacon and onion over base of large casserole dish. Add beans. Top with remaining bacon and onion. Combine rest of ingredients with reserved bean liquid. Pour over beans. Cover. Bake in cool oven set to 300°F (150°C) or Gas 2 for one hour. Uncover. Bake extra ½ hour or until beans are of the desired consistency and colour.

Iron Skillet Potatoes—Serves 4 to 6

2 oz (50 gm) bacon fat or butter
1½ lb (¾ kilo) raw potatoes, thinly sliced
1 onion, peeled and sliced
1 teaspoon parsley
½ teaspoon sage
Salt and pepper

Melt fat in pan over a low heat. Add potatoes, onion, herbs and seasoning. Cover. Cook about 15 minutes. Turn and continue cooking another 15 minutes or until tender.

Molasses Fried Beans—Serves 6 to 8

6 streaky bacon rashers, chopped
1 large onion, peeled and chopped
2 × 1 lb (each ½ kilo) cans baked beans
2 oz (50 gm) sugar
1 tablespoon black treacle
1 teaspoon each garlic salt, pepper and mustard
¼ pint (125 ml) strong coffee

Fry bacon in casserole until fat runs. Add onion and fry till golden brown. Stir in rest of ingredients. Bring to boil. Cover. Simmer 30 minutes, adding a little extra water if mixture appears to be drying out too much.

Refried Beans Mexican Style—Serves 8

2 × 14 oz (each 375 gm) cans red kidney beans
1 small onion, peeled and chopped
1 teaspoon purple-red chili seasoning powder
1 clove garlic, peeled and crushed
¼ teaspoon salt and pepper
2 oz (50 gm) Cheddar cheese, cubed
1 oz (25 gm) butter

Puree beans in an electric mixer or mash by hand. Stir in all remaining ingredients, except butter. Melt butter in frying pan, add beans and cook, stirring occasionally, until mixture has thickened.

Pinto beans were a cowboy favourite—often served straight from the oven with a couple of slices of cornbread. Red kidney beans or haricot beans are used in these recipes

Out on the range sourdough batter was used for a delicious variety of breads and biscuits; cooks were prepared to stake their reputations on their recipes: sourdough biscuits, cowboy style

Bread & Cakes

Molasses Cookies—Makes about 24

3 oz (75 gm) butter
3 oz (75 gm) soft brown sugar
3 oz (75 gm) black treacle
8 oz (200 gm) plain flour
1 teaspoon mixed spice
1 teaspoon cinnamon
1 teaspoon ginger
½ teaspoon each cloves (powdered) and salt
1½ teaspoon bicarbonate of soda
1 tablespoon warm water

Set oven to moderate, 325°F (160°C) or Gas 3. Grease two baking trays. Melt butter, sugar and treacle in saucepan over low heat. Sift flour, spices and salt into bowl. Add melted treacle mixture together with bicarbonate of soda dissolved in the warm water. Mix well with fork. Shape into 24 balls. Place on trays, leaving plenty of room between each as cookies spread. Bake about 15–17 minutes. Store in airtight tin when cold.

Bread Pudding or Slumgullion

Soften old biscuits by soaking in warm water. Add sugar to taste and raisins. Beat to a pulp and pour into a well-greased tin. Bake in moderate oven to a golden brown. Serve with melted golden syrup.

Camp Bread—Makes about 10 'loaves'

8 oz (200 gm) plain flour
2 teaspoons baking powder
Salt
2 oz (50 gm) lard
¼ pint (125 ml) milk

Sift flour, baking powder and salt into bowl. Rub in lard. Mix to firmish dough with milk. Turn out on to floured surface and knead until smooth. Take pieces of dough about the size of an egg. Flatten out to one-inch thickness. Drop into hot, greased pan and fry over moderate heat till brown. Turn over and cook the other side. Make sure pan is well greased all the time. Try eating the camp bread with Burnt Sugar Lick (next recipe).

Burnt Sugar Lick

4 oz (100 gm) sugar
2 teaspoons water
2 teaspoons black treacle

Dissolve sugar in water. Let it turn brown, stirring occasionally. Add treacle. Bring to boil. This is a very good mixture to serve with camp bread if you have a sweet tooth.

Sourdough Bread—Makes 2 loaves

- ½ pint (250 ml) milk
- 2 oz (50 gm) sugar
- 2 oz (50 gm) butter
- 1 teaspoon salt
- 1 oz (25 gm) dried yeast
- 1 tablespoon lukewarm water
- 12 fl oz (300 ml) sourdough starter (see next page)
- 1½ lb (¾ kilo) flour

Warm milk with sugar, butter and salt. Stir and warm until sugar is dissolved. Dissolve yeast in warm water. Beat together milk mixture, yeast liquid, starter and two-thirds of the flour. Add remaining flour to make a stiff dough. Turn onto floured surface and knead until smooth and elastic (about 10 to 15 minutes). Place in greased bowl and turn dough so that it is greased all over. Cover. Leave to rise until double; about 1½ hours in warm place. Punch down by kneading lightly then let rise again for ½ hour. Divide into 2 balls, cover with towel and leave to rest for 10 minutes. Shape into 2 loaves and put each in a greased 2 lb (1 kilo) tin. Cover. Leave to rise until dough reaches tops of tins and feels light and springy when gently touched. Bake in a moderately hot oven set to 400°F (200°C) or Gas 6 for about 40 minutes. Turn out and cool on wire racks.

An Older Version of Sourdough Bread

Fill a keg nearly half full of lukewarm water and add a handful of sugar and enough flour to make a thick batter which can be stirred. Set in a warm place for 1 to 2 days until it becomes sour and has increased to twice its bulk. Boiled or mashed potato can be added to hasten the fermentation. Fill a large bowl two-thirds full of flour and make a well in the centre. Add about half the quantity of the sourdough starter (see next recipe) and also a little soda and salt dissolved in warm water and a little lard or bacon fat. Work in the flour until well mixed and pliable. Dredge the table with flour and then knead.

Put a large spoonful of fat into the heated Dutch oven. Pinch off dough in the size of an egg, roll in your hand then place in the oven and turn over so the entire surface is covered in grease and will not stick together. Let rise by the fire, then place on the coals, cover with the lid and put embers on the top. Make sure you have an even heat so the biscuits will brown evenly. They should have a deep brown upper and lower crust with a delicious interior.

The starter was then topped up with even quantities of flour and water and very carefully tended by the cook until the next time it was needed.

Sourdough Starter

1 oz (25 gm) dried yeast
2 pints (1¼ litres) lukewarm water
1 tablespoon sugar
1¼ lb (600 gm) plain flour

In a large basin able to hold at least 6 pints (about 3½ litres) mix yeast with lukewarm water. Extreme cold or heat will kill yeast so treat it carefully. Add sugar and pour liquid into a well in centre of sifted flour. Gradually stir in. Cover. Let mixture rise until it is very light and fills bowl. Leave, covered, for 24 to 48 hours. The mixture may be kept in the fridge (also covered) 7 to 10 days without attention. Then it should be stirred and equal amounts of flour and water added. To keep starter, pour off amount needed for the recipe, then add equal amounts of flour and water to make up the balance.

Texan Pecan Cake—Makes one cake

3 oz (75 gm) butter
8 oz (200 gm) sugar
1 egg, beaten
¼ teaspoon vanilla essence
8 oz (200 gm) flour
½ teaspoon salt
½ teaspoon baking powder
4 fl oz (100 ml) sourdough starter
4 fl oz (100 ml) milk

Cream butter, sugar, and vanilla together until light and fluffy, then beat in egg. Fold in sifted mixture of flour, salt and baking powder alternately with sourdough starter and milk. Pour into 6-inch buttered tin. Bake about 35 minutes in oven set to moderate, 350°F (175°C) or Gas 4. Carefully turn out onto wire cooling rack and spread top with glaze (see next column).

Sourdough Biscuits—Serves 6 to 8

10 oz (250 gm) flour
1 dessertspoon sugar
1 dessertspoon baking powder
½ teaspoon salt
¾ pint (375 ml) sourdough starter
1 tablespoon butter or lard

Sift flour, sugar, baking powder and salt into large bowl. Pour in starter and mix to firm dough. Grease 12-inch tin or ovenproof dish with butter or lard. Pinch off balls of biscuit mixture the size of walnuts. Place in tin or dish and set in a warm place to rise for up to 30 minutes when dough should have doubled in size. Bake near top of moderately hot oven set to 400°F (200°C) or Gas 6 about 25 to 30 minutes. Eat while still warm, preferably with butter.

Cowboys always had good appetites and cooks worked hard to provide three square—and punctual—meals a day: mealtime for the men of the VOX ranch

Glaze

4 oz (100 gm) brown sugar
2 oz (50 gm) cornflour
¼ teaspoon salt
¼ pint (125 ml) water
1½ oz (40 gm) butter

Combine sugar, cornflour and salt in pan with water. Cook, stirring constantly, until mixture thickens and boils. Boil one minute. Add butter. Cool. Spread over top of cake. Stud with pecans or walnut halves.

Cornbread—Serves 8 to 9

8 oz (200 gm) cornmeal or wholemeal flour
1 tablespoon sugar
1 teaspoon salt
12 fl oz (300 ml) milk
12 fl oz (300 ml) sourdough starter
1 teaspoon cream of tartar
1 teaspoon baking powder
2 eggs, lightly beaten
3 tablespoons melted butter

Combine flour, sugar and salt in mixing bowl. Scald milk. Pour into bowl. Mix well with flour. Cool slightly. Add remaining ingredients and mix. Pour into buttered 9-inch tin and bake 40 minutes in a moderately hot oven set to 400°F (200°C) or Gas 6.

Jalapeno Pepper Cornbread—Serves 8 to 9

8 oz (200 gm) cornmeal or wholemeal flour
1 tablespoon sugar
1 teaspoon salt
12 fl oz (300 ml) milk
12 fl oz (300 ml) sourdough starter
1 teaspoon cream of tartar
1 teaspoon baking powder
2 eggs
4 oz (100 gm) Cheddar cheese, grated
1 large onion, peeled and chopped
1 small green or red pepper, de-seeded and chopped

Make as for corn bread.

Sourdough Flapjacks—Makes about 20

12 oz (300 gm) flour
8 fl oz (200 ml) sourdough starter
¾ pint (375 ml) lukewarm water
2 eggs, beaten
1 tablespoon sugar
2 tablespoons butter, melted
1 tablespoon oil
½ teaspoon bicarbonate of soda

Sift flour into bowl. Gradually add starter and water. Stand overnight if possible, then stir in remaining ingredients. Leave another 10 minutes to bubble. Bake on griddle or in small, heavy frying pan, lightly greased with oil. Use about 2 oz (50 gm) batter for each flapjack, or enough to make a 6-inch flapjack. Serve with jam.

Breakfast, Cowboy Style

Rio Blanco Eggs

Left-over smoked meat, such as cooked tongue or boiled bacon
Dripping for frying
2 eggs per person
Salt and pepper to taste
1 oz (25 gm) Cheddar cheese per person, cut into cubes

Cut tongue or bacon into small pieces. Fry in dripping until crisp. Break eggs into pan and stir round. When almost set, add cheese cubes. Continue to cook until cheese begins to melt. Serve straight away.

Huevos Rancheros—Serves 8

8 tortillas (Mexican style bread) or slices of white bread
Oil or bacon dripping
8 eggs
Butter
1 recipe Huevos Rancheros Sauce (see next recipe)
1 peeled avocado, cut into slices and sprinkled with Lemon juice

Fry tortillas or bread half-minute each side in hot oil or dripping. In separate pan, fry eggs in butter. Season as desired. Place on tortillas or bread slices. Garnish with slices of avocado. Spoon sauce over each.

Huevos Rancheros Sauce—Serves 8

1 oz (25 gm) onion, peeled and chopped
1 clove garlic, peeled and crushed
1 dessertspoon oil
1 can condensed tomato soup
$\frac{1}{4}$ pint (125 ml) water
1 dessertspoon coriander
1 dessertspoon parsley, chopped
1 dessertspoon purple-red chili seasoning powder
Salt and pepper

Gently fry onion and garlic in oil until tender. Add tomato soup, water, herbs and seasonings. Simmer 10 minutes, whisking gently. Makes approximately 1 pint (just over $\frac{1}{2}$ litre).

Campfire Coffee—Serves about 16

4 pints ($2\frac{1}{4}$ litres) cold water
8 oz (225 gm) ground coffee
1 tablespoon beaten egg

Heat cold water into large pot. Mix coffee grounds with the egg, 2 tablespoons of cold water and a dash of salt. Stir in coffee when water boils. Return to boil, stirring occasionally. Turn off heat and pour in dash of cold water. Leave to stand 10 minutes for grounds to settle.

Cattleman's Omelette—Serves 2 to 3

6 rashers streaky bacon, diced
1 tablespoon chopped onion
3 oz (75 gm) raw potato, grated
6 eggs
Salt and pepper
Tabasco
1 tablespoon chopped parsley

Fry bacon in its own fat till crisp. Remove from pan. Add onion. Cook in bacon fat till soft. Add potatoes. Fry till brown. Beat eggs and pour into pan. Add seasoning. When the omelette is nearly cooked, sprinkle with crisp bacon and the parsley. Fold and serve.

Western Music

'Many of the cowboy's best songs were the product of enforced solitude on the range and on the trail—and of the prosaic task of keeping a herd of Longhorns calm through the night.'

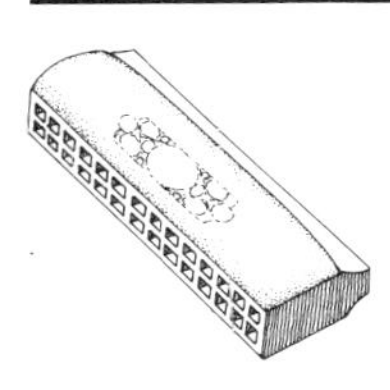

The singing cowboy of the movies—with shirt freshly laundered, teeth brushed and hair shining clean—is a fraud, and so are many of his songs. Not that cowboys didn't sing (there are books full of evidence to the contrary); but their songs were altogether more sturdy than the ditties made popular by stars like Roy Rogers and Gene Autry. True cowboy songs were as direct as the cowboy himself. They may have been gruesome, sentimental or bragging; they were never cute or self-regarding. In fact, as folk-song collectors found, it was often the Devil's own job to get a cowpuncher to give voice in company at all.

Many of the cowboy's best and most characteristic songs were the product of enforced solitude on the range and on the trail—and the prosaic task of keeping a herd of notoriously jumpy Longhorns calm through the night. The cattle soon learned to recognize a familiar voice, and it pacified them. A man who approached a herd without singing, or talking gently, could have a stampede on his hands. And he had to keep himself awake. It was only too easy for a night herder to drift into sleep in the small hours. Moving around and singing helped him to keep going.

Many of the cowboy's songs were about his work, but they're strikingly unlike most worksongs. A sea-shanty helped to co-ordinate a group task; the Negro field-holler enlivened the boredom of dull and repetitive labour. The cowhand's life was anything but mechanical or routine; herding, branding, roping, tending sick cattle—there were hundreds of tasks to be done, a constantly shifting tempo to his day. This freedom and variety is reflected in the wide range of his songs. If there's any connecting thread, it's in the swaying triple-time rhythm which accompanies most of them, and evokes the steady swing of a rider in the saddle.

A song like 'Git Along Little Dogies' is a perfect example of this—and also contains a version of that curious falsetto yell ('Whoopie ti yi yo', etc) which was later formalized into the yodelling of popular

Musicians were in demand all over the West, and particularly in the cow towns: cowboys dance to the music of a three-piece band

A man who could play a musical instrument was always sure of a welcome: cowboys enjoy an impromptu concert outside a bunkhouse

Western-style singers. A mechanically repeated sequence of sounds usually takes shape, sooner or later, as a recognizable melodic phrase. English street-cries, including the surviving rag-and-bone man's call, are an example; so is the Western cook's 'Gettin'-up Holler', the cowboy's human alarm clock. These whoops and cries, high-pitched and penetrating, carried clearly above the drumming of hooves on the trail, when other sounds were obliterated. Many old-timers claimed that white men learned this trick from the Indians, particularly the Comanches, with whom they had a close if uneasy relationship.

The borderline between speech and song is most vividly represented by the 'bragging' chant. This extraordinary incantation was a challenge to the bucking bronc to do its worst. The veteran collector John A. Lomax found it in Texas, and marked his transcription, 'To be declaimed, not sung.' Lomax notes that each phrase was yelled out while the horse was in the air, and the declamation ended only when the rider was thrown off—or when the animal finally surrendered.

The songs of the Old West make any tidy-minded academic folklorist despair. Like the Foreign Legion, the open range attracted men of every race, class and occupation. In the congenial anarchy of their new life they could start again with a new identity and an unknown past. But one thing couldn't be hidden: their musical heritage. The runaway sailor's 'Bury me not in the deep, deep sea' became 'Bury me not on the lone prairie'. The scapegrace Englishman's music-hall memories brought the melody of 'Vilikins and his Dinah' to 'Sweet Betsy from Pike'; the 'Swede from North Dakota' sang about himself in unusually full detail.

Cowboy country was infinitely remote from the polite north-east of America, spiritually as well as geographically. While Jesse James was running riot in Missouri, his fellow-countryman, Henry James, was preparing *Portrait of a Lady* for publication. Though the cowboy was far from the Atlantic seaboard and its urbane culture, his songs were often conventionally Victorian. 'Last-minute repentance' ballads were popular, like 'Young Companions', with its stock-in-trade of sweet old mother, childhood memories and bad company.

During the cowboy's heyday conditions in the West were significantly similar to those which produced the border ballads of southern Scotland in the 16th century. Both areas were beyond reach of established law; might was often right. Far from the cooling and impartial eye of legal process, the line between needless violence and heroism became blurred. Because decisive action of any kind makes a good story, the desperado was transformed into a hero:

Wha ever heard, in ony times,
Sicken an Outlaw in his degre,
Sic favour get before a King,
As did the Outlaw Murray of the Foreste frie?

or:

Now Charlie being an outlaw up on the mountain high,
With both infantry and cavalry to take him they did try,
But he hid amongst the brush that grew thick upon the field,
And received nine wounds before he would yield.

There are differences in period and idiom, but the similarity is striking. Violent action is glorified, and the form of both songs is exactly comparable. The four-line verse with a repeated melody emphasizes the central narrative and the urgent flow of events, and eliminates digression. The moralistic ending of many Western ballads is usually just a conventional gesture.

Like the songs of the English agricultural worker, those of the Western cowboy were intimately connected with his way of life. When this changed, the form also became outdated. The exception is the myth-making narrative ballad—particularly when an outlaw is the subject. From Robin Hood and Outlaw Murray to Jesse James and even to Pretty Boy Floyd:

Now as through this world I've wandered,
I've seen all kinds of men;
Some will rob you with a six-gun
And some with a fountain pen.

As through this world you wander,
As through this world you roam,
You won't never see an outlaw
Drive a family from their home. (Woody Guthrie)

It's easy to see how this tradition became one of the mainstays of the radical folk-song movement in the 1930s, beginning with Alred Hayes and Woody Guthrie and passing down to our time through the work of Pete Seeger and Bob Dylan.

Infuriatingly, the development of the gramophone coincided with the decline of the great cattle drives. As a result, it's impossible to know exactly what the songs sounded like when they were originally sung. Today they're invariably accompanied, usually on a guitar. This instrument almost certainly arrived in America from Spain, via Mexico, so it was probably known in the West. But it's unlikely to have been in everyday use in the early cowpunching days. It was fatally brittle, and both hands are needed to play it; cowboys would have found it an encumbrance. Instrumental music, like the fiddle and banjo style of the Kentucky mountains, is usually characteristic of settled communities. The most common instrument was probably the harmonica, which was easily available as a result of mass production and mail-order catalogues. It could be carried in the pocket and brought out to fill idle moments. The other pocket instrument was the jew's harp.

Cowboys probably accompanied their songs on harmonicas or jew's harps; today the guitar is the most popular instrument: cowboy musician

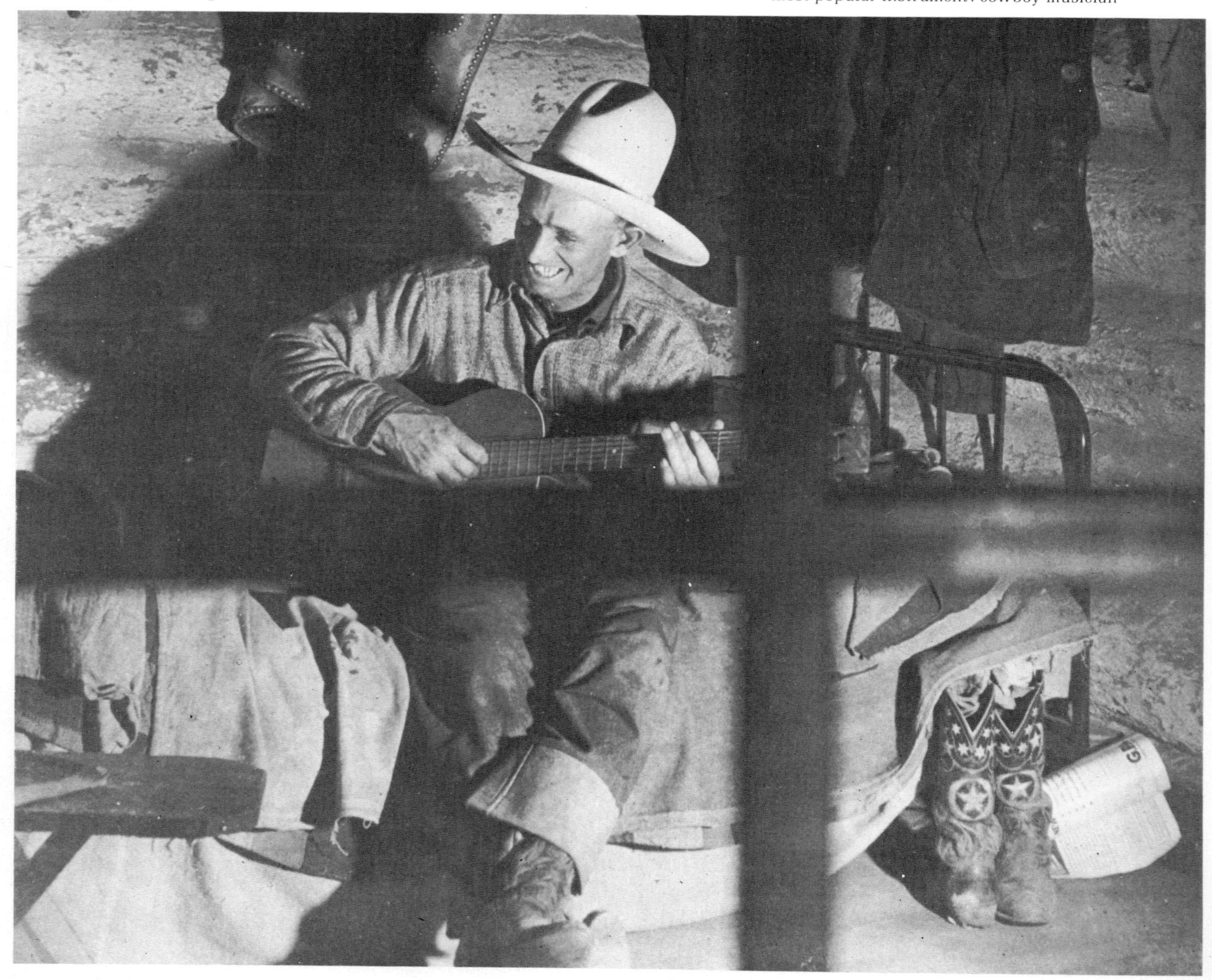

Most cowboy songs are highly rhythmic, implying a strumming accompaniment. The melodies also suggest a simple harmonic substructure, no doubt influenced by revivalist hymns and popular songs. Their simple form makes cowboy songs the most un-'folklike' folksongs in history. Even when an old, rambling English ballad, 'The Unfortunate Rake', turns up as that most beautiful of Western songs, 'The Streets of Laredo', its rhythm is trimmed down to a gentle waltz and a strongly-implied three-chord accompaniment.

This very simplicity is probably the main reason for the songs' enduring popularity. 'Home on the Range' has been sung by generations of Americans (and Europeans) who've never crossed the Texas state line; and has been arranged for brass bands, male-voice choirs, crooners and light-operatic tenors. Its appeal is universal—homesickness—and it's certainly strong. In the case of 'Home on the Range' it was worth a $50,000 lawsuit for a writer to claim authorship. He was unsuccessful; the conclusive evidence was produced by a 90-year-old woman who sang the song from memory, and declared she'd learned it as a young girl in the remote West.

The songs that follow are arranged for the guitar.

Cowboy's Bragging Chant
The Texas cowboy made a speciality of these chants, partly to impress his horse, partly to keep his own courage up. They were meant to make the man sound as formidable or repulsive as possible—like the one that starts: 'I'm wild and woolly and full of fleas'.

The Streets of Laredo
(A Cowboy's Lament)
There are probably hundreds of versions of this song: the dying penitent has been a sailor, a fallen woman and an 18th-century rake. Lyrics varied even in the West, but this—the most perfect—has become the standard version. The mournful sound of 'Laredo' sets the tone for the whole song.

'I see by your outfit that you are a cowboy,'
These words he did say as I boldly walked by;
'Come set down beside me and hear my sad story,
I'm shot in the breast and I know I must die.

'It was once in the saddle I used to go dashing,
Once in the saddle I used to go gay;
First down to Rosie's and then to the card-house;
Got shot in the breast and I'm dyin' today.

'Get sixteen gamblers to handle my coffin,
Let six jolly cowboys come sing me a song,
Take me to the graveyard and lay the sod o'er me,
For I'm a young cowboy and know I've done wrong.

'Get six jolly cowboys to carry my coffin,
Get six purty maidens to sing me a song,
Take me to the valley and lay the sod o'er me,
For I'm a young cowboy and know I've done wrong.

'Oh, beat the drum slowly and play the fife lowly,
Play the dead march as you carry me along;
Put bunches of roses all over my coffin,
Roses to deaden the clods as they fall.'

As I walked out in the streets of Laredo,
As I walked out in Laredo one day,
I spied a young cowboy all wrapped in white linen,
Wrapped in white linen as cold as the clay.

Home on the Range
The one Western song that everybody knows. In pioneering days its appeal lay in the idyllic security reflected in its lyrics. Today its potency is in its nostalgic harking back to a time when the range and the West were free to all comers.

Where the air is so pure and the zephyrs so free,
And the breezes so balmy and light
That I would not exchange my home on the range
For all of the cities so bright. (*Chorus*)

How often at night when the heavens are bright
With the light from the glittering stars,
Have I stood there amazed and asked, as I gazed,
If their glory exceeds that of ours. (*Chorus*)

The Swede from North Dakota

The cowboy singer, Glenn Ohrlin, who is of Swedish descent, learnt this song from his father. It's one of the few examples in which the singer is explicit about his origins. There is a decided hint of the polka about the tune, and the words are both canny and self-mocking.

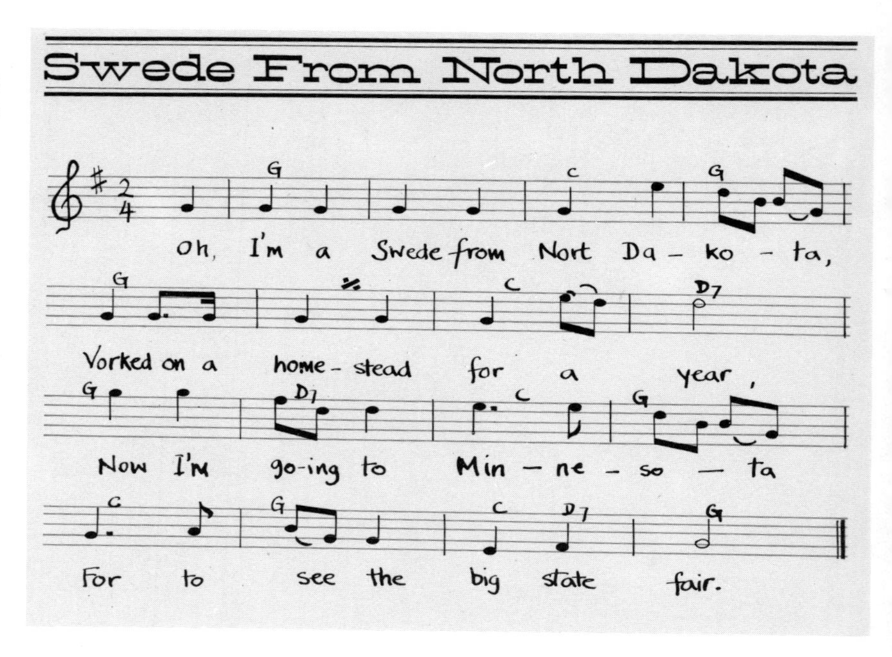

I landed down in Minneapolis,
Dere I vent in one big spree.
Now all the Swedes in Minnesota
Look a little bit like me.

I vent down to Seven Corners,
Vere Salvation Army play.
Dere a voman come up to me,
Dis is vat the voman say.

She said, 'Vill you vork for Yesus?'
I said, 'How much Yesus pay?'
She said, 'Yesus don't pay nothing.'
I said, 'I von't vork today.'

I vent down to Vashington Avenue,
Dress me up all out of sight.
Got me a suit and got me a bottle,
Yesus Christ, I feel for fight.

I voke up the very next morning
In the town they call Saint Paul.
I voke up vit an awful headache,
Guess I get some alcohol.

Going back to Nort Dakota,
Get me a yob on a farm somewhere.
Going back to Nort Dakota,
Oh, to hell vit the big state fair.

The Old Chisholm Trail
Driving cattle north from Texas to Kansas was tough work and there were times when even the most easygoing cowboys resented the limitations and hardships of life on the trail. Their feelings are clearly expressed in this song with its recurrent theme: 'quit punchin' cows' and get the hell out.

I woke up one morning on the Old Chisholm Trail,
Rope in my hand and a cow by the tail. (*Chorus*)

I jumped in the saddle and grabbed holt the horn,
Best durned cowboy ever was born. (*Chorus*)

I'm up in the mornin' before daylight,
And before I sleep the moon shines bright. (*Chorus*)

Oh, it's bacon and beans 'most every day,
I'd as soon be a-eatin' prairie hay. (*Chorus*)

I went up to the boss, and we had a little chat;
I slapped him in the face with my big slouch hat. (*Chorus*)

So, I sold my rope and I sold my saddle,
'Cause I'm tired of punchin' these goddam cattle. (*Chorus*)

Goin' back to town to draw my money,
Goin' back home to see my honey. (*Chorus*)

I'll ride my horse to the top of the hill;
I'll kiss that gal, guldurn, I will. (*Chorus*)

My seat is in the saddle, and my saddle's in the sky;
And I'll quit punchin' cows in the sweet by and by. (*Chorus*)

Night Herding Song
Gentle, rhythmic—a lullaby to soothe the cattle. Even a folksong has to start with someone and this one seems to have originated with a cowboy called Harry Stephens, in the 1880s or early 1890s. He told John A. Lomax that he composed it while working for the Wylie Cattle Company in Yellowstone Park.

Oh, say, little dogies, when you goin' to lay down
And give up this siftin' and roving around?
My horse is leg-weary and I'm awful tired,
But if you get away, I am sure to be fired;
Lay down, little dogies, lay down.
Hi—o, hi—o, hi—o.

Oh, lay still, dogies, since you have laid down,
Stretch away out on the big open ground;
Snore loud, little dogies, and drown the wild sound
That'll go away when the day rolls round,
Lay still, little dogies, lay still.
Hi—o, hi—o, hi—o.

Jesse James
There's an endearing touch of the absurd about James's death: he's said to have been standing on a chair hanging a picture, like any good suburban husband, when he was killed. 'Mr Howard' was the name he'd assumed at the time, his murderer was Robert Ford, an ex-member of the James gang.

It was on a Saturday night and the moon was shining bright,
They robbed the Glendale train,
With the agent on his knees, he delivered up the keys
To these outlaws Frank and Jesse James. (*Chorus*)

The people held their breath when they heard of Jesse's death
They wondered how he ever came to fall;
Robert Ford, it was a fact, shot Jesse in the back
While Jesse hung a picture on the wall. (*Chorus*)

Oh, Jesse was a man, a friend of the poor
He'd never rob a mother or a child;
He took from the rich and he gave to the poor
So they shot Jesse James on the sly. (*Chorus*)

Well, this song was made by Billy Gashade,
As soon as the news did arrive;
He said there was no man with the law in his hand
Who could take Jesse James when alive. (*Chorus*)

Goodbye, Old Paint

This short and repetitive ditty, possibly a version of 'I Ride an Old Paint', was usually accompanied by much stomping of feet and general hilarity. New lyrics were invented to suit different occasions, and there are literally hundreds of verses —some very bawdy. The last four bars allow lots of scope for exuberant harmonizing.

I'm a-leaving Cheyenne, I'm off for Montan',
Goodbye, old Paint, I'm a-leaving Cheyenne.

Old Paint's a good pony, he paces when he can,
Goodbye, old Paint, I'm a-leaving Cheyenne.

Go hitch up your hosses and give them some hay,
And seat yourself by me so long as you stay.

My hosses ain't hungry, they won't eat your hay,
My wagon is loaded and rolling away.

My foot's in the stirrup, my bridle's in my hand,
Good morning, young lady, my hosses won't stand.

Goodbye, old Paint, I'm a-leaving Cheyenne,
Goodbye, old Paint, I'm a-leaving Cheyenne.

Gettin' Up Holler

This call from the chuckwagon was the cowboy's alarm clock. Like the bragging chant, it is intoned speech rather than a song.

Bacon in the pan, coffee in the pot;
Git up now and git it while it's hot.

Git Along Little Dogies
A genuine worksong from the early trail days when cowboys drove the great herds north to Kansas—and beyond. 'Uncle Sam's Injuns' were tribes who'd been confined to reservations away from their ancestral hunting-grounds. The government was obliged to buy beef to feed them.

Early in the Spring, we round up the dogies,
Mark 'em and brand 'em and bob off their tails,
Round up our ponies, load up the chuck wagon,
And throw the little dogies out on the trail.

Your mother she was raised way down in Texas,
Where the jimson-weeds and the cactus grow,
Now we'll fill you up on prickly pear and *cholla*,
And throw you on the trail, the trail to Idaho.

It's whooping and yelling and driving the dogies,
Git along, you little dogies, little dogies, git on.
It's whooping and punching and git along you little dogies,
For you know Wyoming will be your new home.

Whoopee ti yi yo yi yo,
Wyoming will be your new home,
Whoopee ti yi yo, git along you little dogies,
It's your misfortune and none of my own.

Sweet Betsy from Pike
The tune is an old music hall favourite, and even though it describes a hellish trek by covered wagon it retains a kind of cockney chirpiness in the face of all odds. It was vastly popular during the cowboy's hey-day.

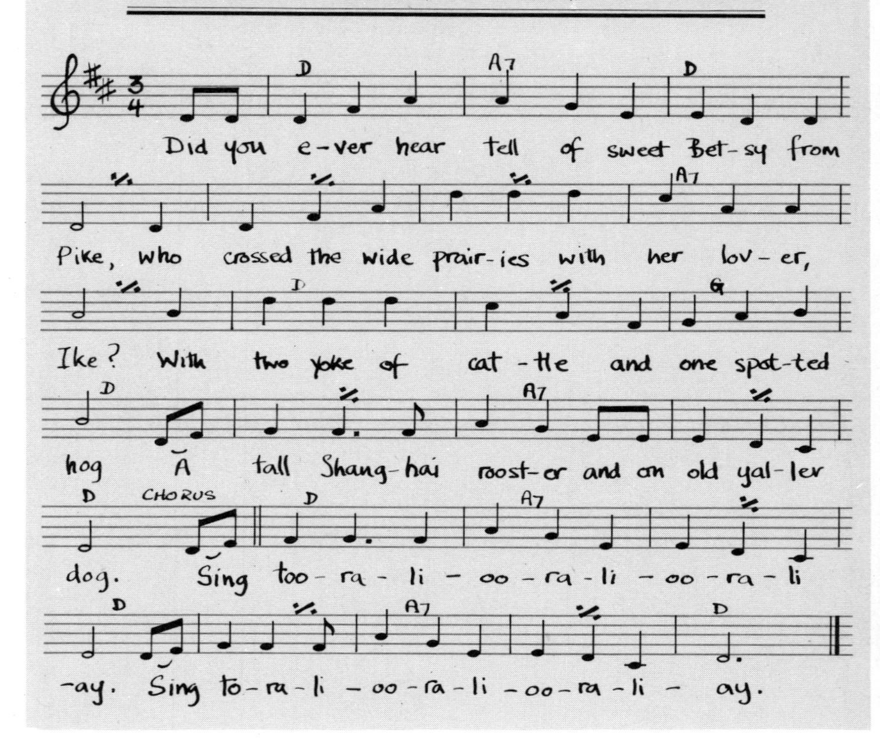

They swam the wild rivers and climbed the tall peaks,
And camped on the prairies for weeks upon weeks,
Starvation and cholera, hard work and slaughter,
They reached Californy, spite of hell and high water.
(Chorus)

They soon reached the desert where Betsy gave out,
And down in the sand she lay rolling about,
While Ike in great wonder looked on in surprise,
Sayin', 'Get up now, Betsy, you'll get sand in your eyes.'
(Chorus)

The Indians come down in a wild yelling horde,
And Betsy got skeered they would scalp her adored,
So behind the front wagon wheel Betsy did crawl,
And fought off the Indians with musket and ball.
(Chorus)

They stopped off at Salt Lake to inquire the way,
And Brigham declared that sweet Betsy should stay,
But Betsy got frightened and ran like a deer,
While Brigham stood pawing the ground like a steer.
(Chorus)

One morning they climbed up a very high hill,
And with wonder looked down upon old Placerville,
Ike shouted and said as he cast his eyes down,
'Sweet Betsy, my darlin', we've got to Hangtown.'
(Chorus)

Long Ike and Sweet Betsy attended a dance,
Where Ike wore a pair of his Pike County pants,
And Betsy was covered with ribbon and rings,
Quoth Ike, 'You're an angel, but where are your wings?'
(Chorus)

A miner said, 'Betsy, will you dance with me?'
'I will that, Old Hoss, if you don't make too free,
But don't dance me hard, do you want to know why?
Doggone ye, I'm chock full of strong alkali!'

Long Ike and sweet Betsy got married, of course,
But Ike, getting jealous, obtained a divorce,
While Betsy, well satisfied, said with a shout,
'Goodbye, you big lummox, I'm glad you backed out.'

Young Companions
A warning against the perils of liquor and the dangers of the Big City; in cowboy country the line between godliness and damnation was clearly drawn.

I had a kind old mother,
Who oft would plead with me,
And the last word that she gave me,
Was to pray to God in need.
I had two loving sisters,
As fair as fair could be,
And oft beside me kneeling,
They too would plead with me.

I did not like my fireside,
I did not like my home,
I had in view far rambling,
And far away did roam.
I bid adieu to loved ones,
To my home I said farewell,
And I landed in Chicago,
In the very depths of Hell.

It was there I took to drinking,
I sinned both night and day,
But still within my bosom,
A feeble voice would say,
'Oh fare you well my loved one,
May God protect my boy,
May God forever bless him,
Throughout his manhood joy!'

I courted a fair young maiden,
Her name I will not tell,
For I should ever disgrace her,
Since I am doomed to Hell.
It was on one beautiful evening,
The stars were shining bright,
And with a fatal dagger
I bid her spirit flight.

So justice overtook me,
You all can plainly see,
My soul is doomed forever,
Throughout eternity,
It's now I'm on the scaffold,
My moments are not long,
You may forget the singer,
But don't forget the song.

I Ride an Old Paint

This lilting waltz, also known as 'I'm Riding Old Paint', was traditionally the last tune played at dances. The poet Carl Sandburg, whose *American Songbag* is one of the classic folksong collections, praised the 'rich poetry' of its imagery. It was especially popular in Oklahoma, and may have originated there.

Old Bill Jones had two daughters and a song,
One went to Denver and the other went wrong.
His wife she died in a pool room fight,
But still he sings from morning till night.

Oh when I die take my saddle from the wall,
Put it on my pony, lead him out of his stall,
Tie my bones to his back, turn our faces to the West,
And we'll ride the prairies that we love best.

Chorus

Ride around the little dogies, ride around 'em slow,
For the fiery and the snuffy are a-r'aring to go.

Acknowledgements—Text Credits

We would like to thank the authors, publishers and agents who have given us permission to use extracts from their works. Credits are listed in the order in which excerpts appear on the page.

The Cowboy and the West: 16—The American West by John A. Hawgood, Eyre & Spottiswoode (Publishers) Ltd. Extract originally from 'A Letter Book of Joseph Eve' in Southwestern Historical Quarterly vol. XLIII, no. 4 (April 1940). 18—The Cattle Kings by L. Atherton, published by Indiana University Press, 1961. 19—ibid. 22—The Great Plains by W. P. Webb, © copyright, 1931, and renewed, 1959, by Walter Prescott Webb. Used by permission of the publisher, Ginn and Company (Xerox Corporation). 26—Cattle by William MacLeod Raine and Will C. Barnes, published by Doubleday, Doran & Company Inc., 1930, copyright 1930 by William MacLeod Raine and Will C. Barnes. 27—ibid. 28—The Great Plains by W. P. Webb; ibid., The Old-Time Cowhand by Ramon F. Adams, Macmillan Publishing Co. Inc., © Ramon F. Adams, 1948, 1949, 1951, 1954, 1959, 1960 and 1961; ibid.

The Long Drive: 33—Trail Driving Days by Dee Brown and Martin F. Schmidt, copyright 1952 Charles Scribner's Sons; A History of the JA Ranch by Harley True Burton published for University Microfilms Inc. Ann Arbor by Argonaut Press Ltd., New York, 1966. 41—Cattle by William MacLeod Raine and Will C. Barnes, published by Doubleday, Doran & Company Inc., 1930, copyright 1930 by William MacLeod Raine and Will C. Barnes. 42—Trail Driving Days by Dee Brown and Martin F. Schmidt; ibid. 43—Cattle by William MacLeod Raine and Will C. Barnes. 48—(lines 15–16) The Old-Time Cowhand by Ramon F. Adams, Macmillan Publishing Co. Inc., © Ramon F. Adams, 1948, 1949, 1951, 1954, 1959, 1960 and 1961; (lines 33–34) A History of the JA Ranch by Harley True Burton; Cowboy Life: Reconstructing an American Myth, edited by William W. Savage, Jr., copyright 1975 by the University of Oklahoma Press; ibid; The Old-Time Cowhand by Ramon F. Adams; ibid. 50—Cowboy Life edited by William W. Savage Jr.; (line 44) The Old-Time Cowhand by Ramon F. Adams. 51—(line 19) ibid.; Cattle by William MacLeod Raine and Will C. Barnes. 51–52—Cowboy Life edited by William W. Savage Jr. 53—ibid; The Old-Time Cowhand by Ramon F. Adams; Cattle by William MacLeod Raine and Will C. Barnes; Cowboy Life edited by William W. Savage, Jr.; ibid.

The Working Cowboy: 54—A History of the JA Ranch by Harley True Burton, published for University Microfilms Inc. Ann Arbor by Argonaut Press Ltd., New York, 1966; Cowhand by F. Gipson, Harper and brothers, New York, 1953. 55—ibid.; The Book of the American West, edited by Jay Monaghan (chapter: Ramon F. Adams), copyright 1963 Simon & Schuster Inc., reprinted by permission of Simon & Schuster Inc. 59, 60, 62—all quotes from The Old-Time Cowhand by Ramon F. Adams, Macmillan Publishing Co. Inc., © Ramon F. Adams, 1948, 1949, 1951, 1954, 1959, 1960 and 1961. 65—October 1973 issue of National Geographic, by courtesy of the National Geographic Society. 73—Cowhand by Fred Gipson.

At Home on the Range: 74—The American Cowboy—The Myth and the Reality by Joe B. Frantz and Julian Ernest Choate, Jr., copyright 1955 by the University of Oklahoma Press. 75—Western Story by Charley O'Kieffe, University of Nebraska Press, copyright © 1960 by the University of Nebraska Press. 76—Before Barbed Wire by Mark H. Brown and William R. Felton, copyright © 1956 by Mark H. Brown and William R. Felton, by permission of Paul R. Reynolds Inc., New York; Sod-House Frontier by E. N. Dick, D. Appleton-Century Co., 1943, courtesy of Hawthorn Books Inc. 77—Before Barbed Wire by Mark H. Brown and William R. Felton. 77–78—Sod-House Frontier by E. N. Dick. 79—The Cattleman's Frontier by L. Pelzer, Arthur H. Clark Co., 1936, by courtesy of the author and publisher. 81—Sod-House Frontier by E. N. Dick. 82—The New Country: A Social History of the American Frontier 1776–1890 by Richard A. Bartlett, Oxford University Press, 1974, by courtesy of the author and publisher. 83—A Bride Goes West by Nannie T. Alderson and Helena Huntington Smith, University of Nebraska Press, 1942. Reprinted by permission of International Creative Management, copyright © 1942 by Farrar and Rinehart, Inc. and renewed 1970 by Nannie T. Alderson and Helena Huntington Smith. 84—Western Story by Charley O'Kieffe; The American Cowboy: The Myth and the Reality by Joe B. Frantz and Julian Ernest Choate, Jr. 85—Before Barbed Wire by Mark H. Brown and William R. Felton; Sod-House Frontier by E. N. Dick. 86—Western Story by Charley O'Kieffe. 86–87—Sod-House Frontier by E. N. Dick. 87—The American Cowboy: The Myth and the Reality by Joe B. Frantz and Julian Ernest Choate, Jr. 89—(lines 20–21) The Trampling Herd by P. I. Wellman, Tandem Publishing Ltd., 1973, by courtesy of the publisher. 90—The American Frontier by C. Merton Babcock, Holt, Rinehart & Winston, Inc., 1965. 91—Rawhide Texas by Wayne Gard, copyright 1965 University of Oklahoma Press.

Man and Horse—An Inseparable Pair: 92, 93, 94—all quotes from The American Cowboy, copyright © 1973 by Harold McCracken. Reprinted by permission of Doubleday & Company, Inc. 95—Frederic Remington's Own West edited by Dr Harold McCracken, published by Promontory Press by arrangement with The Dial Press, copyright © 1960 by Harold McCracken. 98—(line 17) Cowboys by Royal B. Hassrick, published by Octopus Books, 1974, by courtesy of the author and publisher; ibid.; The Book of the American West edited by Jay Monaghan (chapter by Ramon F. Adams), copyright 1963 Simon & Schuster Inc., reprinted by permission of Simon & Schuster Inc.; (lines 43–44) The Old-Time Cowhand by Ramon F. Adams, Macmillan Publishing Co. Inc., © Ramon F. Adams, 1948, 1949, 1951, 1954, 1959, 1960 and 1961. 102—Man on Horseback by Glen R. Vernam, Harper & Row, Publishers, Inc., 1964, copyright © 1964 by Glenn R. Vernam; The Book of the American West edited by Jay Monaghan (chapter by Ramon F. Adams). 103—ibid.; Cowboy Lore by Jules Verne Allen, published by The Naylor Company, 1933 (reprint 1971), by courtesy of the publisher; Man on Horseback by Glen R. Vernam; Before Barbed Wire by Mark H. Brown and William R. Felton, copyright © 1956 by Mark H. Brown and William R. Felton, by permission of Paul R. Reynolds Inc., New York; ibid.; The Old-Time Cowhand by Ramon F. Adams. 106—ibid.

Rustlers and Horse-thieves: 109—The Book of the American West edited by Jay Monaghan (chapter by Wayne Gard), copyright 1963 Simon & Schuster Inc., reprinted by permission of Simon & Schuster Inc. 113—Hot Irons by Oren Arnold and John P. Hale, The Macmillan Company, New York, 1944, copyright 1940 by The Macmillan Company; The Book of the American West edited by Jay Monaghan (chapter by Wayne Gard); The Old-Time Cowhand by Ramon F. Adams, Macmillan Publishing Co. Inc., © Ramon F. Adams, 1948, 1949, 1951, 1954, 1959, 1960 and 1961. 115—The Day of the Cattleman by E. S. Osgood, Phoenix Books, 1929, © University of Minnesota Press. 116—Trail Driving Days by Dee Brown and Martin F. Schmidt, copyright 1952 Charles Scribner's Sons. 117—27 Years a Maverick (reprinted 1968 as Cowboy Life in Texas) by W. S. James. Reprinted by courtesy of Steck Vaughan & Co., Austin, Texas.

Myths and Legendmakers: 118—Cowboy Life: Reconstructing an American Myth, edited by William W. Savage, Jr., copyright 1975 University of Oklahoma Press; The American Cowboy—The Myth and the Reality by Joe B. Frantz and Julian Ernest Choate, Jr., copyright 1975 University of Oklahoma Press. 120—Good Men and True by E. M. Rhodes, Houghton Mifflin Company, copyright W. H. Hutchinson. 123—The Great Plains by W. P. Webb, © copyright, 1931, and renewed, 1959, by Walter Prescott Webb. Used by permission of the publisher, Ginn and Company (Xerox Corporation); The Old-Time Cowhand by Ramon F. Adams, Macmillan Publishing Co. Inc., © Ramon F. Adams, 1948, 1949, 1951, 1954, 1959, 1960 and 1961; ibid. 125—ibid. 126—Great Gunfighters of the Kansas Cowtowns, 1867–1886 by Nyle H. Miller and Joseph W. Snell, University of Nebraska Press, 1967, copyright © 1963 by Nyle H. Miller and Joseph W. Snell; The Old-Time Cowhand by Ramon F. Adams. 131—ibid. 133—(lines 5–6) ibid; We Pointed them North, E. C. Abbott and Helena Huntington Smith, Farrar & Rinehart, Inc., 1939.

The Code of the West: 139—Sod-House Frontier by E. N. Dick, published by D. Appleton-Century Co., 1943, courtesy of Hawthorn Books Inc. 140—A Bride Goes West by Nannie T. Alderson and Helena Huntington Smith, University of Nebraska Press, 1942. Reprinted by permission of International Creative Management, copyright © 1942 by Farrar and Rinehart, Inc. and renewed 1970 by Nannie T. Alderson and Helena Huntington Smith; ibid; The Old-Time Cowhand by Ramon F. Adams, Macmillan Publishing Co. Inc., © Ramon F. Adams, 1948, 1949, 1951, 1954, 1959, 1960 and 1961; ibid. 142—Before Barbed Wire by Mark H. Brown and William R. Felton, copyright © 1956 by Mark H. Brown and William R. Felton, by permission of Paul R. Reynolds Inc., New York. 143—Sod-House Frontier by E. N. Dick. 145—A Bride Goes West by Nannie T. Alderson and Helena Huntington Smith; ibid; (lines 19–22) The Humor of the American Cowboy by Stan Hoig, University of Nebraska Press, 1970, by courtesy of the author and publisher; The Cattle Kings by L. Atherton, Indiana University Press, 1961; The Humor of the American Cowboy by Stan Hoig. 146—The Old-Time Cowhand by Ramon F. Adams; ibid. 147—Cow People by J. F. Dobie, Little, Brown & Co., 1964, by courtesy of the author and publisher. 147–148—ibid.

Practical Skills: 176—quoted in Man on Horseback by Glenn R. Vernam, Harper & Row, Publishers, Inc., 1964, copyright © 1964 by Glenn R. Vernam. 177—ibid. 178—The Old-Time Cowhand by Ramon F. Adams, Macmillan Publishing Company Inc., © Ramon F. Adams, 1948, 1949, 1951, 1954, 1959, 1960 and 1961. 182—ibid.; ibid. 183–184—ibid. 184—Cowboy Lore by Jules Verne Allen, published by The Naylor Company, 1933 (reprint 1971), by courtesy of the publisher.

Chuckwagon Cooking: 185—Round Up at the Double Diamond by Bill Surface, Houghton Mifflin Co., 1974, by courtesy of the author and publisher; Cattle by William MacLeod Raine and Will C. Barnes, published by Doubleday, Doran & Company Inc., 1930, copyright 1930 by William MacLeod Raine and Will C. Barnes. 186—(lines 26–27) Frontier Ways by E. E. Dale, Texas Western Press (University of Texas Press) 1959; The Old-Time Cowhand by Ramon F. Adams, Macmillan Publishing Company Inc., © Ramon F. Adams, 1948, 1949, 1951, 1954, 1959, 1960 and 1961; Frontier Ways by E. E. Dale. 187—all quotes from Frontier Ways by E. E. Dale. 189—Round Up at the Double Diamond by Bill Surface.

Western Music: 'Swede from North Dakota'—copyright 1973 by The Board of Trustees of the University of Illinois. 'The Swede from North Dakota' is reprinted from the book The Hell Bound Train by Glen Ohrlin, published by the University of Illinois Press, Urbana, 1973. 'Jesse James'— from the book American Favourite Ballads and Tunes edited by Pete Seeger, © 1961 Oak Publications. 'Goodbye Old Paint', 'Git Along Little Dogies', 'Young Companion' and 'I'm Ridin' Old Paint'—BY PERMISSION OF BARTHOLD FLES, LITERARY AGENT FOR MARGARET LARKIN, taken from the book The Singing Cowboy published by Alfred Knopf, copyright 1931. 'Cowboy to Pitching Bronco', 'Sweet Betsy from Pike' and 'Gettin' Up Holler' collected, adapted and arranged by John A. and Alan Lomax—TRO Essex Music Ltd. Verses from 'Pretty Boy Floyd', page 203, by Woody Guthrie—TRO Essex Music Ltd.

Picture Credits

We would like to thank the following individuals and organisations who supplied illustrations for the book:

Amon Carter Museum, Fort Worth, Texas: Pages 128–129. Arizona Historical Society: Pages 54, 60 (top), 76–77, 88 (top), 91, 139, 144. Barnabys Picture Library: Pages 70, 110, 158, 160. Brown Brothers: Page 109 (left). California Historical Society: Page 108. Camera Press: Pages 45, 150–151, 152, 153, 156, 157 (top and bottom), 164, 165, 166, 168–169, 170, 171, 182–183. The Cattleman: Page 21 (top). Coffrins Old West Gallery: Pages 6, 17 (centre), 68–69, 74, 76 (bottom), 79, 114–115 (bottom), 115 (top). The State Historical Society of Colorado: Page 75. Culver Pictures Inc.: Page 89. The Denver Art Museum: Pages 96–97. Denver Public Library, Western History Department: Pages 16 (centre), 17 (right), 65 (bottom), 86, 87, 109 (left), 126, 127, 138, 204. Dickinson County Historical Society, Abilene, Kansas: Page 43. Esmark Inc.: Page 21 (bottom). Thomas Gilcrease Institute of American History and Art: Page 49 (top). The Hammer Galleries, New York: Pages 49, 99 (bottom), 148. Harper's Magazine: Page 120. Barney Hillerman Photography: Page 69. Hungarian News and Information Service: Pages 154 (top and bottom), 155. Kansas State Historical Society Museum: Pages 13, 38, 42, 112–113, 135 (right). The Library of Congress, Washington D.C.: 8, 32, 52, 141 (bottom).The Library of Congress, Washington D.C.—Erwin E. Smith Collection of Range Life Photographs: Pages 61, 64, 105. Los Angeles Municipal Art Gallery: Pages 22–23. Dr Harold McCracken, The Buffalo Bill Historical Center, photographs reproduced by courtesy of Dr McCracken: Pages 92, 93, 94 (top and bottom), 119. Montana Historical Society: Pages 17 (left), 39, 57, 83 (top), 116, 141 (right). National Film Board Canada: Page 167. Nebraska State Historical Society: Page 123. Nebraska State Historical Society, Soloman D. Butcher Collection: Pages 82–83 (bottom). North Dakota State Historical Society: Page 80. Oklahoma Historical Society: Page 134 (left). Photograph courtesy of Pan American World Airways Inc.: Page 161. Philip Morris Inc.: Pages 10–11, 14–15, 36–37, 58–59, 100, 104, 188–189, 193, 195, 196–197. Pinkerton National Detective Society: Page 134 (right).

Popperfoto: Pages 159, 162 (top and bottom), 163. Jerry Sinise: Pages 12, 18–19, 28–29, 67 (top and bottom), 71, 180, 184, 185, 194. Texas Western Press, The University of Texas at El Paso publishers of Riders of the Border by José Cisneros: Page 9. Title Insurance and Trust Company Los Angeles, Collection of Historical Photographs: Pages 46–47, 50–51. University of Oklahoma Library, Western History Collections: Pages 16 (left and right), 30, 130. University of Oklahoma Library, Western History Collections (Rose Collection): Pages 34–35, 44, 50–51. University of Oklahoma Library, Western History Collections (A. A. Forbes Collection): Page 198. University of Wyoming, Western History Research Center: Page 202. Wadsworth Atheneum, Hartford, Conn.: Page 132 (right). Walker Art Studio: Pages 19, 58 (top and right), 62–63, 101. Western Americana Picture Library: Pages 33, 60, 72, 78, 81, 88 (bottom), 90, 95, 99 (top), 118, 131, 132 (bottom left and bottom right), 135 (left), 136 (left and right), 137 (left and right), 142–143, 147, 201. Western Ways Features: Pages 2, 27, 55 (top and bottom), 146.
Larry Willcox: Pages 10, 29 (right, centre and left), 56, 66, 121 (top and bottom), 124, 125. Wyoming State Historical Department: Page 106.

Bibliography

Adams, Andy, *Cattle Brands*, Houghton Mifflin & Company, Boston, New York, 1906

Adams, Ramon F., *The Old-Time Cowhand*, The Macmillan Co., New York, 1961

Alderson, Nannie T. and Smith, Helena Huntington, *A Bride Goes West*, University of Nebraska Press, Lincoln, 1974

Allen, Jules Verne, *Cowboy Lore*, The Naylor Company, Texas, 1933 (reprint 1971)

American Heritage, *History of the Great West*, American Heritage Publications, New York, 1965

Arnold, Oren and Hale, John P., *Hot Irons*, The Macmillan Co., New York, 1944

Atherton, Lewis, *The Cattle Kings*, Indiana University Press, 1961

Babcock, C. Merton, *The American Frontier*, Holt, Rinehart & Winston Inc., New York, 1965

Back, Joe, *Horses, Hitches and Rocky Trails*, The Swallow Press Inc., Chicago, 1959

Bartlett, Richard A., *The New Country: A Social History of the American Frontier 1776–1890*, Oxford University Press, New York, 1974

Botkin, B. A., ed., *A Treasury of American Folklore*, Crown Publishers Inc., New York, 1944

Brown, Dee and Schmidt, Martin F., *Trail Driving Days*, Bonanza Books, New York, 1952

Brown, Mark H. and Felton, W. R., *Before Barbed Wire*, Bramhall House, New York, 1961

Burton, Harley True, *A History of the JA Ranch*, Argonaut Press, New York, 1966

The Cambridge Modern History (vol. VII The United States), Cambridge University Press, Cambridge, 1934

Clark, Dan Elbert, *The West in American History*, Thomas Y. Crowell Company, New York, 1948

Clark, Thomas D., *Frontier America: The Story of the Western Movement*, Charles Scribner's Sons, New York, 1969

Crawford, Thomas Edgar, (Dykes, Jeff C., ed.), *The West of the Texas Kid 1881–1910*, University of Oklahoma Press, Norman, 1962

Dale, E. E., *Frontier Ways: Sketches of Life in the Old West*, Texas Western Press, 1959

Dale, E. E., *The Range Cattle Industry*, University of Oklahoma Press, Norman, 1930

Dick, E. N., *The Sod-House Frontier*, D. C. Appleton-Century Co., New York, 1943

Dobie, J. Frank, *Cow People*, Little, Brown & Co., Boston, 1964

Drago, Harry Sinclair, *The Legend Makers*, Dodd, Mead & Company, New York, 1975

Droit, M., *Camargue*, George Allen & Unwin (Publishers) Ltd., London, 1973

Dykstra, Robert R., *The Cattle Towns*, Atheneum, New York, 1970

Elman Robert, *Badmen of the West*, The Ridge Press Inc., 1974

Farrell, Cliff, *The Mighty Land*, Doubleday & Company Inc., New York, 1975

Faulk, Odie B., *Tombstone: Myth and Reality*, Oxford University Press, New York, 1972

Forbis, William H., *The Cowboys*, Time-Life Books, New York, 1973

Frantz, Joe B. and Choate, Julian Ernest, Jr., *The American Cowboy: The Myth and the Reality*, University of Oklahoma Press, Norman, 1955

Furnas, J. C., *The Americans (Social History)*, Longman Group Ltd., London

Gard, Wayne, *Rawhide Texas*, University of Oklahoma Press, Norman, 1965

Grant, Bruce, *The Cowboy Encyclopedia*, Rand McNally & Company, New York, Chicago, San Francisco, 1951

Green, Ben K., *A Thousand Miles of Mustangin'*, Northland Press, Flagstaff, Arizona, 1972

Gribble, L., *Famous Stories of the Wild West*, Arthur Barker, London, 1975

Haines, Francis, *Horses in America*, Thomas Y. Crowell Company, New York, 1971

Harris, W. Foster, *The Look of the Old West*, Bonanza Books, New York, 1955

Hassrick, Royal B., *Cowboys*, Octopus Books Ltd., London, 1974

Hawgood, John A., *The American West*, Eyre & Spottiswoode (Publishers) Ltd., London, 1967

Hendrix, John, *If I Can Do It On Horseback: A Cow Country Sketch Book*, University of Texas Press, 1963

Hoig, Stan, *The Humor of the American Cowboy*, University of Nebraska Press, 1970

Hollon, W. Eugene, *Frontier Violence: Another Look*, Oxford University Press, New York, 1974

House, Boyce, *Cowtown Columnist*, The Naylor Company, San Antonio, Texas, 1946

Horan and Sann, *Pictorial History of the Wild West*, Spring Books, London, 1961

Howard, Robert West, ed., *This is the West*, Rand McNally & Company, New York, 1957

Kolb, S. & J., *A Treasury of Folk Songs*, Bantam Books, New York, 1948

Larkin, Margaret, *The Singing Cowboy*, Alfred A. Knopf Inc., New York, 1963

Lavender, D., *The American West*, Penguin Books, Harmondsworth, 1969

Laws of the Territory of Utah, Tribune Printing & Publishing Co., Salt Lake City, 1886

Lea, Tom, *The King Ranch* (two volumes), Little, Brown & Co., Boston, Toronto, 1957

Lomax, John A. and Alan, *American Ballads and Folk Songs*, The Macmillan Co., New York, 1964

Lomax, John A., *Cowboy Songs & Other Frontier Ballads*, The Macmillan Co., New York, 1938

Lomax, John A. and Alan, *Our Singing Country*, The Macmillan Co., New York, 1949

McCracken, Harold, *The American Cowboy*, Doubleday & Company Inc., New York, 1973

Miller, Nyle H. and Snell, Joseph W., *Great Gunfighters of the Kansas Cowtowns 1867–1886*, University of Nebraska Press, Lincoln, 1973

Miller, W., *New History of the USA*, Paladin, St Albans, 1970

Monaghan, Jay, ed., *The Book of the American West*, Bonanza Books, New York, 1963
Nordyke, Lewis, *Great Round Up*, William Morrow & Co., New York, 1955
Ohrlin, Glenn, *The Hell Bound Train: A Cowboy Songbook*, University of Illinois Press, 1973
O'Kieffe, Charley, *Western Story*, University of Nebraska Press, 1960
Orpen, A. E., *Memoirs of the Old Emigrant Days in Kansas 1862–1865*, William Blackwood & Sons Ltd., Edinburgh, 1926
Osgood, Ernest Staples, *The Day of the Cattleman*, The University of Chicago Press, Chicago, 1929
Paul, Virginia, *This Was Cattle Ranching*, Superior Publishing Co., Seattle, 1973
Pelzer, L., *The Cattleman's Frontier*, Arthur H. Clark Co., Glendale, Calif., 1936
Raine, William MacLeod and Barnes, Will C., *Cattle*, Doubleday, Doran & Co. Inc., New York, 1930
Remington, Frederic, McCracken Harold, ed., *Frederic Remington's Own West*, Promontory Press, New York, 1960
Savage, William W., Jr., *Cowboy Life: Reconstructing an American Myth*, University of Oklahoma Press, Norman, 1975
Seeger, Pete, ed., *American Favorite Ballads*, Oak Publications, New York, 1861
Surface, Bill, *Round Up at the Double Diamond*, Houghton, Mifflin Co., Boston, 1974
Swan, Oliver G., ed., *Frontier Days*, Macrat, Smith Co., Philadelphia, 1928
Ulyatt, Kenneth, *The Day of the Cowboy*, Penguin Books, Harmondsworth, 1973
Vernam, Glenn R., *Man on Horseback*, University of Nebraska Press, Lincoln, 1972
Webb, Walter Prescott, *The Great Plains*, Grosset & Dunlap, New York, 1974
Wellman, P. I., *The Trampling Herd*, Doubleday & Co. Inc., New York, Toronto, London, Paris, 1951
Zurhurst, Charles, *The First Cowboy: and Those Who Followed*, Cassell & Co., London, 1974

Index

Page numbers in italic refer to illustrations

Photosetting and reproduction by Tradespools Ltd., Graphic House, South Parade, Frome, Somerset. Printing and binding by A. Wheaton and Company, Hennock Rd., Exeter, United Kingdom